Findin  ey Are

que

800 East 96th Street,
Indianapolis, Indiana 46240 USA

Mobile Marketing

Finding Your Customers No Matter Where They Are

ISBN-13: 978-0-7897-3976-6
ISBN-10: 0-7897-3976-3

Library of Congress Cataloging-in-Publication Data is on file

Printed in the United States of America

First Printing: March 2010

Trademarks

Warning and Disclaimer

Bulk Sales

Que Publishing offers excellent discounts on this book when ordered in quantity for bulk purchases or special sales. For more information, please contact

U.S. Corporate and Government Sales
1-800-382-3419
corpsales@pearsontechgroup.com

For sales outside of the U.S., please contact

International Sales
international@pearson.com

Associate Publisher
Greg Wiegand

Acquisitions Editor
Rick Kughen

Development Editor
Rick Kughen

Managing Editor
Kristy Hart

Project Editor
Andy Beaster

Copy Editor
Krista Hansing Editorial Services, Inc.

Indexer
Lisa Stumpf

Proofreader
Jennifer Gallant

Technical Editor
Kim Dushinski

Publishing Coordinator
Cindy Teeters

Interior Designer
Anne Jones

Cover Designer
Anne Jones

Compositor
Gloria Schurick

Reviewers
Steve Baldwin
Eric Chan
Rebecca Lieb

CONTENTS AT A GLANCE

TABLE OF CONTENTS

12 Mobile E-Commerce 237

13 Mobile Marketing Privacy, Spam, and Viruses 255

14 The International Mobile Marketing Landscape 277

15 Looking into the Future for Mobile 297

About the Author

Cindy Krum is the CEO and Founder of Rank-Mobile, LLC, based in Denver, CO. She brings fresh and creative ideas to her clients, speaking at national and international trade events about mobile Web marketing, social network marketing and international SEO. Cindy is hosts a weekly radio show about mobile marketing called Mobile Presence on WebmasterRadio.FM. She writes for industry publications, and has been published in Website Magazine, Advertising & Marketing Review, Search Engine Land, ODG Intelligence, and quoted by many respected publications including PC World, Internet Retailer, TechWorld, Direct Magazine, Inc. Magazine and Search Marketing Standard.

Dedication

My favorite thank you and a dedication for all of you, is a quote from Isaac Newton, who said: "If I can see further than anyone else, it is only because I am standing on the shoulders of giants."

Acknowledgments

I would specifically like to thank my editor, Rick Kughen, and my primary tech editor, Kim Dushinski, for all of their help and advice regarding the book. They have been invaluable assets.

I had a number of additional tech editors that helped review my work and act as sounding boards, and I am very greatful for their help. They are: Jen Sable Lopez, Bryson Meunier, Jordan Kasteler, Andy Lustigman, Ken Singer, Eric Chan, Justin Harmon, Barry Bryant, and Greg Hickman.

I would like to include a deep and sincere "thank you" to everyone who has helped me get to this point in my career. As much as I would like to name names, I can't because I know I will forget someone, and feel horrible. Instead I would like to thank the groups and communities that have made my career possible:

- The two conference series, Search Engine Strategies (SES) and SMX (Search Marketing Expo) for always including me in sessions about mobile marketing, and in some cases, creating mobile sessions just for me;

- SEOmoz and BlitzLocal, for always being available to help with logistics, offer sound business advice, act as a sounding board or give words of encouragement;

- WebmasterRadio.FM and WebProNews for giving me a digital form where I can take and give interviews, create an online dialogue and learn from my peers;

- Tech Editors, who worked with me, sometimes with little notice or preparation, to make this book as accurate as possible;

- And all my dear friends in the online marketing community, without whom this experience would have been much less enjoyable.

Starting a company and writing a book in the same year has been quite a challenge; and doing it all in a down economy has been nerve-wracking—to say the least. As I see friends and old colleagues lose their jobs, and successful companies tighten their belts or go under, I feel lucky. In the year that has taken to write this book, I have been surrounded by some of the smartest people in the world. I hope to keep my place in their good graces and some day, pay their good deeds forward.

We Want to Hear from You!

As the reader of this book, *you* are our most important critic and commentator. We value your opinion and want to know what we're doing right, what we could do better, what areas you'd like to see us publish in, and any other words of wisdom you're willing to pass our way.

As an associate publisher for Que Publishing, I welcome your comments. You can email or write me directly to let me know what you did or didn't like about this book—as well as what we can do to make our books better.

Please note that I cannot help you with technical problems related to the topic of this book. We do have a User Services group, however, where I will forward specific technical questions related to the book.

When you write, please be sure to include this book's title and author, as well as your name, email address, and phone number. I will carefully review your comments and share them with the author and editors who worked on the book.

Email: feedback@quepublishing.com

Mail: Greg Wiegand
           Associate Publisher
           Que Publishing
           800 East 96th Street
           Indianapolis, IN 46240 USA

Reader Services

Visit our website and register this book at informit.com/register for convenient access to any updates, downloads, or errata that might be available for this book.

Introduction

I believe that mobile marketing is the marketing of the future. My name is Cindy Krum, and I am the author of Mobile Marketing: Finding Your Customers No Matter Where They Are. This book is intended to be a comprehensive guide for marketers and anyone who wants a clearer understanding of how they can integrate mobile marketing with their existing on- and offline marketing campaigns.

Mobile marketing is a quickly changing industry. My hope is that this book is as comprehensive, timely, and accurate as possible. That being said, the mobile industry is still very inconsistent and, in many instances, opaque, complicated, and variable. It can be difficult to pin down different technological capabilities or get a clear understanding of how different technologies work together. I have done my best to describe the mobile world as I understand it, but I will be the first to admit that I am no technology expert. Many people have a deeper understanding of specific mobile technologies, but few have the breadth of understanding for the entire channel or its potential relationship to other marketing channels. My strength is in my vision and my ability to help companies create unified mobile strategies that create long-term value while still generating an immediate return.

You will find several themes throughout the book. These themes are the core reasons that I have become so passionate about mobile communication and have become somewhat of an evangelist for mobile technology.

- **Empowerment**—The adoption of mobile technology has economic and political ramifications that help people lead better lives and have a voice in their society. Because mobile phones are cheaper that computers, in many places, smart phones are simultaneously a person's first personal phone and first personal computer. Jeffrey Sachs, from the Columbia University's Earth Institute, said that mobile technology has been "the single most transformative tool for development." It has already helped unify communities, stabilize economies, and provide access to information in areas where it was previously unavailable. Mobile technology has been used to monitor and verify election results, coordinate political protests, and enable disaster-management teams.

- **Ubiquity**—We are quickly approaching a time when almost every person in the world has access to a mobile phone. In both developed and developing countries, people rely on mobile phones to conduct business, receive information, and interact socially. Faster mobile network connections are constantly becoming available around the world, deepening our reliance on mobile data above and beyond our reliance on simple voice and text messaging. This ubiquity has broad social and cultural implications that have already had a dramatic impact on many people's day-to-day lives.

- **Relevance**—Mobile marketing messages can be location specific, time specific, and even person specific, making the message highly relevant to the person receiving it. Messages can even be tailored to meet the needs of a person or company at the exact moment that the need arises—all of which exponentially improves the relevance of the message. Mobile technology is also the first communication channel that creates messages that can be saved and opened later—at the exact moment when they are relevant—without the risk of the message being lost or damaged in the process (such as when coupons are clipped or ads are printed).

These themes have fed my passion for all things mobile. They are fundamental differences that make mobile a uniquely powerful marketing technology. People around the globe have allowed themselves to become deeply dependant on a small piece of technology called a mobile phone, and that is what makes it so darn important!

I deeply hope that you find this book very valuable. I have done everything possible to present an unbiased synopsis, supplementing my own knowledge and experience with research and case studies, and calling upon industry experts to review my work whenever possible. This book has taken the better part of a year to research and write, and in that time, things have already changed dramatically. The editorial team and I have done our best to ensure that the chapters are all as current as possible at the date of launch, but if we have missed something, please forgive us. The hope is that the book gives you the foundational knowledge you need to make the right plan, hire the right people, and set the right expectations so that your mobile marketing initiatives succeed. Thanks for reading it!

1

Getting Started with Mobile Marketing

Many elements make mobile marketing remarkable. This type of marketing is uniquely suited to help potential customers find you or learn about your products precisely when they need them. Many customers have their phones with them all the time, frequently as their primary means of communication with the rest of the world. Many people even report that they would be "lost" without their cellphone and find it hard to imagine life without it.

The Potential of Mobile Marketing

Analysts have been saying that it was "the year for mobile" for a long time, and this has created a false expectation. Mobile marketing will evolve just like traditional online marketing did—over time. It will see small surges as technology improves or key demographics change, but overall, we can expect the growth and acceptance of mobile marketing to follow a normal or slightly accelerated acceptance curve, similar to the growth of traditional Internet marketing.

Mobile marketing describes any attempt to appeal to potential customers with some sort of marketing message. Describing it in more concrete terms is difficult, because the term mobile marketing encompasses such a wide variety of activities, including

- Mobile advertising, in which brands pay to display visual ads embedded within the content of another website
- SMS and MMS
- Location-based mobile marketing
- Mobile applications
- Mobile search marketing
- Offline marketing in TV, radio and print
- Online marketing on websites, in searches, and with email

We are building on what we have learned from traditional Web marketing, but the technology will still have to work its way into society, as with every other marketing-laden technology before it. When other technologies were new, many people thought they could live without things such as TV, radio, and Internet. Not until the technologies sufficiently proved their value did they became tightly integrated into our society. There may not be a "year of mobile," but it is definitely the next new marketing opportunity. You must understand it or risk being left behind, because mobile marketing promises to be the most personal, targeted, and actionable marketing available in our time.

The following sections detail what makes mobile marketing something you can't afford not to master.

Mobile Marketing Is the Most Personal Form of Web Marketing

I like to joke that the only thing more personal than a person's cell phone is his underwear. Mobile phones are not shared, like traditional phones or desktop computers might be, so they are a uniquely targeted means of communication. The mobile phone is the most personal piece of technology that most of us will ever own.

- Our mobile phones are with us all the time. They know who we call and who we text, and they can triangulate where we are throughout the day.

- Smart phones have access to our entire address book and calendar. They can see what websites we are looking at and what applications we are downloading.

- Our mobile phones know what kind of entertainment we like. We use them to download and play videos, play games, or listen to music.

- Mobile phones can even hold and distribute digital likenesses of us with cameras, videos, and voice recordings.

Mobile Marketing Is the Most Targeted Form of Web Marketing

We can tell a lot about a person based just on cell phone use. In many ways, the mobile phone and the way it is used can provide powerful demographic and psychographic signals about the owner. People choose different carriers, handsets, or phone features because of their social and utilitarian needs. As marketers, we should use this information to present our audience with the most compelling marketing possible.

We can learn a lot about people from the handset they purchase. Businesspeople frequently choose devices that offer the best corporate email solution and allow simple computing, perhaps BlackBerrys or Treos. The more mod subscribers in the crowd will choose phones that focus more on applications and aesthetics, such as the iPhone or the HTC Dream. Teenagers and the younger crowd will choose phones such as the SideKick, to allow them to stay connected to their friends through text messaging, gaming, instant messaging (IM), and social networks.

Similarly, we can sometimes glean demographic and psychographic information about our audience based on the carrier for their mobile service. Although AT&T, Sprint, and Verizon do not target unique demographic profiles, smaller carriers and service resellers, called MVNOs (mobile virtual network operators) do cater to specific audiences. For instance:

- People who get service from Boost Mobile or Helio tend to be young and male.

- Virgin Mobile users also tend to be young but are more evenly split between the genders.

- People with service through Cricket, Blyk, or MOSH Mobile tend to be thrifty or have a lower income.

- People with service from BeyondMobile tend to be businesspeople.

Savvy marketers should have a good understanding of the demographic and psychographic indicators of their target market, as well as the top visitors to their website.

Mobile Marketing is a More Immediate Form of Web Marketing

Because our mobile phones are always with us, they make any message that we receive immediately available. And because we use our cell phones to stay connected with the rest of the world, we check them often—sometimes habitually or incessantly—which is also very powerful. This immediacy makes mobile marketing an extraordinary marketing option for last-minute or time-sensitive calls to action. The mobile nature of the delivery increases the odds that the recipient is already "out and about" and available to act immediately on information.

Mobile Marketing Is More Actionable Than Other Forms of Web Marketing

Mobile phones combine a number of technologies that close the gap between the "real world" that we live in and the "interactive" world that we market in. The convergence of technology in the cell phone has simplified and streamlined many actions:

- To upload a picture to the Internet, you used to have to take the picture with your digital camera, plug the camera into the computer, download the picture to the computer, and then upload the picture to the Internet. Now you can simply take a picture with your camera phone and immediately upload it to the Web.

- To place a call to a number you didn't know, you used to have to look up a phone number on a computer, and then switch devices and type the phone number into your phone. On a mobile phone, when you've found the phone number, you simply click on it to be connected.

- To make digital copies of music or movies, you used to have to download the files to your computer and then burn them to a CD or transfer them to a player. Mobile phones enable you to download and consume those files seamlessly, all on one device.

Mobile marketing enables us to make our marketing messages more interactive and actionable, which has a direct impact on the bottom line. It simplifies interaction between the brand and the customer, making it much easier for our customers to interact with our brand. It removes some of the barriers that previously prevented people from responding to our marketing message and from taking the call to action.

Mobile as a Direct Marketing Channel

In simple terms, direct marketing relies on the availability of our target market to receive and understand our marketing message directly, so mobile marketing falls neatly into this category of marketing. When compared to other types of direct marketing, the mobile phone offers a greatly expanded opportunity for our target market to receive our direct marketing messages. It has drastically changed our perception of availability, and this has changed how we market our products and services. Mobile marketing enables us to tap into the true essence of direct marketing as never before.

Direct marketing with mobile devices offers a lot of advantages over other types of direct marketing. It is particularly useful because it has these characteristics:

- Cost effective
- Scalable
- Targeted
- Personal
- Shareable
- Portable
- Flexible

- Interactive
- Immediate
- Measurable
- Effective
- Actionable
- Repeatable
- Fun

Mobile marketing also has the power to convert traditional marketing efforts into direct-response campaigns. TV or radio commercials that were previously just one-way broadcast messages—with minimal opportunity for a direct response—can be made interactive and trackable when combined with a mobile call to action.

Instructions telling potential customers to interact with your brand become more powerful when people can act on them immediately—and because most people keep their mobile phone with them at all times, mobile calls to action are more compelling than simply including a Web address or phone number and hoping the viewer will remember it later. When mobile communication calls to action are included, we close the loop and shorten the gap between us sending the message and recipients acting on it. The mobile phone is such a capable response mechanism that all types of direct marketing are lifted to the next level of effectiveness.

Direct Marketing That Is Personal

Mobile marketing is really the most personal direct marketing channel out there because of the variety of communication options it opens for us to reach a specific consumer with a specific message. It leverages the power of standard direct-marketing techniques and makes the message consumable and immediately actionable with one device.

Mobile marketing offers a bevy of creative marketing opportunities because the responses to our calls to action can come in a variety of different media and are uniquely trackable to one specific user. Information you get via mobile tracking can add dimension to your understanding of the customer's preferences and enables you to vary the channels of communication so customers don't feel overwhelmed.

Mobile marketing is also uniquely suited for persona marketing. Persona marketing is based on the idea that your customers can usually be classified into three or four groups, based on their demographic, psychographic (personality, values, attitudes, interests, and so on), and behavioral needs. Customers are grouped based on similarities and are given a name to represent the group. For example, a store that sells professional beauty products might be marketing to the following personas:

> **Katie the Cosmetologist:** Katie is young and either is still in cosmetology school or has graduated in the past two years. She is still testing different products she likes and is easily enticed by sales and promotions. She wants to feel and look like a master stylist in her salon, but she is still working her way up the ropes. She comes into the store about once a week to see if there's anything new or on sale.

> **Sally the Salon Owner:** Sally is a bit older and more set in her ways. She owns or manages a salon. Although she used to be a stylist on the floor, she now spends most of her time on the administration and logistics of running the business. She has products that she buys regularly and in bulk, and she is slow to add anything new to her shopping list. She shops twice a month and is less price sensitive because she isn't interested in trying new products. Promotions that involve bulk purchases or that encourage her to spend a certain amount of money to receive a specific discount are persuasive to her.

> **Susan the At-Home Stylist:** Susan can be almost any age but is usually younger. She is tired of paying salon prices for treatments and services she can easily provide herself at home much more cheaply. She is usually less price sensitive than Katie because she is buying products only for her own use or for a very short list of friends. She is not a professional, so she needs more help knowing what to buy and how to use it, but she still loves a good bargain.

Each of these personas would benefit more from different types of offers and different types of marketing messages. Information collected via a mobile device can be used to categorize customers, and distinct messaging strategies can be created for each persona. Different messages and incentives can be sent to people in each persona over different periods of time, using different communication and response channels.

Direct Marketing That Is Portable

Before mobile email access and text messaging, we relied on our computers for even the simplest text-based communication. If we were in a meeting, in transit, or just away from our computer, we simply could not be reached via text-based communication (short of being passed a note during a meeting). With mobile email and text, even when we're not really available, messages are still put through and are waiting for us the minute we become available, even if only for a second. We are no longer tied to computers for text-based digital communication.

When text-based communication lost its ties to the traditional computer, it opened up a world of marketing opportunities. It enabled us to communicate without interrupting the recipient's day, and it provided recipients the opportunity to consume our message when it was convenient for them and to save it or carry it with them for future reference. Mobile text-based communication—different from other types of direct marketing—gave us the potential for durable, portable marketing messages that could be consumed quickly and politely at the recipient's leisure.

Direct Marketing That Is Persistent

Before everyone had cellphones, most direct marketing was tied to specific locations. Direct marketers reached people at addresses or phone numbers that a group of people usually shared. A marketer's ability to communicate with people largely depended on people actually being at specific places. Marketers were forced to anticipate where people were, at whatever time they wanted to reach them. If people moved, went on vacation, or were just out and about, they were unavailable to receive our marketing messages.

Now, in a world where most adults (as well as many children and teens) have cellphones, we can more easily reach exactly who we are looking for, when we want to market to them. This is because mobile phone numbers are assigned to specific *people* instead of specific *locations*, and they are rarely used by more than one person. Mobile phones go with people when they move, go on vacation, or just go out to run errands.

This means we have more opportunity, as marketers, to reach the people we are trying to market to and less risk that our message will be screened out or lost by those who are not the intended recipient. We can spend less time simply trying to reach the person with our offer and more time crafting a persuasive marketing message and a meaningful call to action.

Direct Marketing That Is Intelligent

The data that we can gather about our customers through mobile marketing initiatives also can inform future marketing campaigns. Mammoth customer relationship management (CRM) systems and preference centers can be built off information available directly from a phone response. These systems can give marketers the opportunity to create deep, enduring relationships with their customers.

A good CRM system should be used to ensure that the right marketing messages reach the right customers exactly when they are most relevant. Triggered response emails and text messages can be set up to respond to any interaction that the user has with the brand, and they can be also be scheduled based on personal specifications that the user indicates in the preference center.

Some companies are already doing this: Some banks send account holders text messages when checks post to their accounts, and some pharmacies send text messages reminding recipients to refill their prescriptions. Other types of companies can leverage CRM systems for similar initiatives or for more creative mobile marketing efforts. Users will appreciate the high level of personalization and the responsiveness that you can show them, and this will help build trust and loyalty for your brand.

If you are using persona marketing in conjunction with your CRM database, you will be able to predict the communication preferences of new users based on the preferences of others in their persona group. If you can accurately predict a user's communication preferences, you can begin sending more effective and targeted messages to new customers more quickly—and you eliminate the possibility that they will become frustrated and unsubscribe from your communication lists.

Is Mobile Marketing Right for You?

Although mobile marketing can be powerful, it is not appropriate for every company. It has unique assets that make it particularly advantageous for some initiatives, but it is not predictable or stable enough for other initiatives. As with any marketing campaign, a mobile marketing effort must be closely considered and evaluated before the work begins. Companies that don't offer the right product or service, or don't have enough resources to get it right, should wait to undertake a mobile marketing project. Understand your audience, know your objectives, and be prepared to fail.

So when should mobile marketing be used?

Brands

Well-known brands generally have different goals than lesser-known companies. Their objectives are more focused on maintaining brand equity and building brand loyalty, which can be done very effectively with mobile marketing. Most of the first forays into mobile marketing were undertaken by big brands that wanted to test the channel. Big brands tend to have bigger budgets that they can use to test new technologies and to reinvent themselves to appear innovative and new.

Big brands also usually have more research and information about their customers, to help segment and direct their marketing efforts. To target their messages appropriately, big brands—especially big brands that have a variety of product lines— should limit their mobile messaging to a specific type of product or service. For example, someone who wants to buy a $30 leather dog collar from Coach is likely very different from the person who wants a full set of Coach luggage. Similarly, a shopper who is interested in Apple software may be very different from a shopper who is interested in an iPod Shuffle.

Brands Case Study 1

Many international car manufacturers have made a good entrance into mobile marketing, the most notable being BMW, which has undertaken a number of great mobile marketing projects. To sell more snow tires in fall 2008, BMW tire centers in Germany sent customized MMS messages to all the people in their customer database who owned BMWs. The message reminded recipients of the importance of snow tires in bad driving conditions. It had a personalized greeting, recommended a specific tire for their car, gave the price, and listed dealerships in their area. The campaign achieved 30% conversion rate, which is no doubt attributable to the targeted nature of the offer to their list of recipients.

Brands Case Study 2

Starbucks is another company that embraced mobile marketing early. Starbucks tried a number of different campaigns, but in 2009, it launched a mobile loyalty campaign in Mexico that saw tremendous success. It started with postcards that encouraged the recipient to text the word "Starbucks" to a short code. When users texted in, they received a 2D barcode (QR codes) coupon that could be scanned off the phone in the Starbucks cafes. The offer changed each time the barcode was scanned, so recipients were encouraged to redeem the coupon multiple times. Starbucks experienced a 60% redemption rate on the first redemption of the coupons, and the program created an engaged audience of recipients.

Brands Case Study 3

NASCAR is another big brand that has had massive success with mobile marketing. NASCAR has gone in a different direction, working directly with carriers such as Sprint to provide fans with special NASCAR features on some handsets that Sprint offers. NASCAR has also had success with text messaging and ring tone downloads, as well as Bluetooth location-based marketing at races. NASCAR has integrated mobile marketing with TV broadcasts during races and with its branded reality show, *NASCAR Angels*. Additionally, NASCAR has experimented with mobile microsites dedicated to helping its audience save gas. This project has included a mobile coupon element that gave participants discounts at ExxonMobile and Auto Zone.

Brick-and-Mortar Establishments

Stores, restaurants, and entertainment venues are in a unique position to leverage mobile marketing because of their ability to target local foot traffic. They can set up location-based Bluetooth broadcasts that send marketing messages directly to the consumer when they are in the area. They can also develop strategies that incorporate outdoor advertising, to allow users to text in for specials, menus, show times, directions, or other information.

In many instances, urban areas are largely segmented by the type of business in the area. Shopping, restaurants, and entertainment venues might be in one area; business and commerce locations might be in another; and transportation services might be in another. This makes targeting your mobile marketing message simple because the potential recipients have self-identified their interests.

The type of messaging that works best for brick-and-mortar stores depends on the product or service being provided. In general, your mobile messaging should be as specific and actionable as possible. If you are a store, give specific deals with expiration dates and instructions for redemption. If you are a restaurant, send out your specials for the evening and include prices. Restaurants can even allow visitors to text in to get on a waiting list, or receive a text message when their table is ready. Concert venues or clubs can let people know important details about the show, such as who will be playing and when, and how much it costs to get into the venue.

Brick-and-Mortar Establishments Case Study 1

In Oswestry, England, in 2007, a text-messaging campaign created by a restaurant called The Venue encouraged diners to text the word "Venue" to a short code to add themselves to a list that would receive special offers and notifications via text. After only two text-message broadcasts, the average number of diners in the restaurant more than tripled. This was ideal for the restaurant because it could send out text messages at exactly the time it wanted to bring in foot traffic. The restaurant also noted that this approach saved time and money compared to the print flyers it had tried previously.

Brick-and-Mortar Establishments Case Study 2

In 2009, T-Mobile launched a Bluetooth marketing campaign that targeted London shoppers as they passed local T-Mobile stores. Graphics in store windows encouraged passersby to activate their Bluetooth. Those who did, or who already had Bluetooth enabled, were sent messages encouraging them to upgrade their phone to one of the T-Mobile exclusive handsets. T-Mobile reported an increase in foot traffic and sales in stores, and noted that customers seemed very interested in the marketing initiative.

Brick-and-Mortar Establishments Case Study 3

In 2007 in Las Vegas, the MGM Grand created a marketing campaign that started with "moving billboards" driving the strip. (These were actually small trucks with billboards on the rear of the cabs.) The billboards advertised the award-winning nightlife at venues within the MGM Grand and encouraged pedestrians to text in to be "added to the VIP list." People who texted in a code were sent a response asking for their first and last name and the number of people in their party. The campaign successfully drove traffic into the casinos and also helped build a database of people who opted in to receive text messages.

Events

Mobile marketing is particularly valuable for things that happen in real time, such as sporting events, concerts, conferences, and conventions. Savvy marketers can reach a targeted consumer base exactly when the consumer has the desire to interact. This type of mobile marketing can make an event run more smoothly, create goodwill with attendees, and enable the organizers to build a mobile marketing database of contact information to use in subsequent marketing efforts. The following are some examples of event-based mobile marketing:

- **Sporting events**—Many stadiums have begun to encourage interaction by creating text-in contests and polling, revealing the results to visitors while they are still in the venue. When visitors text in a response to the prompt, an auto-response can be sent, encouraging them to opt in for team statistics and discounts on tickets, food, and beverages in the venue.

- **Concerts and clubs**—Visitors can also be reached with contests and polls. Attendees can be encouraged to send pictures or text from their mobile phone to a particular short code, and those messages can quickly be displayed on a large monitor in the venue, to add to the experience. Alternately, the venue can encourage visitors to text in when they hear a song that they like so that a link to a downloadable ring-tone or MP3 can be sent back. MP3s and other downloads that are promoted at the event can even be set up with short pre-roll advertise-ments or branded message that remind the recipient about the venue or about upcoming shows.

- **Conferences and conventions**—Marketers have the opportunity to leverage many services that can be consumed on the mobile phone. For example, the event might sponsor or provide such things as free WiFi and text-message notifications. Conferences can offer name badges that mobile phones can scan, to immediately enter new contacts into the phone.

Events Case Study 1

At the Pick 'n Pay Argus Cycle Tour in Cape Town, cyclists were encouraged to enter a contest hosted by Powerade to win prizes at the event. To participate, they had to download a packet of free content to their phone. The content included Powerade ringtones and wallpapers, along with a bar code that would be scanned off the phone to determine whether the recipient had won. The initiative helped reinforce the brand with its target market, but it also did a good job of driving visi-tors to the booth at the event, which increased the sales of other products offered that day.

Events Case Study 2

At the Event Marketing Summit in Chicago in 2009, attendees were encouraged to text "EMSUMMIT" to a short code to interact more with the event. After opting in, attendees could get schedule updates and reminders on their phone, but they could also interact with speakers in real time by texting comments or questions to be displayed on the venue's main screen. A company called Mozes provided the text-to-screen capability as part of a self-promotion campaign at the event, so participants also received text messages reminding them to visit the Mozes booth at the show to enter more raffles and learn more about the technology.

Events Case Study 3

In 2007 in the United Kingdom, at an event called V Festival (sponsored by Virgin Mobile), concertgoers and festival attendees were encouraged to download a Mobile Festival Survival Kit that included a variety pack of different content for their phones. Multiple mobile survival kits were distributed, and they included things such as brightly colored flashing screen savers to help friends find each other in the dark and short animations of a flame, to be held up in place of a lighter during concert ballads. The survival kit also encouraged people to sign up for text messages to alert them when different bands were about to go on stage.

Who Is Mobile Marketing Wrong For?

Believe it or not, mobile marketing isn't the answer for some companies—at least, not yet:

- **Companies without the resources**—The mobile marketing industry is still coming together and remains in flux. Companies that don't have the financial resources to test campaigns and possibly fail should consider waiting until the channel is more solid and predictable. In fact, for some companies, it might be best to wait until there are more tools to simplify the mobile marketing process. Mobile marketing is not for the faint of heart. It requires planning, money, and manpower. Companies should always be prepared to fail and should understand that it might take a couple tries to get it right.

- **Companies without an objective**—The mobile phone gives every marketing medium the potential for a direct response, so having a specific call to action is crucial to the success of a mobile marketing campaign. Calls to action can encourage anything from responding to a print or TV call to action, to signing up for text alerts, placing a call from your site, or requesting directions to your store.

  Calls to action highlight the conversion events in your campaign. Viewers "convert" when they take some action that you suggest or offer. Multiple conversion events should be tracked with each initiative, and each conversion event should be assigned some monetary value to help you determine the return on investment for the campaign. Without a clear call to action, gauging the success of your campaign will be more difficult. Mobile marketing is new and exciting, but that shouldn't be why you initiate a campaign. Your marketing efforts must create some type of value or return on investment to be successful. Always set clear objectives and targets so you can evaluate your success.

- **Companies without the technical resources to handle the response—** Nothing is worse than having a good response to your marketing campaign and having technology fail. Even your first mobile marketing campaign has the potential to be fantastically successful and highly viral, so you must plan for that, too. Before you launch a campaign, make sure that you have process-tested and load-tested all the back-end technology. This includes anything that you will be using to send or receive text messages, take calls, provide downloads, or spark any other conversion events that your campaign might include.

Not only can a technology failure waste time and money, but it will eliminate all the value you created in the communication. Technology failure can cause long-term damage to your relationship with customers, making it much less likely that they will respond to your mobile calls to action in the future.

- **Companies without the human resources and inventory to handle the response—**Determining what the response rate of a mobile marketing campaign will be can be difficult, but it is important to plan for both extremely good and disappointingly bad response rates. If your mobile marketing campaign includes in-person aspects, such as creating foot traffic to a brick-and-mortar establishment, it is important for the location to be staffed and ready to handle any surge in customers.

In some cases, such as with Bluetooth and WiFi broadcasts, when your restaurant or venue has reached maximum capacity, your message can be throttled or stopped completely. In other cases, such as with billboards or banners near your brick-and-mortar store, you have less ability to update the messaging. If you are trying to drive foot traffic into a store for a specific item and you run out of that item, you are in a similar pickle. Basically, if you don't have enough inventory or availability, you should rethink mobile marketing until those are more secure or until you have a very good understanding of the response rate you can expect.

2

Understanding the Challenges in Mobile Marketing

Many different elements must come together to build the mobile marketing experiences that we desire to create for our target audience. The number of possible combinations of handsets, browsers, operating systems, and networks can create exponential problems for mobile marketers who are not ready to face the challenge. And although it is important to understand the many aspects of mobile content delivery, it is also crucial to understand that you won't be able to address every possibility. Focusing on the minutia is more time-consuming than it is worth and likely will stall your project and have a direct negative impact on the ROI.

One of the most important things you must do when planning a mobile marketing campaign is to anticipate where your campaign or message might fail, and adapt to include alternative or contingency messaging. Know how your message will appear in the best-case rendering scenario and in the worst-case rendering scenario. Then do what you can to ensure that there is an elegant degradation between the best- and worst-case scenarios, in which limited rendering technology will cause more complex elements of the campaign to silently fail, in favor of less complex elements. Your message should always be clear and compelling, regardless of the technological difficulties.

The Changing Face of Telecom

Internationally, traditional land-line service providers, Internet service providers (ISPs), and mobile service providers are struggling to address the rapidly changing demands of their consumers. As services such as TV, phone, radio, and Internet become exclusively digital, many companies are fighting to protect their interests and expand their service offerings.

As many households eliminate land lines and switch to mobile phones and VoIP, traditional phone service suppliers are struggling to maintain their sources of revenue. Similarly, as many homes and businesses turn from copper-wire broadband Internet access to wireless broadband, traditional ISPs become more concerned that they will not be able to recoup their investment. Cable TV companies are threatened because people are accessing TV and movies on the computers and mobile phones. Even mobile networks are threatened by pressure from other carriers to decrease the cost of mobile data communication and, further, by subscribers who rely more heavily on data than voice communication. Some mobile subscribers even use their "unlimited data plans" with VoIP technology to totally circumvent the need for carrier-provided voice communication.

All of this unrest should be taken as a clear signal that the telecom industry is on the brink of major change. We are about to enter a period in which consolidation will be the only avenue that will effectively address the consumer's needs. Consolidation will be good, but it will still leave the companies struggling to turn a profit, as the price for data- and IP-based communication continues its race to the bottom.

The good news for mobile marketers is that many of the key players are looking to advertising and marketing as their saving grace. Each of the different companies that provide data-based service can access subscribers' information and track their behavior. When the multitude of different companies consolidate and combine their efforts, they will have access to a great deal of information about their subscribers' digital consumption habits. Traditional phone, broadband, and cable TV service providers are quickly realizing the power that this kind of information has for marketers and are adjusting their business models to include an advertising and content-targeting profit center.

The History of Mobile Network Technologies

To understand and anticipate the future, it is important to understand the past. A very strong correlation exists between the history of traditional Internet marketing and the history of mobile marketing. At first, mobile devices were used purely as a utility, much like the Internet. Not until the technology had thoroughly penetrated the mainstream market did marketers understood the power of the medium.

Mobile marketing can cover a variety of different initiatives, but it began with text and picture message marketing, the creation of mobile-friendly websites, and mobile banner advertising. Now marketers can place advertising within mobile games and mobile videos, and even within a mobile TV broadcast. More creative mobile marketers are also using full-screen interstices, which appear while a requested webpage is loading, in addition to location-based Bluetooth marketing and interactive mobile games and applications to entice their audiences.

Before you can understand the nuances of those types of marketing initiatives, you must understand the evolution of the mobile networks, handsets, operating systems, and mobile browsers. This chapter explains how those technologies have evolved and discusses how all the innovations come together to affect your marketing message.

Mobile phones are only as powerful as the network technology that runs them. A network's speed can have a huge impact on what types of mobile marketing will be successful with your demographic. Understanding how the different network technologies interact will help you make critical decisions about your mobile marketing campaign. Figure 2.1 shows the 15-year evolution of mobile networks. The following sections briefly explain each of the major mobile network technologies.

1G

The first generation of cellphone signals was based on a circuit-switching domain and relied on an analog radio signal transmitted by the phone and picked up by towers. Radio towers used digital signals to connect to other radio towers and then to the rest of the telephone network. Because G1 technology relied on analog instead of digital signals, they were less reliant on the caller's proximity to a cellphone tower.

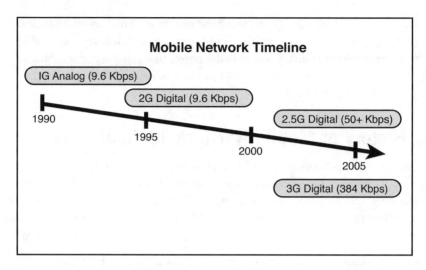

Figure 2.1 *Mobile networks have grown from 1G speeds of just 9.6 Kbps to 3G speeds of 384 Kbps in just 15 years, with 4G networks in the near future.*

2G

2G networks are the second generation of cellphone networks that relied on a digital signal instead of a radio signal. This technology, launched in Finland in 1991, is based primarily on a packet-switching protocol for transferring voice digitally. Phones that ran on a 2G network were smaller and had better battery life because they were not required to emit as strong of a radio signal. The voice quality on 2G phone networks was generally better and more secure because of digital encryption. Because 2G technology relied on a digital signal instead of analog signal, it was able to transmit more than voice, such as text messages and email.

2G technology was good for the carriers because it was more efficient on the spectrum. It allowed carriers to push a higher volume of calls through their network, but it relied more on proximity to a cellphone tower; when a caller moved out of range, calls were dropped entirely instead of progressively degrading. Technologies that are directly related to 2G are code division multiple access (CDMA), time division multiplex access (TDMA), and Global System for Mobile Communications (GSM).

CDMA

Used in North and South America as well as Asia, this subset of 2G technology still accounts for 17% of subscribers in the world. In code division multiple access (CDMA), the system relies on each phone being assigned a specific code, which allows multiple users to be put on the same transmission channel.

TDMA

Most 2G networks relied on time division multiplex access (TDMA) to transmit digital signals that were divided into different time slots instead of codes, as in CDMA. The signals are sent in rapid succession, all while sharing one digital channel. The timing requirements for this type of technology frequently made it unreliable as a mobile phone transmission technology because when callers moved closer to or farther away from a tower, they would misalign the timing requirements of the system and disrupt the transmission.

GSM

Global System for Mobile Communications (GSM) was developed to address some of the shortfalls of TDMA technology. It was originally created in Finland in 1991 and is now used around the world. It requires timing advance commands to be sent to the base station, which sends signals to the mobile phone, telling it whether it should transmit the signal earlier and, if so, by how much. It accounts for 80% of the subscribers around the world. GSM is the most ubiquitous set of standards for mobile phones. Because of its success, many other 2G technologies, including CDMA and TDMA, eventually transferred to GSM. GSM is so widespread that international roaming is now much more simple, because phones can almost always access a signal that they can use.

2.5G

2.5G networks offer some improvements over 2G networks but are not quite as fast as 3G networks. They use a circuit-switching domain for voice communication and a packet-switching domain for data communication. This set of standards enables high-speed data transfer over existing 2G GSM or CDMA networks that have been upgraded, and it usually describes when a 2G network has been upgraded with GPRS for data transmission. Technologies that are directly related to 2.5G are GPRS, EDGE, and iDEN.

GPRS

The first improvement in mobile data transmission, Generated Packet Radio Service (GPRS), can be added to 2G, GSM, or 3G networks. GPRS achieves moderate improvements in data transmission by using TDMA to improve packet switching over the mobile network. As with many other technologies, after its initial deployment, GPRS technology was later integrated into GSM.

EDGE

Enhanced Data Rates for GSM Evolution (EDGE) was launched in the United States by Cingular in 2003. Through optimization of packet switching, it provides better than a threefold improvement over other networks in capacity and performance of data transmission, making mobile computing and data transmission much more valuable. Sometimes referred to as 2.75G, EDGE improved the rate of data transmission over GSM networks. Although it was originally intended for GSM, it can be added to 2G, 2.5G, and GPRS networks as well.

iDEN

Integrated Digital Enhanced Network (iDEN) combined voice compression with TDMA to improve on 1G radio telephony. It is a proprietary subset of 2G technology developed by Motorola and used by Nextel in the United States and Telus in Canada. The technology is important for Nokia and Telus because it allows for push-to-talk radio and dispatch functionality that enables mobile phones to be used as long-range walkie-talkies. Many airports also use iDEN networks to enable their push-to-talk handsets.

3G

The third full generation of mobile technology, 3G networks can provide more advanced services while achieving higher network capacity than 2G technology. In terms of data, they provide mobile phones with broadband- or near-broadband-speed transmission. These networks are functionally similar to WiFi but are meant to cover a much larger area. The first 3G network was launched in Japan by DoCoMo; later the next year, SKTelecom launched another in South Korea. Monet Mobile Networks and Verizon were the first to launch 3G technology in the United States in 2003, and the 3 Network was the first to launch in Europe (the United Kingdom and Italy). (Download: 5.8Mbps, upload: 14.4Mbps).

4G

4G systems represent a collection of wireless standards that are all adapted to be 100% packet and IP based. They will be a complete replacement for current networks and will provide a comprehensive and secure IP solution where voice, data, and streamed multimedia can be given to users on an "anytime, anywhere" basis. 4G networks are designed to give subscribers access to much richer content on their phones, including IPTV, streaming audio and video, digital video broadcast, and video chat, at much higher data rates than previous generations. 4G promises higher network capacity and more simultaneous users per cell. (Download and upload: 15–30Mbps) Technologies directly related to 4G are WiMax, LTE, and Clearwire.

WiMax

WiMax is an IP network designed to move data instead of voice communication. It could replace mobile technologies such as GSM and CDMA or simply can be added to networks with GSM and DSMA to increase their capacity. The WiMAX Forum was formed in June 2001 to promote conformity and interoperability of the standard, called WiMAX. The group describes WiMAX as "a standards-based technology enabling the delivery of last mile wireless broadband access as an alternative to cable and DSL."

Questions still surround the viability of WiMax technology. Sprint and Clearwire are the only large service providers that have committed to using WiMax for mobile technology. Most other service providers that have embraced WiMax are using it as a fixed wireless technology. The WiMax forum anticipates that the WiMax mobile networks will focus less on service to mobile phones and more on service to other wireless Web-enabled devices.

LTE

Long-Term Evolution (LTE) it is an IP data network that optimizes the transmission of data (rather than voice) packets. It is expected to be deployed in 2010, but it competes with WiMax as the 4G standard of choice for network operators. AT&T and Verizon Wireless in the United States and many European carriers have already said they plan to use LTE instead of WiMax because it appears to be more efficient. LTE promises to bring high-speed data access not only to mobile phones, but also to HD TVs, LTE-enabled music players, and much more. Some people believe that WiMax technology will be subsumed into LTE, but that debate is still being played out.

Clearwire

Clearwire is a brand-name wireless Internet service provider (ISP) that operates in the United States, Ireland, Belgium, Spain, Denmark, and Mexico. It provides a unique wireless network that uses WiMax technology with 3G technology to provide 4G wireless network access. Clearwire launched in the United States in 2008, but its goal is to provide nationwide 4G network connections in the future. The company has been testing many different high-speed mobile technologies but has been criticized because it has not adopted the WiMax technology.

WLAN and WiFi

Wireless local area network (WLAN) technology is Internet access that is broadcast from wireless access points, otherwise known as wireless routers or "hotspots." These wireless access points send short-range radio signals that can be accessed by a variety of different devices, such as PCs, game consoles, mobile phones, MP3 players, and PDAs. Many people use the terms *WLAN* and *WiFi* interchangeable, but WiFi is actually a designation to indicate a specific WLAN technology that has been certified by the WiFi Alliance.

Bluetooth

Developed in 1994 but popularized in the late 1990s, Bluetooth technology uses radio broadcast to allow multiple proximal devices to recognize each other and send information between them wirelessly. When multiple Bluetooth devices are linked in a group, it is called a personal area network (PAN). Bluetooth can connect many devices, including mobile phones, computers, printers, digital cameras, and video game consoles, and allow them to pass information back and forth.

VoIP

VoIP stands for voice over Internet Protocol or voice over IP. It is simply a means of using a broadband Internet signal to transmit voice. Skype and Vonage were the first to make this type of communication mainstream. With the addition of a signal converter or a headset on the computer, VoIP calling allows computers to have phone calls with other computers or directly with phones. Because this can be done at a very low cost, many traditional phone service carriers are losing customers to VoIP services. As mobile data networks improve, mobile VoIP is becoming a reality that many mobile careers are reticent to embrace.

FemtoCell

FemtoCell is a technology that is used indoors to boost indoor mobile handset signals by converting a wired broadband signal into a radio signal that mobile phones can pick up. AT&T, Sprint, and Verizon already offer FemtoCell base stations for subscribers' homes, and it is also being deployed in some commercial locations. This type of technology will likely be important for improving access to mobile marketing messages to your demographic when they are inside and mobile signals are weaker.

UMA

Similar to FemtoCell, UMA is deployed through a base station that uses WiFi signals to carry voice and data from mobile handsets to a base station. The base station provides improved access to GSM and GPRS by tapping into unlicensed aspects of the network spectrum. In the United States, this is being promoted by T-Mobile; in the United Kingdom, it is being promoted by British Telecom.

The Evolution of Mobile Devices, Handsets, and Operating Systems

Just as a marketing message is only as powerful as the network sending it, it is only as powerful as the handset that is receiving it. The capability and evolution of mobile computing has always been directly tied to the handset. Before you launch a mobile marketing campaign, you must understand what type of devices will be displaying your marketing message.

The true predecessor of the mobile phone is actually the two-way radios used by sea captains, ambulances, and police cruisers. These set the groundwork for the first mobile phones, which also operated on radio signals through the G1 mobile networks. The first mobile phones were large and cumbersome, and not at all intended for mobile computing. They simply tapped into analog radio frequencies to receive and send calls. The first commercially available cellphones were designed to be permanently installed in cars, drawing power directly from the car battery. Later models—the size of a briefcase—were "transportable" and could be plugged in to the cigarette lighter in the car to get power, but they were quite heavy, usually weighing in at about 15 pounds.

The next evolution of the mobile phone was apparent with the introduction of a truly handheld cellphone, affectionately referred to as the "brick phone." In 1983 the Motorola DynaTAC was the first mobile phone to receive FCC approval in the United States (see Figure 2.2). It

Figure 2.2 *1983: Motorola's DynaTAC 8000X "brick phone" was the world's first commercially released mobile phone. Photo courtesy of Motorola.*

weighed about 2 pounds and cost about $4,000, and had a battery that would last for about half an hour without recharging.

As technology improved, cell phones switched from 1G analog radio signals to a 2G digital signal, which allowed them to become much lighter and smaller. The addition of GSM technology also enabled newer phones to send the first text messages (see Figure 2.3).

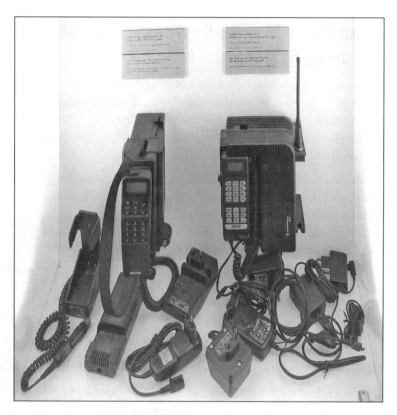

Figure 2.3 *The first phones capable of text messages—two 2G GSM phones with chargers and base stations. Photo courtesy of Clemens Pfeiffer via Wikimedia Creative Commons License 2.5, a freely licensed media repository.*

Mobile computing was actually a reality long before mobile phones were deeply integrated into our society. It began with the first laptops, when the idea of mobile computing was quite revolutionary. Laptops allowed people to take their computer with them instead of having to save information on disks and rely on accessing a desktop PC wherever they went. This was important for people who required a specific set of software to perform certain tasks, but in many cases, laptops were too cumbersome for people to lug around on a daily basis. Despite the drawbacks of these first laptops, they were the genesis of all other types of "mobile" data technology.

Mobile computing hit a new plateau with the evolution of personal digital assistants, otherwise known as PDAs. Businesspeople commonly used PDAs to keep track of their calendar and address book. The first PDAs were not Web enabled, but usually included simple software to help their owner keep notes, set reminders, and perform simple calculations.

As time moved on and technology improved, mobile carriers began offering PDAs that were both voice and data enabled. In 1993, IBM and BellSouth launched the Simon Personal Communicator, the first mobile phone to add PDA features. It was a phone, pager, calculator, address book, fax machine, and email device, and was the predecessor to what we now call the smart phone.

The term "smart phone" was coined long after the first smart phones were commercially available. There is no agreed-upon definition for the term "smart phone," but it generally refers to a phone that has an operating system that allows applications to be added or removed, that can take and send data, and that can access Web content. The first true smart phone was the Nokia 9210, which offered an open operating system and a color screen, as well as email, text, and voice communication capabilities (see Figure 2.4). Palm also offered a series of Palm Pilots that ran the Palm operating system, had PDA features, had a full QWERTY keyboard, and were capable of sending data and voice transmissions.

Figure 2.4 *The first true smart phone—the Nokia 9210. Photo courtesy of Nokia.*

In 2001, Research In Motion (RIM) released the first BlackBerry. The BlackBerry was the first smart phone that really focused on improving the usability of mobile email communication. It ran the Symbian operating system, which could accept third-party applications, and it was widely adopted by business professionals who needed access to their email when they were not in the office. In 2002, Handspring launched the first Treo, and Microsoft launched the first Pocket PC, which ran the Windows Pocket PC operating system, now referred to as Windows Mobile. Both of these handsets offered a full QWERTY keyboard, making text and email communication much easier.

The Windows Mobile operating system now runs on many devices and is frequently used by Palm instead of its own operating system. In general, Windows Mobile devices provided much of the same functions as the previous smart phones, with a much nicer interface, similar to the desktop version of Windows. The Windows Mobile operating system also provided simplified versions of Microsoft software, such as Word and Excel, which were quite handy for power users.

Although these original smart phones were important to the advancement of mobile computing and quite useful for businesspeople, they were not widely adopted. These first smart phones and voice-enabled PDAs were quite expensive (between $400 and $800), and many of the functions were considered unnecessary for the normal user. In terms of mass adoption, the "candy bar" phone first offered by Nokia in 2003 was very popular; it offered some of the advanced features of the more capable phones yet sold for only $150 (see Figure 2.5). Text messaging or navigating the Web on this phone required users to type letters using the traditional phone keyboard. Users pressed number buttons multiple times, to represent different letters in the alphabet. Many users, and especially teens, became quite adept at this kind of text communication, but it was less than ideal.

Figure 2.5 *The first widely adopted and lower priced smart phone was Nokia's "candy bar" phone. Photo courtesy of Nokia.*

The first SideKick was launched in 2002 as a means of targeting more capable phones to the younger generation. It offered a full QWERTY keyboard, which made it much easier to send text and email. It had a large monochrome screen that slid up to reveal the keyboard, and it had a touch-pad that worked much like a mouse on a computer. It could surf the Web with the ability to render HTML, and it also introduced "chat," otherwise known as instant messaging, which had previously been accessible only on traditional computers. This was the first smart phone to be considered "cool" and was popularized partially because of its appearance in multiple rap and hip-hop music videos.

The Razr (see Figure 2.6), launched in 2004, was the next phone to be considered "cool." It had fewer capabilities than the SideKick, but it also had a much lower price point, which made it accessible for a larger demographic. Unlike the SideKick, it had a slim profile and was intended mostly for calling and texting. By 2007, the Razr was the single most widely distributed handset in the world.

The first-generation iPhone was launched in the United States in 2007 (see Figure 2.7). Considered a "multimedia smart phone," the iPhone made mobile computing much easier and more interactive than any previous phone, and it raised the bar in terms of the phone "cool factor." In 2008, the second-generation iPhone was launched, adding GPS and other services to the mix. The third-generation iPhone will launch later in 2009. Apple has seen the same success with the iPhone that it did with the iPod, creating a wide-spread cult following and truly raising the bar for the rest of the industry. In a pure evaluation of revenue, Apple is now the third-biggest manufacturer of cell phones worldwide, after Nokia and Samsung, and in 2008, the iPhone 3G surpassed the Razr as the most widely distributed handset in the world. The iPhone runs on its own Apple operating system that is easy to use and fun.

Figure 2.6 *The Razr had fewer capabilities than the SideKick but was much more affordable. Photo courtesy of Motorola.*

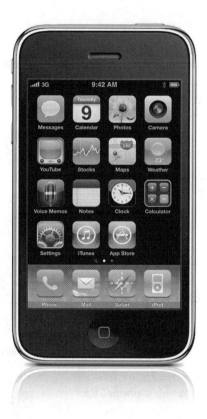

Figure 2.7 *The Apple iPhone revolutionized smart phones. Photo courtesy of Apple.*

The iPhone is considered the first true Web browsing phone because it can display full HTML Web pages almost exactly as they would be displayed on a traditional computer. It is highly customizable and has a large screen that adjusts itself based on whether you are viewing it in landscape or portrait mode. The iPhone has done so much to change the landscape for mobile marketing that I've dedicated an entire chapter in this book to understanding the technology (see Chapter 4, "Everything You Need to Know About the iPhone"). It is one of the best things that has ever happened to mobile marketing.

Since the launch of the iPhone, many carriers have begun offering iPhone clones that purport to offer a similar mobile experience, especially in terms of providing true Web browsing. In 2008, Google, T-Mobile, and HTC joined forces to launch the Dream, which was the first phone to run the Android operating system, created by Google. The Dream phone and Android operating system were meant to rival the iPhone in terms of Web browsing, the capacity for third-party applications, and the "cool" factor. Palm launched the Palm Pre in mid-2009, which also is intended to compete directly with the iPhone (see Figure 2.8). Despite much fanfare, it missed the mark, and none of the iPhone clones have yet to prove much of a threat to the iPhone.

Figure 2.8 *The Palm Pre is considered by many to be an iPhone clone. Though it has many nice features, it hasn't proven to be much of a threat to the iPhone.*

The History of Mobile Browsers

One of the hardest parts of working on the mobile Web is working with the mobile browsers, but each year the situation improves. To understand the evolution of mobile Web browsers, you only have to look to the evolution of traditional browsers.

The two technologies are similar and thus follow a familiar path in terms of milestones and innovations. Mobile browsers became a reality about 10 years after traditional browsers did, so all the major benchmarks in the evolution of mobile browsing occur 10 years after they did for traditional browsing.

In their genesis, both mobile and traditional Web browsers only rendered text and were navigated through text commands because they had no mouse devices. Because of many browsers that interpreted HTML slightly differently, Webmasters had difficulty anticipating how a website would look on different browsers. As browsers improved and consolidated, pictures and color were incorporated with the text, and directories and portals were created to help us move around the Web and find new websites. With the traditional Web, we got to a point where there were only three or four major browsers, and they all rendered HTML in a similar way. Unfortunately, mobile browsers have yet to hit that milestone.

Mobile browsers in 2009 are about where traditional browsers were in 1999. There has been some consolidation and movement toward a more similar rendering standard across all mobile browsers, but mobile Web rendering can still be unpredictable and difficult to control or get perfect.

Mobile browsers must overcome a number of hurdles that traditional browsers didn't have. Mobile browsers can potentially be loaded on an infinite number of handsets, each with different specifications, including screen size, available memory, input technologies (keypad, scroll wheel, touchscreen, and so on). With some phones, the browsers must work in both landscape and portrait mode, and different carriers may choose to block some handset technology not blocked by others. Some phone manufacturers also assign different functions to various buttons on the devices, further complicating mobile browsing.

It is also important to note that because mobile phones are constantly being improved and replaced, mobile Web browsers tend to go through more versions within a primary version number than traditional Web browsers do. On a traditional computer, users have to download a new browser each time there is an update, but mobile phones are shipped with a browser preloaded, so it is easier for the browser companies to distribute updated software whenever they have a new version. It is common for one mobile Web browser to already have many different versions that predate it.

The good news is that the situation is improving by leaps and bounds every year. The list of mobile browsers for which Web developers must develop is getting shorter, and the mobile browsers are coming ever closer to a unified rendering standard. The launch of true Web browsers in 2007 on mobile phones has already done a lot to change how people use their phone and think about Web access. Furthermore, an increasing number of digital devices, such as game stations, GPS units, and MP3 players, include a Web browser or, in some cases, a mobile Web browser.

Following is a list of common Web browsers in use today:

- **Openwave**—Credited with the launch of the first mobile browser in 1997 (but then operating under the name UnwiredPlanet), Openwave is still a popular mobile browser. It represented 29% of the mobile browsers in the world in 2008. The first OpenWave browsers supported only WAP, but the browser has updated to support HTML and other, more complex coding languages. It is a reliable mobile browser that is native on many mobile phones.

- **Nokia Browsers**—Nokia's first mobile browser launched in 1999 and was capable of rendering only WAP websites. It frequently accessed only WAP content provided directly from the mobile carrier. The original Nokia WAP browser was licensed to other handset manufacturers to help encourage the adoption of WAP programming standards. Subsequent versions of the mobile browser adapted with the technology to render full HTML and XHTML. Nokia browsers represented 34% of the mobile browsers in the world in 2008.

- **Opera Mobile and Opera Mini**—Opera launched its first mobile browser in 2000. It was unique, in that it was not tied exclusively to any operating system, but it could be added to any phone that allowed third-party applications. Opera currently offers two browsers, Opera Mobile, which is intended for larger, more capable smart phones, and Opera Mini, which is intended for smaller, less capable phones. Opera browsers are also frequently preloaded on phones that run the Windows Mobile or Symbian operating systems.

- **Blazer**—Blazer launched its first mobile browser in 2000, supporting WAP, HTML, and iMode. This mobile browser was developed specifically for the Palm operating system and is found on Palm OS Palm and Treo handsets. It was one of the earlier mobile browsers available and was one of the first to support WAP and HTML instead of exclusively WAP.

- **Internet Explorer Mobile**—Launched in 1996 as Pocket Internet Explorer, Internet Explorer Mobile is the default mobile browser on all Windows Mobile, Windows CE, and many Palm devices. From the beginning, Internet Explorer supported HTML rendering and only later added WAP rendering with the release of the Pocket PC 2002 operating system. Internet Explorer Mobile also represents a large portion of the native mobile browsers available on phones today.

- **BlackBerry Internet Browser**—This browser was created by Research In Motion (RIM) to run exclusively on the BlackBerry operating system on BlackBerry phones, It should be noted however, that not all BlackBerrys run this browser, because in some cases, RIM has allowed carriers to place alternative browser as the native browser on the phone, omitting the BlackBerry Internet Browser. This browser has gone through various editions and upgrades, but historically it has been one of the less powerful mobile browsers. The BlackBerry browsers could originally render only WAP sites, but HTML capability was added with the launch of Symbian 4.0 in 2005. The browser improved with the launch of the BlackBerry Storm, but the browser still lacked sophistication in its mobile Web rendering.

- **Mobile Safari**—Mobile Safari is the primary browser that runs on the Apple operating system on the iPhone. Mobile Safari offers a similar Web browsing experience to the traditional Safari browser. Mobile Safari was the first Web browser that could really claim to provide a true Web browsing experience on a mobile phone.

- **Mobile Chrome**—This is the primary browser for phones that run the Android operating system developed by Google. This browser is similar to the desktop version of Chrome, in which Google pioneered a combined address bar and search bar that could understand whether searchers were trying to find a specific Web page or perform a search. Like mobile Safari, Mobile Chrome is a true Web rendering browser.

- **SkyFire**—SkyFire is a browser developed for the Windows Mobile and Symbian operating systems. SkyFire launched in beta in 2008 and offers much promise, but at the time of this writing, it has not yet been taken out of beta. It is another true Web browser that can run QuickTime and SilverLight, and it was the first software for Windows Mobile phones capable of running Flash.

3

Mobile Targeting and Tracking

In marketing, tracking and targeting are crucial to the success of your campaign. Although these are sometimes discussed separately, the intensely personal nature of the message and the heightened ability to track your customers' interaction demands that the two be considered together in mobile marketing. In the mobile world, targeting refers to both identifying key demographics and psychographics of your intended audience, and adapting your marketing message to meet their needs. Tracking refers to any attempt to capture and evaluate data about the effectiveness of the mobile marketing campaign.

Targeting Your Mobile Customers

As discussed elsewhere in this book, not everyone is an ideal candidate to receive your mobile marketing messages. For the most part, people with smart phones and true Web browsing phones are far more likely to be compelled by any type of mobile marketing message. In terms of age group, that means only about 8% of Baby Boomers, 18% of Millenials, and 10% of Gen-Xers are likely to be compelled by your mobile marketing messages. Table 3.1 shows what types of smart phones each of these demographics tend to use.

Table 3.1   Mobile Phone Usage by Generation[1]

Millenials (18% Own a Smart Phone)	Gen X-ers (10% Own a Smart Phone)	Boomers (8% Own a Smart Phone)
Blackberry: 39%	Blackberry: 40%	Blackberry: 39%
iPhone: 20%	iPhone: 11%	iPhone: 10%
Sidekick: 15%	Sidekick: 5%	Treo: 10%
Treo: 12%	Treo: 8%	Sidekick: 10%
Blackjack: 10%	Blackjack: 3%	LG enV: 3%
LG enV: 9%	LG enV: 3%	T-Mobile Wing: 3%
T-Mobile Wing: 5%	T-Mobile Wing: 3%	Nokia N95: 3%
Nokia N95: 4%	Nokia N95: 3%	Helio Ocean: 4%
Helio Ocean: 4%	Other: 19%	Other: 19%
Other: 14%	Not sure: 13%	Not sure: 10%
Not sure: 7%		

[1] Online survey of 4,000 mobile users in the United States between the ages of 16 and 64, conducted in January 2009 by Frank N. Magid (http://localmobilesearch.net/news/hardware/survey-half-mobile-users-accessing-content-weekly).

These statistics might be slightly disappointing to mobile marketers who assume that the entire world is active on their mobile phones. Unfortunately, although the price of smart phones and mobile data plans continues to drop, many people still either can't afford a smart phone or don't see the value in owning one. A whole other group of people own smart phones but don't use them to access mobile content, as illustrated in Figure 3.1.

What is the primary reason why you do not access the Internet on your mobile?

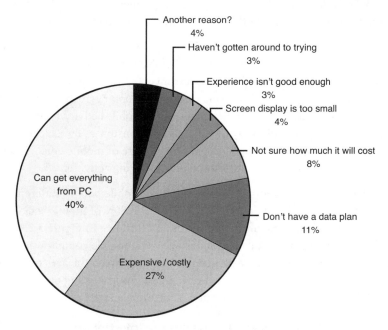

Figure 3.1 *For many reasons, some mobile users don't access the mobile Web on their mobile phones. Chart courtesy of Internet2Go, localmobilesearch.net.*

Age and Gender

According to a 2008 study by m:Metrics, the best demographic you can reach with mobile marketing is men between 18 and 34 years old. This demographic actually had a 9% click-though rate for mobile. Although women in this age group were quite active, they were less likely to click through on an advertisement. A comScore study from 2009 also reports that 70% of iPhone users are male.

Still, women are an important demographic in mobile marketing and should not be ignored. A 2009 study called "Women and Digital Life" reported that females between 12 and 24 named their mobile phone as the most important piece of technology in their life—even more important than a personal computer or laptop. The younger part of this demographic surpassed their older business professional counterparts in terms of mobile Internet usage.

Busy mothers can also be quite a lucrative demographic to target with mobile marketing, partially because they are 43% more likely to download mobile content. A 2009 study by GreyStripe actually renamed part of the "soccer mom" demographic to "iPhone moms." This makes sense, because the report shows that 29% of iPhone owners are women with children. Because they are often the purchase decision makers for the household, they control the purse strings —and are also frequently out of their homes, away from other types of marketing channels.

Some marketers worry that there is a trade-off between different types of mobile activities; for example, if people begin to get involved with one type of mobile activity, such as applications, they will become less involved with another mobile activity, such as online mobile social networking or mobile shopping. As it turns out, the opposite might be true. In a multiplier effect, more mobile activity might beget more mobile activity. A 2009 study of 2,000 mobile consumers by ExactTarget found a correlation between growth in participants' use of mobile email, instant messaging, text messaging, and mobile social networking activities.

As you might expect, different age groups use their mobile phones differently. According to the Magid study referenced in Table 3.1, 80% of mobile social networking activity is by people under the age of 34. As shown in Figure 3.2, a 2008 study showed that the highest demographic accessing mobile content was between the ages of 20 and 29. The second-largest group was between the ages of 30 and 39. Teenagers between 16 and 19 were the third largest group, beating out only those 40 to 49 and those 50 and above for their use of the mobile Internet.

Mobile Users Accessing the Internet on Their Mobile Devices, by Age, Income and Gender

Question: Do you access the Internet on your mobile device? (yes, no)
Base: U.S. mobile user ages 16+ (n=1,001)

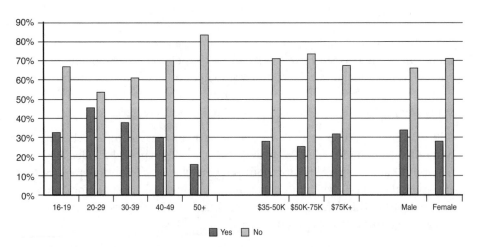

Figure 3.2 *A 2008 study showed that the largest portion of the mobile market that accesses the mobile Internet is between the ages of 20 and 29. Chart courtesy of iCrossing.*

According to GreyStripe—one of the top mobile gaming companies—47% of its mobile gamers are between the ages of 18 and 24, 23% are between 23 and 43, and only 14% are between 13 and 17. Text messaging is the most popular method of communication for people who are ages 13 to 24, and, according to a 2009 post on the Mobile Marketing Blog, their acceptance of this medium is actually growing at a faster rate than email, phone calls, and even social media. A 2008 study by Nielson shows that 35% of those age 13 to 17 actually remember receiving a text message ad, whereas only 10% of those 55 and older do (see Figure 3.3).

Recall of Any Text-Message Advertising Amongst Texters, by Age and Ethnicity (Q2 2008)

	Recall Any Text Ad
All Subs	16%
Ages 13-17	35%
Ages 18-24	18%
Ages 25-34	16%
Ages 35-54	12%
Ages 55+	10%
White	13%
Hispanic	23%
African American	24%
Asian/Pacific Islander	20%

Source: Nielsen Telecom Practice Group

Figure 3.3   *You might have guessed it, but this study proves that mobile users between the ages of 13 and 17 are the most likely to remember your text message advertisement. Image courtesy of Nielson Telecom Practice Group.*

Income

Mobile consumers tend to be more affluent than their nonmobile counterparts, and the more affluent mobile users tend to rely more heavily on mobile content than those lower on the income scale. According to a 2009 comScore study, mobile consumers with an annual household income of more than $100,000 tend to access business information three times more than those with an income of less than $100,000 per year (see Figure 3.4). They are also two times more likely to consume content from mobile news or mobile shopping websites.

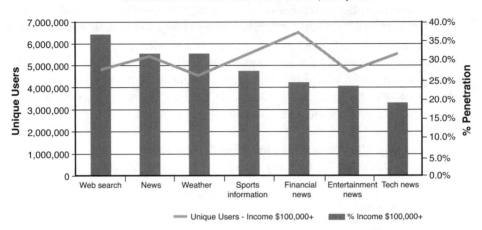

Figure 3.4 *As you might expect, mobile users with annual incomes $100,000 or higher are two times more likely to consume content from mobile news or mobile shopping websites. Chart courtesy of comScore, Inc.*

The same survey found that people who are accessing mobile content spend about 39 minutes per week with some type of mobile content, presumably either mobile Web content or mobile applications. They spend 38 minutes per week on text messaging and 44 minutes per week on mobile phone calls.

Surprising, a 2008 comScore report, "All about iPhone," shows a recent significant increase in the number of people in the lower income brackets (between $25,000 and $50,000 annual income) purchasing iPhones, rising 48% between June and November 2008. Forty-three percent of iPhone users earn more than $100,000 annually, and that demographic is more likely to use mobile search than to participate in any other type of mobile behavior. Forty percent of iPhone and iTouch users actually report using the mobile Internet on their mobile phones more than they do on their traditional computers.

Psychographic Mobile Targeting

Psychographic data is harder to collect than demographic data, but it is important for mobile marketing because it helps the marketer understand the mindset and values of the consumer. Psychographic data describes things such as lifestyle, ideals, and behaviors (sometimes psychographics are also described as IAO variables, for interests, attitudes, and opinions). Because this type of information is more difficult to measure, it is also more difficult to quantify in statistics. Psychographic information is usually elicited from surveys that companies or market research firms give potential customers. Think of your customers' psychographic profile as a quantitative evaluation of your potential customers' self-concept.

Mobile phones have become so ubiquitous that no specific psychographic groups are associated with ownership of a mobile phone. However, differences do exist in the way various groups think about mobile technology. This can offer insight about potential psychographic qualities of consumers. In 2009, Carol Taylor, director of user experience at Motricity Marketing, identified five types of mobile consumers:

- **Up-to-date**—These people are driven to stay current with news, weather, and events at all times. They like to be informed, and others look to them as beacons of information. They use their mobile phone as a resource to stay them connected with real-time information about the world around them.

- **Social and curious**—These people are sometimes described as connectors because they enjoy bringing others together, networking, and planning events and outings. They use their mobile phones to keep up with their friends' lives and to stay connected to the people they care about.

- **Busy and productive**—This group of people is very concerned with all information related to their own personal efficiency and their ability to cope with a busy schedule. They use mobile phones because they are more portable, accessible, or convenient than using traditional computers. They are interested in anything that can help them manage their multiple priorities and meet the demands of their busy day.

- **Latest and greatest**—These people want to be the first to try something, even if there is no guarantee that they will be satisfied with it. They always want to use the newest technologies and applications, and to be a part of the newest social networks and communities. Friends look to them for reviews and recommendations of new technologies.

- **Just the basics**—This group of people is not really interested in the phone, except for the fact that it makes their life easier. They are not impressed by the newest technology or the marketing appeals of most applications. They are not early adopters, and they look to reviews and recommendations to find the tools and applications that they want to use on their mobile phone.

Using these groups, you might be able to improve your ability to segment and target your messages to your target market. In most cases, you will be able to identify some or all of these groups within your target audience, but if you don't feel that any of these psychographic groups are representative, you might need to conduct your own research to determine what motivates your target market's decisions.

Geographic Mobile Targeting

Different geographic regions have adopted and used the mobile channel at different rates, based on differences in the mobile network infrastructure, network speed, handset availability, laws, billing rates, and cultural norms. Many of these differences were discussed earlier in Chapter 14, "The International Mobile Marketing Landscape."

With mobile marketing, geographic segmentation is very much about the situation the customer's location might indicate. When people are in different geographic locations, they generally have different needs and different motivations. Mobile marketing campaigns will be more effective if you can anticipate with some precision where the recipients will be when they receive your marketing message. With location in mind, you can adapt your message to suit the needs of your potential customer when at work, at home, in the car, when commuting on public transportation, while running errands, or while out for a night on the town.

Understanding and anticipating your customers' physical location also gives you insight into their physical surroundings—you'll know whether it's noisy or crowded, whether they are near a computer, or even whether they're in a location where they might lose their cellphone signal, such as in a subway train. Different cities and regions have different norms. For instance, if you are targeting people during rush hour in Houston, you can expect that they will be in their car, but if you are targeting people during rush hour in London, you can expect that they will be using some form of public transit.

The geographic situation might also provide information about your target markets' social and temporal concerns. Are the mobile users you're trying to reach out with friends? Alone? Just killing time? In a rush? Do they need to get directions? Do they just want coordinate effectively with their families? When you answer these types of questions, you can more easily develop a compelling marketing message that your customers will actually act on.

Device and Carrier Targeting

In some cases, it makes sense to target different carriers or devices. This can be so for several reasons:

- Your content is specifically formatted for particular devices.
- The effort is part of a campaign that is co-branded with a device or carrer.

- You believe different devices or carriers will reach the appropriate demographic or geographic group more effectively.

If you have decided that device or carrier targeting is a good idea for your initiative, it is important to determine which device or which carrier is the best to work with, so you should start with the statistics. Statistics about the iPhone and smart phones in general abound, but not a lot of statistics have been publicly made available about other specific handsets or carriers. For these statistics, it is usually best to go directly to the carriers or handset manufacturers to get information about the demographics that they reach. If you are working with a carrier, you should be able to get the demographic data directly. If you have trouble getting demographic information from the carriers, sometimes you can find media kits online, work directly with the media contact for the carrier, or gather information about the demographics through information intended for potential on-deck advertisers.

Beyond statistics that you can compile from various sources, it might be a good idea to do your own market research, either surveying your existing customer base or working with market research firms to survey potential customers. Whether you are conducting your research in person, online, or on a mobile phone, it is important to keep your questions as short and clear as possible.

You can conduct your research in many ways. In some cases, you will want to conduct simple one- or two-question surveys; in other cases, you will have a long list of questions to include. Remember that people will be more likely to take the survey if you offer some incentive, such as a coupon or a gift. The longer the survey is, the more important the incentive becomes. In some cases, you might need to hire a market research company to help with the surveying, by developing questioners and recruiting sample groups.

In addition to formal surveys, if you or your brand is active in social networks, it might be possible to do crowdsourcing to find out more about who your target market is and what they care about. Crowdsourcing simply refers to the practice of taking casual, nonscientific surveys of your customers by asking them questions on social networks. This is especially valuable if you have done a good job attracting your target market to your social profiles on venues such as Twitter and Facebook.

Figure 3.5 shows a simple survey that the clothing company H&M performed on Facebook just before the Back-to-School shopping season in 2009. Within nine minutes of the question being live on Facebook, 660 people said they liked the question (and presumably responded), and 100 left comments. This type of market research is quite cheap and reaches your most active demographics.

Figure 3.5 *Crowdsourcing is simple and effective on Facebook.*

Tracking Your Mobile Performance

Tracking is one of the most important aspects of any marketing campaign. One of the joys of mobile is the sheer amount of information that you can track, if you set up your campaigns correctly. Tracking, also sometimes referred to as analytics, is the process of capturing and evaluating the performance of your marketing campaigns. Different tracking and analytics platforms can be put in place to capture information about the success of your campaign. Before you get deeply into the discussion of what mobile tacking options are available, here are some points to keep in mind:

- In my opinion, you should never spend more on your analytics platform than you do on your analysts. As a consultant, I have seen many companies spend hundreds of thousands of dollars on expensive analytics platforms, but with no dedicated personnel who are qualified to review or interpret the data. In many cases, these companies simply use the platforms to generate simple automated reports that review very basic success metrics. If you are not diving deeply into your metrics on a regular basis, many of the free solutions should fulfill your needs.

- With mobile marketing, it is very important to understand how the tracking system works and what exactly it is reporting on. Some platforms are much better than others about telling you exactly what different statistics mean. Never take statistics for granted or assume that you know what they mean or how they were collected.

- Even the best data is slightly "spongy" and inexact. This is simply because a variety of different technological issues or circumstances can cause a reporting suite to interpret data the way it does. I generally recommend that companies use more than one reporting suite whenever possible, because it can help you get a clearer idea of what is actually happening—and it's also good to have a back-up reporting suite, in case something happens to the other one. Generally, one paid service and one free service is fine.

- Begin with the end in mind. When you are shopping for different tracking and analytics platforms, you should already know what type of information you will need available, how you will want to segment it, and what decisions that information will be expected to inform.

Some of the more common methods of mobile tracking are included next. The different methods and metrics are also covered in more depth in each of the chapters dedicated to that particular aspect of mobile marketing. It is important to note that the following suggestions are just some the most common tracking options; feel free to be more creative when developing your tracking scheme.

Text and Picture Message Tracking

Text and picture messaging is one of the most difficult things to track because different mobile carriers track text messaging slightly differently. Most SMS platforms (also known as SMS gateways, SS7 providers, or SMS aggregators) have a tracking system included as part of the service, which can be helpful but still frustrating. By collecting cell IDs and attaching commands to the SMS message, you can get different types of information. However, not all carriers support all commands, so it is a good idea to segment your campaign by carrier first, before any other segmentation.

One of the first things you will want to track in an SMS or MMS campaign is the size of your list and its growth. This statistic is simply represented by the total number of recipients to whom you can send text messages. This number should be constantly updated based on new opt-ins and opt-outs, and you should track this number over time so that you can see the growth in the list.

You should also compare the rate of opt-ins and opt-outs against the average growth rate of the list over time (see Figures 3.6 and 3.7). In many cases, if you are sending too many messages or your messages are not as valuable as subscribers hope, your opt-out rate will increase with every message. Conversely, if you are doing a good job of offline promotion, you should see a steady growth or even spikes in your opt-ins. This is particularly important if you are tracking the success of mobile coupons, because it enables you to compare the total ROI of a campaign, taking into account the actual in-store redemption rate of the coupon, as it compares to the loss in total subscribers.

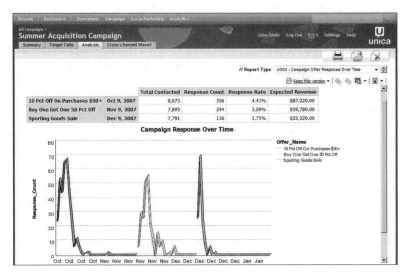

Figure 3.6   *The Unica reporting suite can track and compare the success of multiple promotions over time.*

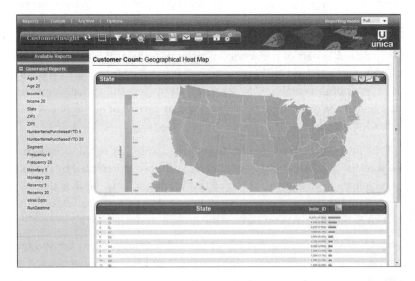

Figure 3.7   *Here's another example of the reporting available with the Unica reporting site.*

In some ways, tracking the impact of an SMS or MMS campaign is much like tracking an email campaign. In addition to tracking your list growth, you want to track the following information whenever possible:

- Messages sent

- Messages received

- Links clicked (if applicable)

- Conversion from links (if applicable)

Encouraging recipients to click on an HTML link in your text message makes it much more trackable. To track the initial Web response, it is good to send the responses to a unique mobile landing page that can be accessed only from the text message campaign. All subsequent onsite activities should be tracked, including downloads, purchases, enrollments, sign-ups, and subscriptions.

Unfortunately, you generally can't track the open rate of text message campaigns because there is no way to embed JavaScript or HTML that will execute when the message is opened. Without tracking the open rate, you are left tracking the number of messages that are successfully delivered, and then the actual responses.

Unlike text (SMS) messages, the open rate of picture (MMS) messages can be tracked. Whenever the MMS is opened, it references the HTML image. In MMS messages, generally only the HTML part of the message can be used to measure opens because many phones still do not decode HTML in the text part of a MMS.

GPS tracking can be integrated with SMS, and market research firms can use this to gain a deeper understanding of not only how people interact with their mobile device, but also how people interact with others in their real-life activities. The process, called reality mining, can be particularly useful for market research companies that want to understand how the use of the mobile phone relates to location and situation. For instance, what causes people to text-message? Or what causes people to use a mobile application instead of searching the Web?

As GPS technology is more readily integrated into more mobile phones, tracking people via GPS becomes simple enough and cheap enough that it could conceivably be integrated into some marketing campaigns. With this type of tracking, the GPS in the phone is queried on a regular interval and then automatically sends an SMS to a tracking system that analyzes the data. This can be done through a remote request or as part of a downloaded application.

This geographic data collected for each person who is being tracked can later be analyzed to determine things such as the route people took, stores visited, or the duration of their stay in any one location. If you want to integrate GPS tracking into your marketing campaign, you must notify whoever is being tracked and get two forms of opt-in permission. Because this method of tracking is so invasive, it is a good idea to send the people being tracked periodic messages, reminding them they are being tracked and allowing them to opt out of future tracking.

Systems such as this can also facilitate navigation around an airport, a tourist attraction, or a city. Other types of companies are using this type of tracking to help people keep track of loved ones or locate missing phones.

GPS tracking is probably too invasive for most marketing campaigns, but it could be integrated in creative ways to incorporate the phone with real-life activities such as races or scavenger hunts. To make the tracking more palatable, consider sending people who agree to be tracked coupons or incentives on a regular basis, to ensure that they are adequately rewarded for providing that amount of personal data.

The term *reality mining* is a play off the phrase *data mining*, which is the practice of compiling customer information from a variety of different sources and perspectives to create a summarized vision of your customers' wants and needs. Reality mining takes it a step further, tying in real-life actions instead of online behavior and purchase decisions. It is relatively new in terms of market research. The most notable study so far was conducted at MIT for the 2004–2005 school year and provided contiguous information about the interaction of 100 students. Sadly, the results of this study have not been made widely available, but we can expect more studies like this one to be performed in the future.

To date, reality mining is primarily used for broad market research projects, but in the future, this kind of intensely personal tracking might be integrated into mobile marketing campaigns. Any type of marketing campaign that requires this much access to personal information must ensure that data is highly secure and that participants are well rewarded for their information.

Mobile Web Tracking

A variety of mobile Web analytics programs have recently come on the scene and are now competing with some of the more established mobile analytics platforms. Many of the first mobile analytics services were created by mobile ad serving companies such as AdMob and Bango, who needed to report Web traffic and click-through rates for their advertisers. Now enough independent mobile analytics programs exist that it is no longer necessary to use a mobile ad network to get reliable information about the traffic on your mobile website.

When you are looking at mobile tracking, the first decision you have to make is whether to use a mobile-specific analytics program or adapt your existing Web analytics platform to track mobile customers. In an ideal scenario, you should be using both and comparing the data to get a deeper insight, but that's not always a workable solution. With two types of Web analytics operating at the same time, you always have a backup if something happens with one of them. The information in the upcoming sections should help you decide how to set up your mobile Web analytics and tracking.

Mobile-Only Web Analytics

Many traditional Web analytics platforms rely on JavaScript tracking code that is embedded on a Web page, or cookies that are stored in the phone memory. Unfortunately, many phones, and even some smart phones, do not execute JavaScript or reliably store cookies, so a mobile-specific tracking solutions is necessary. Also, in some cases, mobile-specific coding languages can cause problems with traditional Web tracking services. So until the new methods of feature phone tracking are developed, mobile-only Web analytics will be important for companies that are targeting less sophisticated phones.

Some of the top mobile-specific Web analytics platforms are described here, along with their services and offerings:

- **AdMob**—AdMob has historically been the gold standard in mobile analytics (see Figure 3.8). The company began as a mobile advertising company and offered comprehensive analytics to help their advertisers understand how well their campaigns were performing. People found the analytics information so valuable that AdMob began offering the platform for free to anyone with a mobile website.

  AdMob will also provide statistics for traditional Web visits when any website is visited, but it is intended specifically for mobile analytics. As you can see in Figure 3.8, the AdMob platform lets you filter information by specific dates and shows information such as visits, pages views, page views per visit, and time spent on the site. It also shows information such as which carrier is sending the most traffic and what the most popular location or activity is on the site.

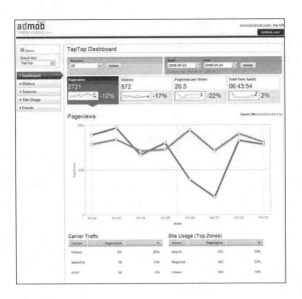

Figure 3.8 *AdMob is one of the most well-known and respected mobile-specific Web analytic platforms in the world.*

- **Bango**—Bango is one of the most well-known mobile analytics programs because it has been around for longer than most of its competitors (see Figure 3.9). As with most mobile analytics platforms, Bango can track activity on both mobile only and traditional websites. It tracks basic Web statistics, such as visits, new and unique visitors, page views, page views per visit, time on site, and conversions.

Figure 3.9 *Bango can track both mobile-only and traditional website traffic.*

Bango Analytics considers itself a real-time reporting solution because it can report on any action that happens on your website within the hour. This can be very important if you are in the midst of a short-term or location-specific promotion, because it provides the capability to tailor different aspects of your campaign on the fly and respond to different statistics as they become available.

One of the most important features Bango offers is the capability to track individual users' behaviors, whether they are connecting via a mobile network or WiFi, even if the connection changes during the interaction (see Figure 3.10). Each mobile device is attached a unique ID, which makes it much easier to segment specific users by their behavior, to import information about specific customers into a customer relationship management (CRM) system, or to integrate it with a loyalty campaign.

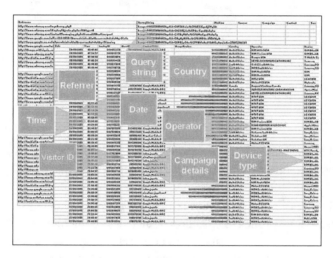

Figure 3.10 *Bango enables you to track the behavior of individual mobile users.*

As with most analytics platforms, Bango enables you to filter your data by page, country, operator, device, time, or date, but it also can monitor and pass URL-based tracking parameters to help supplement native functionality or launch new campaigns quickly.

One of the nice features of Bango is that it warehouses all the raw data that it collects about your website instead of batching it into a one-time report, sending it, and then eliminating it from its server. That means you can continually drill down into historical data, or potentially even create custom metrics from the warehoused information.

Bango's analytics program is quite robust in term of working and integrating with other traditional Web analytics programs though APIs. This is nice because it enables you to consolidate your traditional and mobile data without having to hand-stitch two disparate sets of data together. As shown in Figure 3.11, Bango can use the API to work directly within other reporting suites, such as Omniture, or even proprietary internal tracking systems.

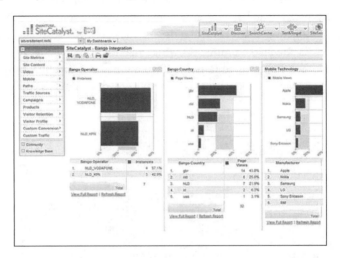

Figure 3.11   *Not only does Bango enable you to track both mobile-only and traditional Web activity, but it also enables you to roll them into combined reports.*

- **Mobilytics**—Mobilytics is a comprehensive mobile tracking suite that includes a lot of the basic features. It includes all the traditional Web metrics, such as visits, unique and new visitors, page views, pages per visit, time on site, and goal and conversion tracking. Mobilytics also has configurable dashboards that enable you to edit how data is presented to you. It also provides the capability to segment traffic based on a variety of different factors, including but not limited to reporting on traffic source, search engine, search term, carriers, countries, phone models, phone manufacturer, and phone capability. The platform can also be used to report on mobile PPC campaigns and mobile ads.

Figure 3.12   *Mobilytics is an all-around tracking suite that enables you to track both mobile and traditional Web campaigns. (Data has been intentionally blurred in this image to protect the privacy of these users.)*

Traditional Web Analytics That Include or Can Be Adapted for Mobile

Now that mobile Web access has become much more common, you can use traditional Web analytics programs such as Google Analytics and Omniture to see how much mobile traffic is making it to your mobile website. The following is a review of the most popular traditional Web analytics suites that can be used or adapted to track mobile Web visitors.

Google Analytics

Google Analytics is a free analytics platform offered by Google. Different from Google Webmaster Tools, it enables you to track and segment Web traffic in a comprehensive, easy-to-use platform. The tracking is easy to set up because it simply involves including the same piece of tracking code in pages throughout the website. This is easily done by adding the tracking code to the header of the website, if it is consistent throughout the website.

If you subscribe to the Enterprise level of Google analytics, you have access to mobile-specific tracking, and that works on phones that don't support JavaScript. The only additional setup is the insertion of a small snippet of code that sits on the server.

In the nonpremium, free version of Google Analytics, you can easily segment out iPhone traffic from other Web analytics. If you need to track other phones, you can also use Custom Segmentation to show you the browser/operating combinations to drill down to find things such as the following:

- How much traffic you are getting on specific phones

- What keywords are driving traffic in mobile searches

- What your mobile bounce rate is

- How many page views per visit your mobile site gets

- What pages are most important to your mobile users

The best option is to set up custom segments for each phone, or each group of phones that you want to track. After segmentation is set up, you can easily move between the results for specific handsets or specific types of phones (see Figure 3.13). (The segmentation rules can get very complicated and, thus, are not included in this example in full.)

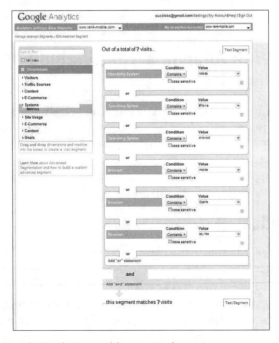

Figure 3.13 *Google Analytics enables you to do custom segmentation so that you can see results for specific handsets or specific types of phones.*

To set up segments that will group all mobile phones so that they can be reported on together, you must set up the Advanced Custom Segments. In this dashboard, include all mobile browsers and operating systems. To set up segments for specific phones, you simply need a list of the top handsets so that you can enter the browser/operating system/screen resolution/color-rendering combinations that each phone has and create them as a custom segment. A full list of mobile phones with these specifications is available at www.phonescoop.com/phones/index_all.php.

The one difficulty with Google Analytics Custom Segmentation is that you cannot set up segments in anticipation of the traffic coming to your website. For instance, if no devices with a 300¥300 screen resolution have ever visited your website, that option will not be available in your custom segmentation options. See Table 3.2.

Table 3.2   Mobile Phone Specifications for Custom Segmentation

Mobile OS	Mobile Browsers	Mobile Screen Resolutions	Mobile Color Rendering
Mac OS X	Opera Mini	300×300	Older Phones:
BlackBerry OS	Skyfire	320×194	1-bit/2 colors, black and white
Symbian OS	Safari	320×204	2-bit/4 colors, grayscale
Google Android	Mozilla's Minimo	320×240	3-bit/8 colors
Windows Mobile	Google Android	320×256	4-bit/16 colors
Mobile Linux	Thunderhawk	320×320	5-bit/32 colors
Palm OS	Microsoft IE for Mobile	320×400	6-bit/64 colors
MXI	Blazer	320×480	
	NetFront Browser	324×352	
	LG Dare	352×416	Most Smart Phones:
	Sprint Instinct	360×120	8-bit/256 colors
		360×480	12-bit/4,096 colors
		360×640	16-bit/65,536 colors
		384×288	18-bit/262,144 colors
		400×240	24-bit/16,777,216 colors
		432×240	
		450×854	
		480×272	
		480×320	
		480×360	
		480×640	
		480×800	
		480×845	
		480×854	
		480×860	
		480×862	
		480×864	
		640×200	

Table 3.2   Mobile Phone Specifications for Custom Segmentation

Mobile OS	Mobile Browsers	Mobile Screen Resolutions	Mobile Color Rendering
		640×240	
		640×320	
		640×480	
		800×352	
		800×480	
		854×480	
		1,600×1,200	

You can also set up a segment that works the opposite way, pulling out traditional computers and leaving everything else in. That gives you less specific data but is a quick way to get mobile information without a lot of setup or hassle with the analytics platform. An example of how you might do that is included in Figure 3.14, although not all the necessary rules are included.

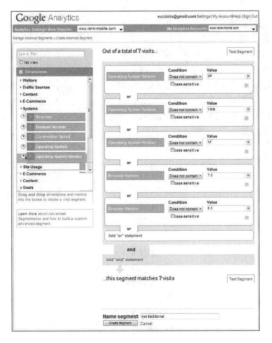

Figure 3.14   *You can also use Google Analytics to pull out data on traditional browsers and operating systems while leaving mobile traffic in.*

Omniture

Omniture is one of the longest-standing and most well-known traditional analytics platforms. In 2008, it added mobile analytics to its SiteCatalyst platform. Omniture also enables you to segment visitors based on device type, device manufacturer, and cookie support, but it adds location, video, and audio formats into its segmentation capability (see Figure 3.15). The mobile portion of SiteCatalyst offers essentially the same reporting and roll-up capabilities for mobile as it does traditional Web traffic. As mentioned earlier, SiteCatalyst can also interface with Bango Analytics to pull in more mobile specific data through the API. See Figure 3.16.

Figure 3.15   *SiteCatalysts enables you to segment visitors based on a variety of factors. (Data has been intentionally blurred in this image to protect the privacy of these users.)*

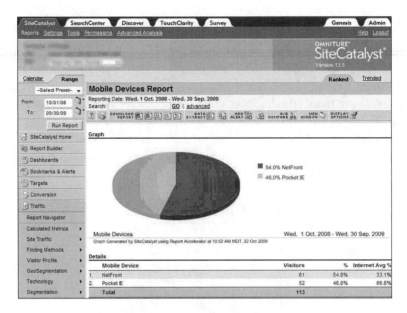

Figure 3.16 *A Omnitures SiteCatalyst graph showing mobile device access to a specific page. (Data has been intentionally blurred in this image to protect the privacy of these users.)*

To provide location information, Omniture works with a platform called WHERE by ULocate. The WHERE platform works with a variety of different systems to deliver location-aware news, weather, events, restaurant reviews, and social networking opportunities to people while they are on the go. It provides information about the users' location while they browse your website from their mobile phone.

WebTrends

WebTrends Analytics 9 is another traditional analytics platform that has begun to offer mobile analytics information. Their platform reports on traffic from mobile browsers, search engine bots, operating systems, and browsers. WebTrends is slightly newer to the mobile analytics game, but it has made public commitments to stay updated so that it provides an easy and reliable source of mobile analytics data. JavaScript is used to track smart phones that support it, and an API is used to collect data from phones that don't support JavaScript.

comScore

comScore is another company that offers a traditional Web analytics platform that includes mobile reporting, although it is actually better known for its publication of reliable industry statistics about the growth of different marketing channels. In 2008, comScore acquired m:Metrics, a company that offered the mobile analytics platform MeterDirect but was also focused on providing comprehensive statistics on the growth and adoption of the mobile marketing channel.

Through m:Metrics, comScore now can provide its subscribers with a variety of mobile research and statistics, as well as some site information through its analytics platform. Since the acquisition, meter direct has been adapted, so the mobile offerings comScore provides now include the following:

- **MobiLens**—This tool draws together content merchandising and consumer behavior with mobile devices to show how different devices respond to your mobile marketing.

- **Mobile Metrix**—This platform provides continuous tracking of your mobile audience's user behavior and compiles information such as gender, age, and income with handset and operator information.

- **Ad Metrix Mobile**—This analytics platform was created specifically for advertisers and publishers to measure mobile display advertising campaigns.

- **Plan Metrix Mobile**—This platform brings together mobile Web analytics and real-life personal characteristics of users. It includes information about device type and carrier information, along with traditional media consumption, lifestyles, interests, and attitudes.

Mobile Email Tracking

Email is very different when it is displayed on a mobile phone instead of a traditional computer, so information about mobile email should be evaluated slightly differently. As it turns out, many people are not acting on commercial emails when they are on their mobile phones. Instead, they are using downtime to scan their emails, delete SPAM, and mentally flag items that require follow-up or seem important. When you review the response rate for mobile emails, it might be low, but the presentation of your email in a mobile device could ensure that it is even seen on a traditional computer at all.

As with any email campaign, you should be tracking the number of emails sent, received, opened, and bounced, as well as the response rate to those emails. Because email cannot be directed to a mobile device in one instance and a traditional computer in the other, the email might be received on a traditional computer, a mobile device, or both places. This can make measurement a bit complicated; the following companies should be able to help with mobile email optimization and tracking.

- **ExactTarget**—ExactTarget is a traditional email platform that was one of the first to begin integrating mobile delivery into its email solution. Its platform enables you to integrate your system with a variety of different platforms, including SalesForce.com, Microsoft Dynamics, WebTrends, CoreMetrics, Google Analytics, and Omniture.

  The ExactTarget system also lets you send different responses based on specific customer behaviors, otherwise known as triggered responses. It also enables you to create content libraries and send content in emails that is dynamically generated, based on different demographics or filters. When they are set up in the system, each different behavior, triggered response, or dynamic email can be tracked and evaluated to determine the relative success of the different segments.

- **mobileStorm**—As with other email platforms, mobileStorm enables you to create and segment subscription lists and monitor the success of your campaign. In addition, mobileStorm specializes in mobile marketing, so it offers a variety of other products and services that companies can use to set up mobile-friendly email campaigns, track their success, and personalize responses. These campaigns can work independently or in tandem with SMS campaigns, and the two can be combined to grow your subscribers' lists.

  mobileStorm can also help you set up autoresponses on email and SMS campaigns, to manage the opt-in and opt-out process seamlessly, and help you track and manage the mobile and traditional coupons that you send. If you are marketing an event, the system also includes a handy RSVP manager.

- **Pivotal Veracity**—Pivotal Veracity is another traditional email provider that can help with mobile email delivery (see Figure 3.17). It focuses on deliverability and rendering, both of which are crucial to the success of mobile email. In terms of tracking, their platform provides advanced analytics and custom weighting, to gain a deeper understanding of how different responses impact your bottom line. The platform focuses on the capability to preview how your email will look on a variety of different phones. After deployment, it helps track the deliverability and click-through rate for traditional and mobile landing pages.

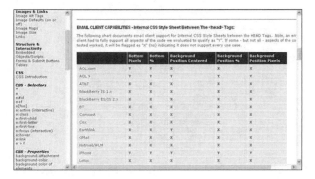

Figure 3.17   *Pivotal Veracity delivers diagnostics, which include information about two Blackberry renderings and the iPhone.*

Application Tracking

As companies begin to spend more money developing interactive applications, it has become more important to track how users are interacting with the applications and what impact the applications are having on branding and engagement. The following companies might be able to help you track the success of your mobile applications.

Flurry

Flurry is an application-only mobile tracking system that was one of the first independent application tracking platforms available. It can monitor applications from a variety of different platforms, including iPhone, Android, BlackBerry, and JavaME (see Figure 3.18). It can both monitor the sequence of actions that people take within an application and use dynamic parameters to evaluate user-generated content and other interactive portions of the application.

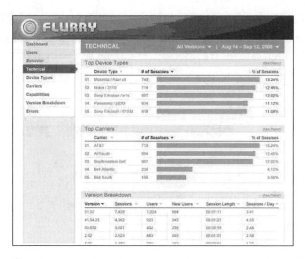

Figure 3.18   *The Flurry mobile reporting suite shows access to the mobile website by top devices and carriers.*

Google Analytics

In addition to tracking mobile Web activity, the same tracking code and platform can be used to track customer behavior within an application. The system currently works with Android and iPhone applications and is reported in much the same way Web traffic is presented.

Omniture

In addition to its Web traffic reporting platform, Omniture offers a tool called Omniture App Measurement that helps companies track the success and behavior of people on their iPhone, Android, and BlackBerry applications. This solution is also part of SiteCatalyst and uses the WHERE platform to determine where users are when they are accessing your mobile applications. This kind of usage information can be critical when determining how and where to promote your applications.

WebTrends

WebTrends also offers analytics for mobile applications, although the company is not very precise about what is included. The project might need further development before it rivals other mobile analytics tracking programs; this service does not appear to be a major push for them yet.

Offline Tracking, Text Message Tracking, and Phone Call Tracking

One of the biggest benefits to mobile marketing is that it enables you to add a direct response to all your traditional media campaigns, making them immediately trackable. Other chapters discuss this kind of tracking in much more depth, but basically this requires a text-messaging prompt in the offline marketing message, as shown in Figure 3.19.

Figure 3.19 *An SMS call to action in traditional media makes it immediately track-able.*

The best way to use mobile marketing to track traditional media marketing efforts is to utilize different response codes in different campaigns. For instance, in the Sponsor A Dog campaign, which was run throughout the London Tube, a poster in one location told people in one place to text "DOG" to the short code, and different posters told people in another location to text something else, such as "DOGS," "PUP," or "LOVE," to the short code. This strategy presegments the data, making it easier to understand where your campaigns are succeeding and where they are not, to prioritize future ad placement.

All the top text message and phone system providers will be able to either provide statistics about your campaign or, ideally, provide an analytics platform that you can use to evaluate and segment the data on your own.

Within the platform, you can also segment responses by the time of day or the area code associated with the response. If you include clickable phone numbers in any of your marketing efforts or promotions, you can track the response in a similar way, providing different phone numbers with different promotions so that tracking the success of each initiative or each location is simple.

Offline behavior can also track the effectiveness of a mobile marketing campaign. This is especially true in the case of mobile coupons and redemption codes, when a promotion is sent to a mobile device, but the trackable behavior actually happens when the coupon is redeemed in the store. You can segment your users in a variety of ways and then track their response. One of the most common tests is to send recipients in different zip codes different redemption codes, and then systematically evaluate how far your customers drive to redeem the coupon. This kind of analysis can help inform a company's decision to open a new location.

Loyalty Tracking

One of the most important and complex opportunities in mobile tracking is the capability to track a multichannel marketing effort in a unified way. A comprehensive multichannel effort includes a variety of on- and offline media, including print, TV, radio, email, location-based mobile marketing, SMS, MMS, applications, billboards and banners, and Web traffic. The following companies can help you set up and track a multichannel marketing campaign.

Unica

One of the top analytics companies for drawing all types of analytics information together is Unica. Figure 3.20 shows Unica's capability to segment customers by their loyalty status and show the value of each segment.

The system has a variety of different products and unique feature that enable you to anticipate opportunities to cross-sell customers when they will be most interested in your products, based on their previous behavior and see a visual representation of your customer data. The system helps you manage customers' different touchpoints and determine, in real time, which messages will be the most compelling and successful.

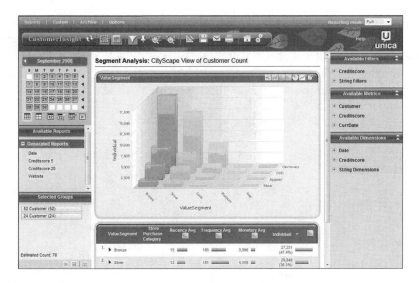

Figure 3.20   *The Unica dashboard enables you to segment customers by loyalty.*

mobileStorm

In addition to their email and SMS solution, mobileStorm provides a multichannel product that enables you to track six types of campaigns in the same platform. mobileStorm is slightly less comprehensive than Unica because it doesn't report on Web traffic, but it does allow you to track email, SMS, voice, fax, RSS, and video. Its database management capabilities enable you to create custom Web forms and mobile forms to gather data from your website and integrate the mobileStorm system into your existing CRM through APIs. It can also help you track phone numbers of subscriptions and removals from the lists, or even create suppression lists as you target various segments.

Responsys

Responsys offers another option for tracking cross-channel marketing efforts that include mobile marketing. This multichannel product is called InteractCampaign. When it is coordinated with InteractProgram, you can create a very dynamic tractable campaign, full of multichannel and cross-channel triggered responses. This seamless integration of cross-channel marketing with triggered responses means that if a customer responds to a mobile ad in one way and an online ad in another, the customer could automatically be sent a promotional email that combines the learnings from both the online and mobile responses.

As you develop your mobile marketing campaigns, keep this list of mobile tracking and analytics tactics and platforms in mind. It is important to stay current on the new mobile tracking and analytics services that are available because they change and develop; mobile marketing is still relatively new, and tracking is important, so likely a lot of innovation will arise in this aspect of the game.

Everything You Need to Know About the iPhone

4

The iPhone has done for mobile phones what the iPod did for MP3 players: It has set a new bar and changed the game. The success of the iPhone has been so dramatic that its revenue has actually eclipsed Apple's revenue from the sale of Mac computers and iPods. In the United States, the iPhone has been the first or second most popular single handset (not handset family) since the second quarter of 2008, and with the launch of a new phone in 2009, it is not likely that they will be out of the top three anytime soon. As of February 2008, the iPhone OS was the fourth most popular operating system on the Web (the entire Web, not just the mobile Web), with a 0.30% market share, behind Windows (90.69%), Mac OS (7.84%), and Linux (0.92%). It is now officially available in more than 88 countries around the world, but it is also being shipped and modified to work in other countries where it has not yet officially launched.

The iPhone has undoubtedly become a status symbol, but it is also quickly becoming a necessary utility. The iPhone is making mobile computing and mobile Web access a reality that is not hindered by caveats and special circumstances, as with other mobile Web experiences. Many iPhone loyalists will tell you that they now rely heavily on the iPhone for day-to-day activities that used to require a full-sized computer or laptop. Mobile computing is rapidly becoming necessary for everyday life, as mobile calling did only 10 short years ago. Soon enough, people will not remember how they got by without the mobile Web at their fingertips at all times.

The revolution caused by the iPhone has also done a lot to expand the reach and potential of mobile marketing. This chapter outlines what makes the iPhone different and particularly valuable for mobile marketers, and how it has changed the future trajectory of the mobile marketing landscape as a whole. It also delves into the demographics and psychographics associated with the iPhone and how that information can be used to improve any mobile marketing campaign. The next section reviews what functions are used the most on iPhones and provides tips for tailoring a campaign to leverage those activities for the iPhone audience. This chapter then explores the limitations of the technology will be explored. Finally, we end with case studies about companies that have uniquely integrated the iPhone into their marketing mix.

The iPhone has a lot of features that other mobile phones have, such as the capability to store and play MP3s and videos, the capability to download third-party applications, and the capability to surf the Web. Beyond what many other mobile phones offer, the iPhone has a sleek touchscreen, accelerometers that can respond to motion and the physical orientation of the device, and a far superior Web browser when compared to anything else on the market. The new features and more usable interface make the iPhone a more robust and compelling marketing channel, and the statistics spell that out.

For the most part, companies are having the most luck reaching the iPhone audience with ads disguised as apps. According to Mobclix, Inc., the average iPhone user has installed 5 to 10 applications on the device, compared with fewer than 2 apps per device for the overall smart phone market. In some cases, companies are even buying existing iPhone apps and retooling them to fit their branding needs instead of creating a new application. For many companies, this can be a great strategy that saves time and money.

The integration of the search, mapping, and calling features is important for marketers who are trying to drive foot traffic to a specific location or store. The iPhone enables users to search for anything and then have results displayed on a map, with the option to click through and call.

iPhone User Demographics

Many misconceptions and assumptions have been made about the iPhone user demographic. According to Nielsen Mobile, as of 2008, only 39% of iPhone users had an annual household income of more than $100,000. The survey included only users who were older than 18, but of those surveyed, the largest age demographic was age 25 to 34, with 33% of the pie, not, as many might have assumed, those age 18 to 24. The next-largest demographic consisted of those age 35 to 44, at 20%. Ages 18 to 24 were actually the third-largest group, making up only 15% of the demographic, closely followed by ages 55 to 64, at 14%. Another 2009 study by ComScore reports that 43% of iPhone users have an annual income of more than $100,000.

The demographic group that is most interested in the iPhone has enough disposable income to afford the phone and enough activities in their life to justify the expense. iPhone users may have different psychographic values and incentives, but the iPhone is appealing enough to justify the expense for each set of values. According to Nielsen Mobile, 36% of iPhone users pay more than $100 per month for their cellphone bill—but luckily, 15% say that their company pays the bill for them. Twenty-four percent of people surveyed reported using the iPhone for business and personal use and paying the bill themselves, and 61% said they use the phone only for personal use.

Although we have less information about the 18-and-under demographic, it is clear that they are using iPhones, too. For teens, the demographic indicators usually relate more closely to the parent than the child. Teens with iPhones tend to come from households with an annual income of more than $100,000. The parents tend to be working professionals who encourage their children both academically and socially. For these young users, the iPhone is a means of staying connected with their parents and friends, but it is also a study aid and a utility. They use the phone for social networking and entertainment, but they may also be downloading applications that help them prepare for exams or perform well on standardized tests. The iPhone is also useful for scheduling extracurricular activities.

Teen users are impressed with bells and whistles, but they are also interested in productivity and efficiency (like their parents). Applications or messages that help them stay organized and manage multiple deadlines are ideal for them. The 30Boxes calendar application and similar tools appeal to them because they are simple to use and effective at keeping them organized.

iPhone User Psychographics

The iPhone is the newest "it" phone. Its "cool" factor is desirable for a variety of user demographics (age, gender, and so on). The many features and the usability of the device make it appeal to the values and needs of a variety of psychograph groups, which are grouped according to personality, values, attitudes, interests, and lifestyles. Early adopters, Apple enthusiasts, and technophiles were the first group to embrace the iPhone; they were followed by business users, and, lastly, gamers and the college crowd. Similar psychographic sets can be targeted with innovative mobile marketing messages on the iPhone, so we also explore strategies for appealing to each of the psychographic sets.

The First Wave of iPhone Adoption

Early adopters are almost always enthusiastic about new technology, especially when the hype reaches fever pitch, as it did for the iPhone. Early adopters have to know whether the new technology is worth the hype so that they can inform their friends and maintain their reputation as innovators in their social group.

The first wave of iPhone adoption was also pushed by Apple enthusiasts and the technophiles, who are not always in agreement when it comes to technology and values. Apple enthusiasts tend to value usability and form equally, whereas technophiles are generally willing to sacrifice form and user-friendly design if it improves usability. Apple enthusiasts are usually willing to embrace anything Apple, but technophiles are frequently put off by the proprietary policies and technology that Apple generally embraces. Despite their apparent differences, both groups embraced the iPhone and did a good job of evangelizing the product for the second and third waves of adopters.

Appealing to these groups means being edgy and taking risks. You must create something new that the early adopters, technophiles, and Apple enthusiasts will test and evangelize to their friends. The best example of something that would appeal to these early adopters is the Air Mouse application. It translates movements detected by the accelerometers in the Phone and sends them as mouse movements, keyboard strokes, or media controls over a WiFi network to a computer. The application automatically assesses what type of device is being used and updates the buttons that it shows on the iPhone screen. This makes the application great for this psychographic group, whose members are probably interested in turning one of their many computers into a media center that is attached to a TV and sound system, and using a long-distance remote to control everything.

The Second Wave of iPhone Adoption

The second wave of iPhone adoption was led by professionals who realized that the device could be useful for business. The visual voicemail feature appealed to their need for efficiency, as did the capability to sync their "push" email activities from their phones to their computers (and vice versa), (which wasn't part of the original release but was quickly added). Businesspeople also liked true Web browsing on the handset because it helped them make the most of their down time or daily commute: A truly usable mobile Web expanded their day and allowed them to accomplish more in less time. Businesspeople were willing to pay the higher cost for the phone for its additional functionality and efficiency.

Appealing to this demographic with your marketing message is simple: You must focus on efficiency. How does your product or service improve their ability to do their work, meet their deadlines, and still be social? The iPhone appealed to both the need to be an efficient businessperson and the need to have a life outside of work. An example of something else that would appeal to this crowd is the UrbanSpoon application. A simple restaurant locator, it also creates efficiency by allowing users to set their location, the type of food they want, and the price they want to pay. Users can choose to set all or none of those three options; the application then gives them restaurant suggestions, complete with reviews, addresses, maps, and phone numbers. This appeals to the efficiency needs of the businessper-son, while the design and implementation offer some whimsy and the promise of down time away from work.

The Third Wave of iPhone Adoption

The last major groups to embrace the iPhone were college students and video game enthusiasts, or "gamers." This group really valued the entertainment potential for the iPhone, as well as the capability to engage in social networking and connect with friends through text and picture messaging. They wanted the device because it was cool and entertaining, and could play music. In some cases, it also allowed stu-dents to postpone the purchase of a laptop, instead relying on the iPhone and a desktop computer or a computer lab for more time-intensive computing. The iPhone was functional and fun, and for most, it was a status symbol.

Gamers are similar but are much more interested in the capability to test games and applications on the iPhone. They are impressed with the clarity and screen resolu-tion and the capability to incorporate motion and sound into game play, as well as the ability to play games against friends over WiFi networks. Gamers are also inter-ested in the true Web browsing because it allows them to access more games, inter-act on gaming forums, and read game reviews.

Interactivity is key for reaching these psychographic groups with your marketing message. One-dimensional mobile marketing campaigns will not make the impact that interactive ones will. This group knows the capability of the iPhone and likes to see it used to the full extent. To them, that is a sign that the brand or company "gets it." This group probably grew up with computers and the Internet as a part of day-to-day life, both at home and at school, so they are not easily impressed. They value messages and technologies that provide entertainment, ensure their position in the social hierarchy, and help them stay connected.

The best avenue for reaching these psychographic groups might be an application such as Shazam, which can use the microphone on the phone to listen to a song and then identify the song; the viewer can learn more about the song or the band, recommend the song to a friend, forward it to a social network, or buy the song. This application does a great job of innovatively using the native technology of the phone to provide an interactive, viral, and cool experience on the iPhone.

How Are iPhones Used?

iPhone users are much more willing to engage mobile media than users of any other handset, which makes them a perfect target market for mobile marketing. The most important characteristic that makes iPhones different for mobile mar-keters is how they are used (see Figure 4.1). People use their iPhones dramatically differently than most other smart phones. According to Nielsen Mobile, an iPhone user is 10 times more likely to watch video on their phone, nine times more likely to play games on their phone, seven times more likely to stream music on their phone, five times more likely to access the Internet, and three times more likely to use an instant messaging service.

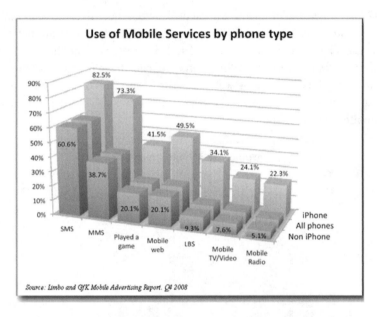

Figure 4.1 *iPhone usage compared to usage of all other mobile phones. Chart courtesy of Marketing Charts (www.marketingcharts.com).*

The iPhone has brought mobile Web access and mobile search to the masses. The fact that 95% percent of iPhone owners regularly surf the Web, even though 30% had never done so before acquiring the device, is quite telling. The iPhone represents only 8% of the mobile handsets but roughly 75% of the mobile search, and iPhones now account for one out of every 333 Web hits worldwide. The desire for Web access and Web search was always there—it was just being slowed by the bad user experience that other mobile phones provided.

iPhone users are more engaged with the full range of capabilities in the phone than other smart phone users. Research conducted by iSuppli Corp in 2007 indicates that they spend about 72% of their time on the iPhone doing things other than making phone calls. The cleaner, simpler interface results in 76% of iPhone users using the device to access their email, compared to only 35% of other smart phone users.

The demand for the non-phone features of the iPhone is so strong that Apple actually sustains a non-phone handset option, otherwise known as an iTouch. This is another way that the iPhone has been totally revolutionary—Apple realized that the non-calling features (apps, music, video, and so on) are more important to some users. In fact, phone capability can be totally absent if the non-calling features are compelling enough to the users. Since non-phone based mobile handsets have many of the same capabilities of more traditional smart phones, these types of devices must also now be taken into account in mobile maketing efforts.

This level of engagement makes iPhone users much more likely to see, recall, and even respond to ads (see Figure 4.2). In the same study, iSppli found that half of iPhone users had responded to a mobile add. After seeing a mobile ad, iPhone users also are twice as likely as non–iPhone users to "click to call" and are 25% more likely to click a link to a mobile website. A surprising 25% of the iPhone respondents surveyed said that they had purchased a product or visited a store as a result of a mobile advertisement.

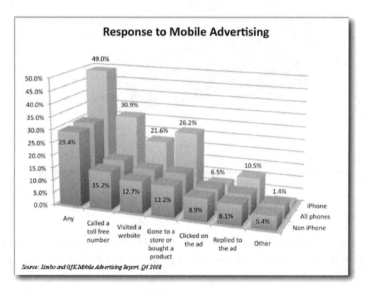

Figure 4.2 *Response to mobile marketing—iPhone users versus all other smart phone users. Chart courtesy of Marketing Charts (www.marketingcharts.com).*

Tips for iPhone-Specific Marketing

Many tips and tricks are associated with using the unique features of the iPhone to make your marketing campaign stand out from others. A successful iPhone campaign will naturally be viral if you really can make the most of the device.

SMS Messaging

Text message marketing on iPhones is essentially the same as text message marketing campaigns with any other types of phones. It is important to note that iPhones cannot send or receive picture messages. Any images that you want to send to someone's iPhone must be sent over WiFi, as an attachment or via a text message link, where the user can download the image from the Web to the phone. This can be particularly problematic for mobile couponing that leverages MMS, but I expect Apple's oversight to be remedied in future generations of the iPhone.

Accelerometers

These are the motion sensors in the phone that can determine the orientation of the phone and how quickly it is moving. Motion sensitivity can be incorporated into a variety of different iPhone marketing campaigns to make the experience more interactive. Whenever you incorporate motion into your marketing campaign, the best practice is to also include a button that will achieve the same goal as the accelerometers without the motion, in case the accelerometers are broken or the viewer doesn't feel comfortable making the motion necessary to execute the command.

Touchscreen

Although many phones are beginning to incorporate touchscreens, the iPhone touchscreen is slightly different. It responds to extended touch and movement, where many other phones respond to only simple taps. This makes it possible for applications to incorporate the capability to drag and drop items to different parts of the screen easily, as if the user were using a mouse. For marketers, the touch screen on the iPhone opens up lots of possibilities when creating applications and games, making them more interactive and engaging.

GPS

Second-generation iPhones are equipped with GPS capabilities. Both the first- and second-generation phones have a business search feature that will plot businesses on a map and give the user turn-by-turn directions. The key difference is that, with the first-generation iPhone, users may have to input the desired address; with the second-generation iPhone, they don't.

The key to leveraging the GPS feature is really in leveraging local search engines, especially Google Local. Your business must be listed correctly in as many local search results as possible, with as much information as possible. In addition to the basic information, such as your address and phone number, be sure to include your hours of operation, major cross streets, simple driving directions, and even a picture of the front of your building, as users would see it from the street. These will help people who are using the GPS search on the iPhone find your brick-and-mortar store more easily.

Submitting your business to local search engines other than Google Local is also crucial. Many iPhone applications interface with the GPS capability of the phone, but they pull search results from other local search engines, such as Yahoo! Local or Yelp. A good example of this is UrbanSpoon. One of the most recognizable mobile search applications, UrbanSpoon helps people find a restaurant. It searches a database of restaurants and reviews from a mixture of Yelp and Yahoo! Local, so to be listed in UrbanSpoon, a business either must be listed in one of those two local search engines or must work with UrbanSpoon directly (there's a submission form on their site, too.)

WiFi

In general, iPhones are much more suited for receiving location-based mobile marketing messages that are sent through WiFi than are other phones. The most important consideration for attracting the attention of iPhone owners with broadcast WiFi marketing is to ensure that iPhone users have enabled WiFi on their phones. This can be a simple process, but many subscribers keep their WiFi turned off unless they have a specific use in mind, because it drains the battery. In some cases, it may be enough to incorporate reminders into billboards and displays in and around your location, but in other cases, it may be more important to give specific instructions about how to change the settings on the phone to receive the message.

Voice Recognition

Many phones incorporate voice-recognition programs to help subscribers place phone calls to people in their address book without having to dial the phone number or find the contact in their address book.. The iPhone, however, takes voice recognition to the next level, by allowing applications to tap into that voice recognition software as well . Applications that can interact with voice and audio recordings expand the interactivity of the device, and can be used in mobile marketing to create a more engaging experience. Having users say a brand name or make a specific sound while they are interacting with a branded application can add an element of whimsy to any iPhone application.

Bluetooth

Unfortunately, the Bluetooth capabilities of the iPhone are a bit more limited than those on other handsets. Many mobile phones can send files, including pictures and text to other phones or to computers via Bluetooth, but the iPhone cannot. The iPhone is set up only to receive and transmit audio, so it can send voice and music;

it is also limited there, because the iPhone Bluetooth cannot transmit in stereo. In terms of location-based marketing, WiFi is more appropriate for the iPhone audience.

QR Codes

QR Codes are small square dot matrices, sometimes called 2D bar codes. These codes can be included on billboards, packaging, print media, or even on computer screens. Users with QR enabled phones can captured the bar code by taking a picture of it with their digital camera. Once that is done, the QR code can actually cause the phone to perform different actions, such as opening a web page, displaying a branded message or adding a contact to your address book.

iPhones don't currently come with a QR code reader natively installed, but it is expected that the next-generation iPhone will. If you think QR codes might be a good way to reach your iPhone demographic, especially if you are in a region that hasn't fully embraced the technology, it is important to give viewers instructions about how to scan the QR code. The instructions should include a recommendation for a good QR code–reading application, an explanation of how the application should be used, and what happens when the QR code is scanned. Explaining the value of the scan is important in driving adoption of the technology.

iPhone Meta Tag for Page Width and Zoom

Some developers are adding a specific meta tag to the header section of their website code of iPhone-specific websites or to make their traditional websites more iPhone friendly. The meta tag tells the site to display at a certain width and zoom level by default when it is displayed on a iPhone. Debate about this meta tag is circulating in the development community because different developers recommend different widths. If you are developing Web content specifically for an iPhone, include this meta tag and try it at different widths.

```
<meta name="viewport" content="width=480" />
```

Innate problems arise when setting that specific width, the most obvious being that when you turn the phone back from landscape to portrait, it must display at a different pixel width. If you want the screen to automatically be set by the width of the phone, you can add the following meta tag:

```
<meta name="viewport" content="width=device-width; user-scalable=no"/>
```

You can also use the meta tag to change the scale that the website displays in, to show at less than full screen but still more zoomed than the iPhone default . By changing the `initial-scale` part of the meta tag from `1.0` to `0.5`, you are telling the site to display at half the size of the phone screen, so you ensure that if users are scrolling right to left, they will have to scroll only a maximum of double the size of the original screen. This is particularly good if you have a site that has two columns of even width. If you have a three-column site and the columns are evenly sized, you can set the `initial-scale` to `0.33`, so that they when they open the site, they see only the first column.

```
<meta name="viewport" content="width=device-width; initial-scale=1.0;
➥maximum-scale=1.0;">
```

iPhone Meta Tag for Double Tap and Pinch

If you have built content specifically for an iPhone, there may be no need for the "double tap" and "pinch" features used on the iPhone to zoom in and out. You can add code to the meta tag after the width to disable these features.

```
user-scalable=no
```

The full meta tag would look like this:

```
<meta name="viewport" content="width=580; user-scalable="no"/>
```

iPhone Meta Tag for Launching Your Site as a Standalone Application

Another meta tag enables users to launch your website as a standalone application, without using the Mobile Safari Browser. This essentially mimics the look of an app, so it is most valuable if you have application-like content on your website but you don't want to bother with selling or submitting the app. If you use this strategy, it is especially important to somehow encourage users to add your site or app to their home screens and then use it like an application. These types of applications may run a bit slower than traditional applications from the App Store because the resources are being downloaded in real time over the Internet instead of being pre-loaded on the phone. Still, they can be quite impressive.

```
<meta name="apple-mobile-Web-app-capable" content="yes" />
```

Limitations of the iPhone

Although the iPhone has done a lot to improve the technology available to receive mobile marketing messages, it still has some limitations.

Slow Connection Speeds and Jailbroken Phones

The most notable exception to all the hype is slow connections. Despite the promises of 3G connectivity, not all areas where the iPhone is sold have universal 3G coverage—in fact, many don't. This can also be a problem when users are connecting to a network that is not with the intended carrier, as with "jailbroken" phones (phones that have been unlocked, thus allowing the phone to work on any carrier network). The number of jailbroken phones is growing, and they generally rely on an EDGE network to connect. When you are testing your marketing campaign, it is best to test it at both 2G and 3G rates; unless people are around a WiFi signal, they may still be downloading your content over an EDGE or GPRS network.

Buttonless Design

The sleek, buttonless design is nice, but it has a direct disadvantage to text communication. Many users report trouble typing and resent not being able to copy and paste or even effectively move the cursor back without deleting. If you are developing an application or an interaction that relies on text responses to be typed quickly, you will only frustrate your users. This can be a problem for text-in contests and polls that include a time element to the participation. If you are targeting the iPhone demographic, it might be better to require shorter responses. Prompt people with multiple-choice questions instead of open-ended ones so that they can just press one letter and send the message, or send people to a Web page where responses are already typed and users only needs to click on a radio button to participate.

Limited Battery Life

For all its capabilities, the iPhone has a limited battery life, which can be problematic for both users and mobile marketers. If you are marketing with mobile games, video, or anything that will be transmitted over a WiFi signal, this will make the battery in the iPhone drain more quickly. Be conscious of this when you are developing applications, videos, and any other rich media content. If the interaction takes a long time, you should allow users to save what they are doing and consider integrating some kind of low battery warning system that will let viewers know that they should plug in their phone to continue the experience.

Inability to Forward Text Messages and Contacts

The iPhone has no good way to forward text messages or contacts to other people, which can be limiting if you are initiating a viral campaign. If this is the case and it is important that text messages or contact information be forwarded to friends, many viable workarounds exist. If your audience is on Twitter or Facebook, you can encourage them to post the message there instead of forwarding it to a friend on the phone. You can also leverage services such as Facebook, Linked In, and Plaxo to help participants send contact information or spread your viral message on social networks.

No Custom Ringtones

Custom ringtones cannot be added to the iPhone. This is probably one of the biggest oversights, because ringtones are popular with the iPhone demographic and are a big driver of revenue for many carriers and mobile marketers. If you are promoting music or a brand with a jingle, it would be nice if you could offer your customers custom ringtones for their iPhone, but it simply can't be done at the moment. The speaker on the handset is good for playing music, but its performance as a speaker phone is lacking. Looping in the phone functionality might be a clever way to incorporate music into your campaign, but the volume of the speaker system could hinder the experience.

GPS Battery Drain

Active use of the GPS can also drain the battery quickly. This can be particularly cumbersome if you are working with an application or initiative that uses the GPS in the phone for a long period of time, such as one that gives turn-by-turn walking instructions. If this is the case, you should always give users an option that allows them to conserve battery life. For instance, if you are providing directions to your location, you could provide all the directions at once instead of generating them on the fly, as most navigation systems do.

Case Studies

The following case studies show how several companies have targeted marketing efforts at iPhone users.

Nationwide Insurance

In 2009, Nationwide Insurance launched a great interactive mobile campaign aimed at building goodwill with its iPhone-using customer base and attracting new customers to the service. The campaign focused on a mobile application called Accident Toolkit that the company developed to help customers submit an auto claim and expedite the repair process after an accident. Nationwide believed that this application would help them stay true to their tagline and prove, in a new way, that "'Nationwide is on your side.'"

The application pulled together a number of the iPhone functions to make submitting a claim and responding to an accident much less stressful (see Figure 4.3). It used GPS position to automatically record the location of the accident, and it then provided contact information to help users notify local authorities or request emergency services, if necessary. It encouraged users to collect all the pertinent information about the accident, including the other party's name, address, phone number, license plate, and insurance company, and store that in the phone. Users could even use the iPhone to take and store pictures of the accident with the other accident records on the phone. After all the records had been taken, the application again used the GPS to help the user contact local towing services or approved body shops, to get the car off the road and into repair.

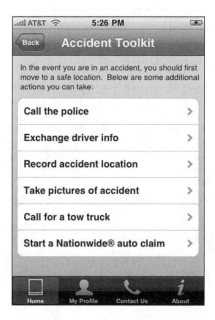

Figure 4.3 *Nationwide's Accident Toolkit is a prime example of a successful mobile marketing campaign aimed at iPhone users.*

Nationwide did a great job of promoting this application, by including it on national and local TV commercials and direct mail, encouraging customers to add the application. They also used display advertising to promote the application on top websites such as Facebook, Web MD, and Weather.com. Nationwide also used social media sites such as Facebook and Twitter to disseminate information about the application. On the viral side of things, it helped that the application was not limited only to Nationwide customers, and it did everything but submit the claim for people who had different insurance providers. This was a great way to expand their reach and brand awareness, and some users likely switched from a different insurance provider to Nationwide.

Reebok Shoes

Reebok wanted to tap into the mass personalization phenomenon that has taken over the younger demographics, so they created an iPhone application to let users create a custom pair of sneakers. Users could choose from three different classic

Reebok sneakers to customize, and then choose the material and the color of different aspects of the shoes. They then had the opportunity to send the designs to friends or share them with the entire world by putting them in the marketplace.

The application also incorporated the iPhone mapping feature. All public designs were geotagged and placed on a map (see Figure 4.4). Subsequent users could see the designs that were popular in their area and either buy them or further customize them to their own taste. The app also incorporated the touch sensors and the accelerometers, requiring the user to touch the part of the shoe that they wanted to modify and shake the phone to add color.

Figure 4.4 *Reebok's mobile marketing campaign allowed users to create custom shoe designs and then geotag them on a map.*

Dockers

Dockers was one of the first companies to use the accelerometers of the iPhone to interact with people who viewed their mobile Web display ads. The ad was launched on an iPhone-only display network that places ads within free iPhone applications. The interactive banners were deliberately placed in game applications that men between 30 and 39—their key demographic—would be interested in playing. The idea was that if they were already interested in playing a game for entertainment, they might also be interested in interacting with an advertisement for entertainment.

The ad featured Dufon, a well-known freestyle dancer, wearing Dockers clothing. In between levels of play, viewers were encouraged to shake the phone to make Dufon dance (see Figure 4.5). The experience looped in music with the dancing and encouraged the viewer to shake the phone again for an encore. The beauty of the campaign was that the ad was interactive if the viewer wanted it to be, but did not force interaction. The banner was a successful standalone advertisement that could be clicked on for more information, just like any other banner. The music and dancing simply added to the level of engagement, displayed different views of the clothing line, and solidified the brand message that you must "Dress to Live."

Figure 4.5 *Dockers created a fun mobile app that encouraged users to shake the iPhone and make Dufon dance.*

WebMD

WebMD created an application for doctors that included a free drug reference database and drug interaction checker (see Figure 4.6). It also allowed doctors to specify a specialty so that they could receive news and alerts based on their specialty. This was an effort to build a mobile community of medical professionals around the application, to help WebMD create brand awareness and affinity among doctors and expand their professional network. The campaign was part of a joint effort between WebMD and Medscape CME (Continuing Medical Education). Medscape provided the targeted news feeds, as well as opportunities for doctors to participate in CME training and accumulate credits that were all tracked as part of the Medscape system.

 Note

A similar effort called ReachMD launched a competing application, pulling in on-demand XM radio content to an iPhone application that also provided CME testing and engagement.

Figure 4.6 *WebMD created Medscape, an iPhone app that provides a drug interaction and reference database for physicians.*

Mobile Advertising

Mobile advertising is the subset of mobile marketing that involves promoting your product or service with text or graphical marketing messages displayed on sites other than your own. Some believe that mobile advertising is "the next big thing" because it can improve the experience for the user and create a badly needed source of revenue for mobile carriers. Only time will tell, but if we look back at the traditional Internet, it certainly is easy to see that various types of ad serving and ad networks have played a crucial role in the evolution of the channel. Mobile advertising is still in its infancy, but it does show a lot of promise.

Mobile advertising has some unique advantages over traditional Web advertising. The improved capability to track and target mobile advertising should create more profitable and actionable mobile advertising campaigns for marketers. The advertising environment on a mobile phone is also much less crowded, because mobile pages frequently have room to show only one or two advertisements; this should further improve the impact of those ads.

The biggest benefit to mobile advertising, however, is the strikingly high click-through and conversion rates that are possible. Traditional online banners perform at an average of .02% to .05% click-though, whereas Bango, one of the top mobile analytics platforms, claims that mobile banners get an average of 1% to 3% click-through. After click-through, the conversion rates average almost 5 times higher than their nonmobile counterparts.

A Glossary of Mobile Advertising Lingo

If you are familiar with online advertising campaigns and campaign management, you are probably reasonably familiar with the lingo and specific language to describe different elements of an online or mobile advertising campaign. If not, a list of common online advertising lingo and acronyms is included below:

- **PPC**—Pay-per-click marketing, a business model in which advertisers are charged for their advertisement only when someone actually clicks on it. Ads are usually shown alongside search results in a search engine. This model is described in more detail later in this chapter.

- **CPM**—Cost per thousand (CPM), the amount that an advertiser pays per thousand impressions.

- **eCPM**—Effective cost per thousand (eCPM), how advertisers refer to the cost of getting 1,000 impressions.

- **Impression**—One instance in which an advertisement is shown online. The number of impressions can be used to evaluate the branding effect that an advertisement might have. It is important to note, however, that an impression is a measure of exposure, not engagement.

- **Click**—A statistic that describes how many time users actually clicked on an advertisement. This is a measure of engagement, not exposure.

- **CTR**—Click-through rate, a relative measure of engagement based on the number of clicks per impression. A high CTR is valuable because it indicates that viewers are finding your advertisement compelling. In other words, viewers are seeing your ads and clicking on them.

- **Conversion**—A visitor to your mobile content takes an action that you want him to take—whether it's buying your product, downloading your product, or signing up for information or services that you offer. When this happens, the visitor is said to have "converted."

- **Acquisition**—A visitor signs up for alerts or emails, or in some way indicates that he or she wants to receive messages from you in the future. Also known as customer acquisition.

- **CPC and CPA**—Cost per conversion and cost per acquisition. These ratios measure the number of conversions or customer acquisitions that you received as a result of the advertising campaign, compared to the amount that you spend to place an advertisement. These are important statistics for understanding how much you are spending on each conversion or acquisition. These statistics can be figured individually, for each conversion event, or can be aggregated, for all the possible conversions in the campaign.

- **ROI**—Return on investment. This is a measurement that is similar to CPC and CPA, but incorporates all the costs associated with running the advertising campaign, including any agency management fees, design fees, and the cost of the time your staff has spent managing the campaign. ROI is discussed later in this chapter.

Different Types of Mobile Advertising

Mobile advertising can take a lot of different forms, but it is usually consumed when viewers are on the mobile Web, are using mobile applications, or are playing mobile games. When an advertisement is clicked, you generally have the option of driving the click to your website, to a mobile specific landing page, or to a download page. The click might also place a call through the mobile phone. Essentially four types of mobile advertising models are used:

- **Mobile banners and display**—As with traditional banners, mobile banners are graphics placed on a Web page. After clicking one, the visitor is linked to a specific offer or full-page advertisement. Mobile banners are usually sold on a CPM (cost per thousand impressions) basis. Mobile site owners agree to show the advertisement on their sites in return for payment from the mobile ad network. Mobile display ads can also be included in games and downloadable mobile applications for additional targeted exposure. In the mobile market, a fair average CPM is between $25 and $75, but this varies widely based on the market in which you are working. See Figure 5.1.

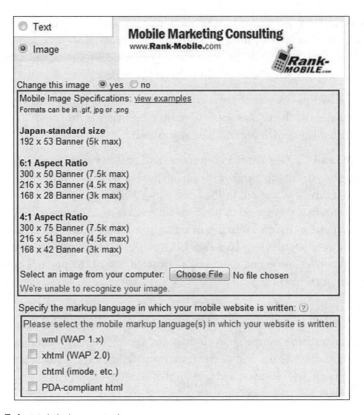

Figure 5.1 *Mobile banner ads.*

- **Mobile pay per click**—Similar to traditional pay-per-click advertising (PPC), mobile PPC ads are text and image advertisements offered by search engines and, usually served alongside organic mobile search results. PPC advertising is displayed when the ad is relevant to the searcher's query. Mobile PPC ads cost the advertiser money only when they are clicked. Advertisers choose a set of keywords that are relevant to searches for their products. Then text ads are served based on an advertiser's bid on a search query and the calculated relevance of the landing page to the search query. In addition to being targeted based on a user's search query, mobile PPC advertising can be targeted by location and carrier.

- **Contextual mobile ads**—Contextual mobile advertising is similar to mobile PPC. Advertisements are offered by the mobile search engine through a bidding model that combines the advertisers' willingness to pay for position with the relevance of the ad to a search query. Contextual mobile ads can be in the form of text or images, and are displayed on a mobile website instead of in mobile search results. In this model, mobile site owners consent for relevant advertisements to be shown on their websites in return for a portion of the profits that the ad network receives from those particular ads. See Figure 5.2.

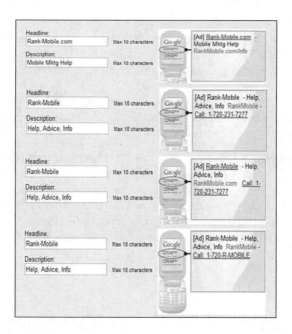

Figure 5.2 *Google AdWords mobile text ad options.*

- **Idle screen advertising**—Mobile advertisements are served while the user is waiting on a page or application to download or some other process to finish.

Although ads can be included on any mobile site, mobile advertisements are most commonly included on mobile news and information portals, social networks, and gaming sites. These types of companies invest heavily in the development of their mobile websites, whether they are news portals, social networks, or online game sites. They anticipate that their mobile websites will be generating high amounts of mobile traffic that they can monetize by selling advertising on the website. Frequently, these companies are giving away their mobile content for free, so their only way to make money is to sell advertising.

A BRIEF HISTORY OF MOBILE ADVERTISING

In the year 2000, D2 Communications, a Japanese mobile-marketing company, began delivering mobile banner ads, but most mobile advertising companies in the United States began delivering graphical banner ads only around the year 2005.

In the United States, mobile advertising was first pioneered by mobile carriers on their carrier decks, when they began offering text-based sponsorship on their portals. The ads were sold predominantly by carriers, were usually based on a CPM model, and were sold to companies and brands that had mobile-specific websites. Carriers did not push this type of marketing because they preferred long-standing content syndication agreements and didn't have the technology to deploy, target, and manage large-scale advertising networks.

Around the year 2000, third-party mobile advertising companies such as AdMob, JumpTap Millennial Media, Rhythm NewMedia, Third Screen Media, and Medio began creating ad networks that served mobile text and banner advertisements on third-party sites, in Europe and the United States. As phones became more sophisticated, the medium flipped from being mostly text based to mostly image based; now, in 2009, more than 97% of mobile ads are images.

On-Deck Versus Off-Deck Web Advertising

The experience between on- and off-deck Web access is becoming very similar, but on- and off-deck mobile Web access are still fundamentally different. As discussed in previous chapters, on-deck Web access is Web access that the carrier provides though a branded portal, sometimes called a WAP deck. Marguerite Reardon, a staff writer at CNET News, explains the unique business model for on-deck Web access quite well:

> Most mobile operators offer subscribers a menu or "deck" filled with the carriers' own content that has been supplied through deals they have made with news organizations, record labels, TV networks and other content producers. Carriers generate revenue by charging for subscriptions to packages or premium content. They also get a cut of revenue when users download content from their decks.

Off-deck Web access is access to the Web-at-large through a mobile browser that the carriers do not control. To be included on a carrier deck, you have to work with a carrier or one of its agencies; to be included in the off-deck mobile Web, all you need is a website that a mobile browser can access.

Carrier decks are limited versions of the mobile Web that the carriers have created for their subscribers. In the on-deck world, each carrier has different advertising guidelines and brokers deals with individual content providers. The content or proceedings of these agreements are rarely made public. That being said, it is nearly impossible to summarize or even postulate what strategies would be most effective to become syndicated in the various carrier decks.

Even though studies show that more mobile Web traffic is moving off-deck, being listed well on a carrier deck can be an important way for mobile marketers to drive traffic to their mobile offerings. Nisheeth Mohan, product manager for mobile solutions and technology at Keynote Systems, wrote this in 2009:

> Nielsen Mobile did a study several years ago in which it reported that "mobile games promoted on a carrier's New, Featured or Best Seller decks saw 90 percent more downloads than when those same games were not promoted. Furthermore, titles that got top shelf placement on the first page of the carrier's deck achieved 53 percent more downloads than when those titles appeared on subsequent pages of the deck." The revenue impact to a content provider is huge.

> Note that in 2008, ring tone revenues were projected to be more than $500 million by BMI and mobile gaming was expected to hit $5.4 billion in 2008, according to Jupiter Research.

> Clearly, it is worth some time and effort to monitor your carrier deck placement. You also probably know that this isn't easy.

> Early knowledge of changes in placement in the deck— both of your content and that of your competitors—can help you with revenue projections, product planning and quality control strategies.

> Unfortunately, most monitoring strategies today are pretty rudimentary.

> Someone—and probably several people—in your company have to manually go through carrier decks on different phones to check your placement; the process is slow and tedious.

> I talked to one deck provider who related a company strategy of mandatory weekend sessions where employees sat with a variety of cell phones and a checklist to confirm their content positions.

> Worse, you can't just do it once. Ongoing vigilance is critical to make sure that you are on top of your visibility—and monitoring those games or ringtones that outrank you on a deck.

The methods for ranking products or advertisements in the carrier decks vary from carrier to carrier and have never been made particularly transparent. In some cases, it is mainly a function of the syndication agreement that was created with the content provider. In some other cases, it is based on popularity and social ranking systems, such as star ratings.

Content syndication agreements can also be confusing because, in some cases, content providers make deals directly with the handset manufacturers (instead of carriers) to ensure that their content is accessible to subscribers in all the networks where a particular phone is sold. As an example, Nokia created a service called Media Center on all of the N95 phones. The service included direct links to Sony, News Corp., and CNN for mobile video distribution. This agreement ensured that access to the Media Center was available on any N95 handset, regardless of what carrier sold it.

On-deck advertising has been successful in the past but has a limited life moving into the future, at least in the United States. Few people have deep access or understanding of how best to work with the multiple carriers. On-deck advertising is frequently a complex trial-and-error process that is laden with long negotiations and content exclusivity rights. In the long run, on-deck carrier solutions do not appear to be particularly scalable or desirable. As marketers, it is important to understand that the target demographic ford mobile marketingis alreadyfamiliar with traditional Web access. In the Long term, they will see little value in accessing a limited or filtered version of the Internet that is provided by the carrier deck. In the consumers mind, carriers simply don't have enough resources or expertise to re-create the Internet-at-large on their branded portals.

The content syndication and licensing that is crucial in the on-deck business model blurs the lines for mobile advertising. Some say that advertising includes only text and image ads that are delivered on a CMP or PPC basis; others argue that the syndication and licensing agreements are simply permits to promote or advertise branded content on the carrier deck. The rankings of on-deck mobile content can be seen as advertisings for your mobile products and services, in the same way that traditional search engine listings can be considered advertisements for Web products or services.

Frequently, carriers are reticent to work directly with advertisers because in many cases, it would require them to share statistics about their network that they would rather keep quiet. Generally, carriers and handset manufacturers do not create and maintain their own ad networks or technologies. Instead, they work with existing mobile ad networks EndPocket, AdMob, or ThirdScreen to leverage their ad-serving platforms and inventory. Nokia is the most notable exception, offering advertising through a company called Nokia Media network.

In mobile advertising, carriers have a unique advantage over third-party advertising partners because they can serve ads based on specific demographic information about their users, pulled directly from their customer database. As a response to this, in 2008, many of the third-party advertising partners began offering sophisticated analytics programs to track the success of advertisements on their networks and provide advertisers with as much information as possible about their advertising campaign. Carriers also can offer incentives for viewing advertisements on the mobile phone, such as free minutes or free downloads. Brands that want to do this have to work directly with the carriers.

When determining what ad network you want to work with and what carrier deck you want to show your ads, you should evaluate the traffic and demographic information associated with the carrier. The most recent Web traffic data can be accessed from mobile Web reporting agencies, such as ComScores' m:Metrics or Nielsen Mobile. Table 5.1 shows a 2009 mobile carrier report card for the top seven U.S. mobile carriers. Information such as the number of subscribers or the percent of revenue that data service represents for the carrier should also be available directly from the carriers themselves. However, third-party reporting services should always be used when they are available. Additionally, both carriers and ad-serving networks should be able to provide demographic information about their audience, including age, gender, income, and location.

Table 5.1   2009 Mobile Carrier Report Card

Carrier	Subscriber Base	Net Adds	Avg Monthly Churn	Service Revenue	Data as a % of Service Revenue	Avg Revenue Per User
Verizon Wireless	86.7 million	1.3 million	1.5%	$13.1 billion	27.9%	$50.74
AT&T	78.2 million	1.2 million	1.6%	$11.7 billion	27.2%	$50.11
Sprint Nextel	48.1 million	(261,000)	2.7%	$6.4 billion	28.0%	$53.52
T-Mobile USA	33.2 million	415,000	3.1%	$4.8 billion	19.5%	$48.29
US Cellular	6.2 million	47,000	1.9%	$982 million	16.0%	$52.54
MetroPCS	6.1 million	684,000	5.0%	$727 million	N/A	$40.40
Leap Wireless	4.3 million	493,000	3.3%	$514 million	N/A	$42.21

Data courtesy of Strategy Analytics, Inc.

With the popularity of the Apple AppStore, many American carriers, including T-Mobile and Verizon, have begun to rebrand their WAP decks as "app stores" in an attempt to drive more traffic and sales through their on-deck portals (see Table 5.2). For the most part, the rebranded carrier portals still follow the same complicated content syndication systems, which still presents a huge barrier to development and entry into this market, but you can expect to see more similar moves from the carriers in the future. The success of the AppStore and the Android Marketplace can largely be credited to the accessibility that they presented for application developers to submit and promote their own applications.

Table 5.2   On- and Off-Deck Carriers for Top 7 U.S. Mobile Carriers

Carrier	Mobile Carrier Deck	On-Deck Mobile Ad Network	Native Off-Deck Search Engine
Verizon Wireless	Mobile Web Games and Apps Store	ThirdScreen Media	Google
AT&T (Except iPhone)	AT&T MEdia Net	Yahoo!	Yahoo! oneSearch
AT&T (Just iPhone)	The AppStore	N/A	Google
Sprint-Nextel	—	EndPocket	Google
T-Mobile USA	Web2Go (App Store) Web'n'walk (UK)	Yahoo!	Yahoo! oneSearch
US Cellular	—	JumpTap	JumpTap
Metro PCS	—	—	—
Leap Wireless	Cricket's Mobile Web Portal	—	—

Data courtesy of Strategy Analytics, Inc.

For more information about the difference between on- and off-deck mobile environments, please reference Chapter 2, "The Brief History of Mobile Marketing."

Combined On- and Off-Deck Solutions

The difficulty of working with carriers and advertising on carrier decks has driven many mobile advertisers off-deck, and unless the carriers' business models change, this trend is likely to continue. Just as the lines between on- and off-deck Web access have become blurred, so have the lines between off- and on-deck mobile advertising. In many cases now, mobile ad-serving networks provide access to audiences that are both on- and off-deck. This is especially true of the search engine ad networks, such as Google, Yahoo!, and JumpTap. The trend has also been pushed by ad networks that sell advertising within free downloadable applications; when viewing the ad, the subscriber is neither on-deck or off-deck.

The lines between on- and off-deck Web access are further blurring, as many carriers have opened up their carrier decks, sometimes referred to as a "walled garden" WAP decks to the rest of the Internet. Some carriers are working with top search engines to provide both on- and off-deck search for their subscribers; sometimes it is unclear whether subscribers are searching for or requesting on- or off-deck information. This confusion and obfuscation should be taken as an indication that the carriers do not have a clear plan regarding how their carrier decks and on-deck content will compete in the long-run.

Working with mobile ad aggregators is the best way to bridge the gap and get your advertisements seen both on- and off-deck. According to Deepa Karthikeyan, a data analyst at Wireless Data Services, the top aggregators in the United States in 2009 were AdMob, Google (AdSense), Yahoo! Mobile, ThirdScreen Media, and Amobee. (Ms. Karthikeyan's methodical research also contributed to some of the vendor descriptions at the end of this chapter.) Many of these mobile ad aggregators have networks that span both on- and off-deck, and allow advertisers to include the carrier as a targeting or segmenting feature on their platform.

Creating Effective Mobile Advertising Campaigns

There are four key elements to creating an effective mobile advertising campaign:

- the creative
- the landing page
- the targeting
- the evaluation of success

Mastering each of these tasks will ensure that you create a valuable campaign, and that you are able to learn from your successes and failures, in order to improve the performance of the campaign.

Authoring Effective Mobile Ads

Users first see the content, or "creative," for a mobile advertisement, which entices them to click through to visit your mobile website and download your mobile application or sign up for your mobile alerts. The creative can be text or display advertising, video, or animation. Regardless of the medium, the creative's only goal is to get people to click on the advertisement.

In mobile advertising, you have a limited amount of space in which to convey your marketing message. In addition, the ads are being displayed on very small screens, so complicated graphics or calls to action could make ads less effective. Creative for mobile advertising should almost always be different than the content or creative for traditional Web advertising.

If you are authoring text for a text-only creative, it is a good idea to use common SMS and Web abbreviations, otherwise know as txt spk, to convey your message. This form of shorthand includes words such as DK for "don't know," Gr8 for "great," and <3 for "love," and will help you get across more in less space. Using txt spk could also make your target audience feel like your brand speaks their language, if they are part of a demographic that is highly fluent in text spk. A more complete list of these abbreviations is included in the back of this book.

If you are building banners or other mobile display advertisements, it is important to focus the graphic on your call to action. Mobile advertising is still new enough that many viewers could be easily confused by seeing a brand message from a company when they are on a different brand's website, so clarity is key to generating a good click-through rate (CTR).

Constructing Effective Mobile Landing Pages

After you have crafted the appropriate message, you need to determine where the ad will link to on your website. If you are doing a basic branding campaign, you can send users directly to the home page of your site. If you are promoting a specific product, service, or application, the click should take the user directly to the page where they can purchase or interact with the offer.

In some cases, it may be advantageous to create separate landing pages for your ads instead of simply landing the visitors on existing pages on your site. This allows you to tailor the message specifically to the ad that the user was interested in. Your landing page should further promote the offer and explain how it can be redeemed. Landing pages should also be linked back to your mobile site so users can become more familiar with your mobile content after they take advantage of the offer.

Tests should be run before and after a campaign launches to ensure that the ads are being displayed correctly and tracked appropriately. It is also important to test your landing pages. As with testing a mobile website, it can be quite complicated to ensure that your advertisement will work perfectly on every browser, handset, and carrier combination. Tools are available to help you do this; Chapter 10, "Mobile Website Development," covers them more completely. If you determine that your ads or landing pages are not rendering well on a certain handset or across a certain carrier network, you can usually use ad network tools to block the ads from being shown in those places until the landing pages or downloads have been fixed.

Effectively Targeting Your Mobile Advertising Campaigns

The most important thing you can do to ensure the success of your mobile advertising campaign is to target your ads appropriately. Mobile advertisements should be as relevant, clear, and actionable as possible. Most ad-serving platforms offer a number of ways to target advertisements, to prevent your ad from being shown on sites or to users that will not likely click through or convert. It is up to you to test and determine the most powerful combination of the following criteria for your brand and your advertisement: demographic segmentation, time segmentation, handset groups, carrier groups, and location segmentation.

Demographic Segmentation

Almost every ad platform allows you to segment your mobile advertising based on demographic factors such as age, gender, and income level. The segmentation works based on the information that the ad network has about the website, application, or game that will be running the advertisement. If you use a platform to target women, your ad will appear on websites that also target women. If you use a platform to target a lower-income demographic, the ad network will put your ad on websites that target lower-income buyers. If you are working directly with carriers or advertising on a mobile social network, it is easier to get specific demographic data because targeting is done based on information that members of the social network supplied voluntarily or from information about members that the carrier requires.

Time Segmentation (Day Parting)

Segmenting your advertisements by time of day, otherwise known as day parting, can be especially powerful for mobile advertising. Some ads and products will be more effective at driving clicks and conversion at specific times of day. In a CPM model, it is particularly important to show ads when they are most relevant to the viewer. This is important because, unlike PPC, in a CPM model, you pay for the ad impression, even if it does not successfully generate any click-through.

Day parting can be especially valuable in mobile advertising campaigns for brick-and-mortar stores. A mobile marketing message for a brick-and-mortar store is intrinsically more actionable because it is being displayed on a portable device. Adding a temporal awareness gets the message even closer to the real-time, as-needed marketing messages that we strive for in mobile marketing. For example, advertisements promoting a lunch special should run when people are planning their lunch, but should not run all day or into the night. Similarly, if you are promoting a TV show or movie that will be on at night, it is best to day-part ads to show during the evening commute, when people are planning their evening.

If you are promoting mobile content or entertainment, day parting is less crucial but can still be valuable. Use your Web analytics to determine when your website is getting the most traffic; then segment your advertising campaigns based on that information. It might be acceptable to keep some ads running around the clock, but focus most the impressions you are getting on the times that your website appears to be most relevant to existing users.

Handset Groups

In some cases, your mobile offering, your advertisement, or your landing page will be built to work on a specific cell phone or mobile handset. This is particularly common if you are working directly on a carrier deck, or if you are promoting a mobile game or application that has been built for a carrier-specific platform. In some mobile ad platforms, you will be able to target specific handset models, such as the BlackBerry Curve 8350i. In other cases, you will be able to segment your targeting only by handset groups, such as all BlackBerry or all Razr handsets.

Carrier Groups

In other cases, you might want to segment your advertising campaign by carrier. This happens naturally if you are advertising on a carrier deck, but it can also be valuable for off-deck mobile advertising. If you are a mobile telecom company trying to get people to switch carriers, you would want to send one message to people who are accessing the mobile Web from other carrier networks, and another message for customers who are already on your network, to encourage them to add new products and services to their plan.

Location Segmentation

Some ad networks also allow you to segment your ads based on the location of the recipient. Most ad networks cannot actually detect a person's location, so they have to be more creative to provide location-based ad targeting. In most cases, when you select to segment your ad serving by location, the ad networks simply set it up to show on websites that are targeted at a specific location. For instance, if you are targeting customers in Chicago, the ad will show on a page that is explicitly about Chicago-based events, locations or activities. In other cases, if you are working with a carrier or a mobile social network, you can get more information about Web visitors and where they live, but you still will probably not be able to tell specifically where they are at any given time.

Evaluating Success

If your mobile advertising is for brand awareness only, your success can be evaluated by the total number of impressions and the click-through rate of your ads. If you want users to take an action or make a purchase while on your mobile site, success should be measured in terms of return on investment (ROI).

ROI = (Gain from Investment – Cost of Investment)/Cost of Investment

ROI is the success metric for mobile advertising because it allows advertisers to determine whether each dollar spent on advertising earns more than a dollar back in value or return. The best ROI is driven by a combination of effective targeting, messaging, and landing pages. In many cases, it is a good idea to set up a test budget so that you can try various types of messaging, creative, and targeting to see what is most effective for your campaign.

Often your call to action for mobile users receiving your advertising is to sign up for news and updates or to download an app instead to make a purchase. To determine the ROI for these types of initiatives, each action that you want users to take from their mobile phone should be assigned a monetary value. In most cases, users can take more than one desirable action on your mobile site, so each of these actions should be given a different value. These values should represent the financial reward that each action provides.

If you are having a hard time determining the relative value of each conversion, you can start by ordering the conversion from most valuable to least valuable. Then determine whether there are multipliers between the different levels of conversion. For example, is conversion #1 three times more valuable than conversion #3, or is it ten times more valuable than conversion #3? After you set up these relationships, you need only determine the actual monetary value of one conversion to assign the values to the rest of the conversions.

Many elements of mobile marketing can be very subjective, but ROI gives everyone in your group a clear idea of how the campaign is performing. When you begin a mobile advertising initiative, it is a good idea to set ROI goals that you and your marketing team can work toward, and make them widely known to everyone on the project. If you are launching your first mobile advertising campaign, it is fine to set the ROI goals low, or even at a break-even level, because you are still learning the medium. After you have launched a couple mobile advertising initiatives, you should begin to set the ROI goals a bit higher, to ensure that your campaigns are constantly improving and that your team is actively engaged in the success of your ad campaign.

Case Studies

The following case studies illustrate successful and creative use of mobile advertising campaigns. You will see that each of the examples features compelling advertising creative and landing pages that are combined with a good understanding of their target market and desired conversion goals.

Land Rover

To reach an affluent male demographic between ages 34 and 54, Land Rover launched a mobile advertising campaign to promote the Range Rover Sport, Land Rover LR2, and Land Rover LR3 (see Figure 5.3). They wanted to create awareness and excitement about these SUVs, to ensure that men in the target demographic considered them when researching their next car purchase. Land Rover worked with AdMob to run targeted text and image ads on premium mobile sites such as CBS and AccWeather. They targeted the ads based on gender and age. Land Rover also decided to send ads only to the most sophisticated smart phones, assuming that this would ensure they were hitting the right income bracket. Those mobile ads took consumers to a mobile site where users could look up dealers and click to call the dealer of their choice. Consumers also could watch videos, view images, download wallpapers, or submit their email address to be mailed a digital brochure.

AdMob was able to drive 73% of traffic to Land Rover's mobile site. In this campaign, Land Rover had 45,000 views of their video, 128,000 views of their image gallery, 7,400 wallpaper downloads, 5,000 dealer look-ups, 1,100 click-to-calls, and 800 brochure requests.

AirAsia

To take advantage of the mass penetration of mobile Web access in Asia, and to increase awareness of their brand and their promotions, AirAsia launched a campaign with Yahoo! Mobile. In a short period of time, their mobile advertising campaign achieved a high click-through rate and drove a considerable amount of traffic to the AirAsia mobile site. In one month, the click-through rate from mobile advertising was 1.78%, and the average cost per conversion was only 56¢.

Adidas

In an attempt to extend its "Basketball Is a Brotherhood" campaign, Adidas worked with AdMob to create an integrated mobile campaign that leveraged AdMob's ad-serving network. In it, graphical ads were deployed to encourage viewers to click on the ad to call Kevin Garnett, a prominent basketball player that was featured in their TV ads. When viewers clicked to call, they could receive a custom voicemail message from Kevin Garnett, view mobile videos, or see images of top players' shoes. The campaign was well received, and a high percentage of users clicked to call more than once. The mobile advertising campaign drove sign-ups more efficiently than the TV, traditional Web advertising, and even in-store efforts.

Figure 5.3 *A Land Rover mobile advertising campaign. Photos courtesy of AdMob.*

Visa

During the Olympic games in 2008 in Beijing, Visa participated by sponsoring coverage of the games on Yahoo!'s website. They also launched mobile banners on the Yahoo! Mobile network to drive traffic to their mobile website. Once on Visa's mobile site, viewers could learn more about the Olympic athletes, read news stories and expert analysis, view images, and see the TX broadcast schedule for the games. The campaign received an above-average mobile click-through rate.

Mobile Advertising Networks

The following is a list of mobile advertising networks. The services, policies, and so on are different for each, so check them out thoroughly before making a choice for your business.

- AdMob—www.adMob.com
- BuzzCity—www.BuzzCity.com
- Itsmy.biz—www.itsMy.biz
- Third Screen Media—www.ThirdScreenMedia.com
- ZestADZ—www.zestadz.com
- 4th Screen Advertising—www.4th-screen.com
- AditOn—www.aditon.com
- Amobee—www.amobee.com
- Celltick—www.celltick.com
- Digital SIDEBAR—www.digitalsidebar.com
- Frog2Frog—www.frog2frog.com
- Ad Infuse—www.adinfuse.com
- Admoda—www.adModa.com
- Decktrade—www.deckTrade.com
- Google AdSense and AdWords—www.adWords.Google.com and www.adSense.Google.com
- Medio MobileNow—www.Medio.com
- Mojiva—www.Mojiva.com
- JumpTap—www.JumpTap.com
- Yahoo! Mobile—www.SearchMarketing.Yahoo.com
- Add2Phone—www.add2phone.com
- GoldSpot Media—www.goldspotmedia.com
- Microsoft Mobile Advertising—http://advertising.microsoft.com/uk/Mobile
- Utarget.FOX—www.utarget.co.uk
- Unanimis—www.unanimis.co.uk

6

Mobile Promotions and Location-Based Marketing

One of the best opportunities in mobile marketing is the capability to build brand awareness and goodwill with your target market. Mobile promotions help customers feel appreciated and, thus, feel more loyal to your brand. With the appropriate customer-tracking systems, loyalty programs can be layered in to create an even closer connection between your customers and your brand. This kind of deep connection can help drive sales, but it will also help create brand evangelists who will endorse your brand to all their friends, which is quite powerful. Mobile promotion is also an ingenious way for companies to reach out to their customers and create a mobile presence without creating and maintaining a mobile website.

The most common mobile promotions begin with SMS, MMS, and proximity marketing messages. These can be followed by coupons, discounts, or promotions that are sent directly to the customers' mobile phones. The coupons or discounts can then be redeemed in a variety of ways. After customers have opted in to your mobile communication, loyalty programs can be developed to optimize your customer interaction at the most granular and personal level. This chapter focuses on using SMS, MMS, and location-based marketing to build a list of potential customers who are interested in receiving marketing messages from you. It then details how to drive sales with mobile coupons and promotions, and finally, how to leverage loyalty programs to create a custom communication strategy to reach your most loyal customers.

Introduction to Mobile Promotions

A 2008 study by Jupiter Research estimated that retailers send out nearly three billion mobile coupons per year worldwide. Mobile couponing, or mCoupons, have yet to be widely adopted in the United States, but they have seen much more success in Europe and Asia. In the United States, problems with delivery and redemption are still being worked out. Despite the complications, mobile couponing is a great way to drive foot traffic to brick-and-mortar stores.

The goal of mCoupons is basically the same as that of traditional coupons: They should drive revenue by encouraging higher volume and repeat sales. They can also help increase product awareness and move overstocked inventory to make room for new, more valuable products. Mobile couponing can be much more tailored to the needs of the specific consumer and less costly than traditional print coupons. For the user, they are also nice because mobile coupons don't have to be clipped and carried around to be redeemed.

The most important consideration when you are developing mobile couponing strategy is the ease of use for the consumers. If the process for sign-up, delivery, and redemption of a coupon is too complicated or time consuming, users will not participate. To develop an effective mobile couponing strategy you must understand the three elements of mobile couponing: coupon messaging, coupon targeting, and coupon delivery and redemption.

What Products Are Right for Mobile Couponing?

Before you get started with mobile couponing, you must assess your goals and expectations. Some products and services are more appropriate for mobile promotions than others. Mobile promotions provided by retailers are much more intuitive than promotions provided by manufacturers. This is because when you are working with a specific retailer, you can ensure that they will have the necessary equipment and training to redeem mobile coupons or discounts at their counters. Because coupons offered by manufacturers can be redeemed at any location that sells the product (for instance a 50¢ off coupon for Velveeta Cheese), there is no way of ensuring a problem-free redemption of the coupon.

Some companies have tried to surmount this obstacle, but their efforts have seen varying success. CellFire, Hothand Wireless, and SingleTouch Interactive have three different models whereby participants can interact with a database of manufacturer coupons (online or through a downloadable application), to choose the manufacturer coupons that they would like from their mobile phone. After coupons are selected, the information is sent to their loyalty account, and redemption happens automatically when the user scans his or her loyalty card at the register.

Mobile coupons from retailers are much simpler. Besides knowing that the retailer will be able to redeem the coupon, there is a lower likelihood that your customers will have more than one or two coupons to redeem during any one transaction. This makes the redemption of the coupon a simpler process and, thus, more rewarding for the consumer and the retailer.

Mobile Coupon Messaging

The most effective and easily redeemable mobile coupons are sent via SMS or MMS. Although it is not yet required by law, the Mobile Marketing Association stringently suggests that users must opt-in to this kind of marketing because their carrier may charge them for the receipt of your text or picture message. This charge must be taken into account when you are crafting your messaging, because the offer must provide enough value to justify the charge to their bill. In the case of text messages, the charge can be around 10¢–15¢ but for picture or multimedia messages (MMS), the charge can be as high as 50¢.

Most mobile coupons are sent via text message, which creates a number of constraints for the marketer. You have only 160 characters (or 70 non-Latin characters), including spaces, to convey your message. Coupons should always provide a clear offer and expiration date. Simple offers with quick expiration periods will promote a faster response, but longer expiration periods will provide a better rate of redemption. Ideally, you should also provide a mechanism for recipients to opt out of future coupons and messages from your company.

Mobile Coupon Targeting

One of the first challenges with mobile couponing in the United States is that there is no consensus regarding the best way to encourage potential customers to opt-in to your marketing messages, thereby ensuring that you are marketing to a targeted list of recipients. Many of the options are still too complicated or intrusive, but there is a clear incentive for companies to find the right balance, and that will probably happen soon. In general, companies can use numerous methods to encourage potential customers to opt-in to your mobile communications and mobile coupons, and a combination of all the methods is usually desirable.

- **Text message opt-in**—The consumer initiates the opt-in process by texting a keyword to a short code after being presented with the option through some other form of marketing.

- **Invitation opt-in**—If you already have a database of customer phone numbers, it is generally acceptable to send them one message, requesting that they opt-in to your mobile couponing program. This message should include your company name and instructions for responding to the text message to opt-in. If recipients do not explicitly opt-in they should not be sent further marketing messages. If they do opt-in, a follow-up message should be sent with an initial coupon thanking them for signing up. You should also be sure to include information about how they should respond if they want to stop receiving text communications, as well as a link to view your terms and conditions.

- **Online opt-ins**—With this method of targeting, people interested in your product or services simply sign up to receive your mobile marketing messages and coupons through your website. They submit their phone number, and then messages and coupons can be sent to them directly from your database. This is just like sending coupons by email, except that the coupons are sent to the user's phone via SMS or MMS. The best practice is to send a text message immediately after the online form has been submitted, thanking users for signing up, verifying that you have permission to send coupons, and including other marketing messages via text messages. If users are signing up for both email and text messages, you will need to send an email confirmation, to complete the opt-in for the email program, and a text message confirmation, to complete the opt-in for the text message program.

- **Point of sale opt-in**—Billboards and displays in stores can be used to encourage users to opt-in to a mobile couponing program. These messages usually have instructions that tell the shopper to text-message a specific word to a short code that is provided on the signage. Alternately, retailers can collect mobile phone numbers through a specialized device at the purchase counter, or a clerk can input them directly into the company's system at the register.

- **Phone call opt-in**—A quick and frequently overlooked method of building a targeted list of mobile coupon recipients is to integrate the opt-in process with your phone system. When potential customers call in and are put on hold, you can include a message that encourages them to opt-in to your mobile couponing program while they are on hold, simply by pushing a button on their phone. Although this works only if the caller is calling from a cellphone, it is quite easy to implement because the phone system can automatically detect the caller's mobile phone number and store it to a database. The hold message would simply say something like, "Press 1 to get mobile coupons sent directly to your cellphone." Again, the first message sent to the phone number should be a coupon thanking customers for opting in and giving instructions about how to opt out if they want to stop receiving the messages.

- **Email opt-in**—If you are doing email marketing, you should also include information about your mobile couponing program in each of the emails that you send, encouraging the recipients either to go to the website to opt-in (include a link to the opt-in page) or to opt-in via text message immediately.

- **Microblogging opt-in**—Microblogging platforms such as Twitter and Pounce are another way to send mobile coupons and promotions to your clients with minimal overhead or complications. Brands can simply create accounts with the microblogging platform of their choice (Twitter is the most popular in the United States). Users can then opt-in to messages from your company by "following" your brand on the platform. Short messages are then broadcast via the platform to all your followers, and they have opted in to your mobile marketing messages via their default agreement with the microblogging platform.

Users can opt-in to receiving your messages via the Web or directly to their mobile phones as text messages. After a brand account has been set up, you can build your list of followers by searching for people who are interested in your product or service. When you friend someone on these networks, many follow you in turn. Automated responses can also be set up using programs such as Twitter-Hawk, and they can be tied to the use of specific key phrases or specific actions taken on the platform. It is advisable to include a personal appeal to your messaging instead of simply relying on automated responses or only including marketing messages in your Twitter feed.

Mobile Coupon Delivery

Mobile coupons can be sent using a variety of technologies. The most common method of mobile coupon delivery is through SMS or MMS based on a list of contracts you already have. Mobile coupons can also be delivered via location-based technology, described in more detail later in the chapter. Regardless of the method of delivery, any mobile couponing delivery should be directed through a database or preference center that identifies potential customers and whether they have opted in to mobile communication. This is also discussed later in this chapter.

Coupon Delivery via Text Messaging (SMS)

In 1991, a Finish company called Radiolinja (now known as Elisa) offered the first mobile data service; the first text message was sent in 1993. Text messaging, otherwise known as Short Message Service (SMS), wasn't used much for marketing in North America until after 2000.

SMS messages can be sent from phone to phone or from computer to phone, or they can be sent from a phone to a "common short code," usually abbreviated to simply "short code." See Figure 6.1 and 6.2. A short code is a five- or six-digit phone number that can be dialed as a destination for a text message. Text messages are then sent to a computer communication system instead of a phone. Short codes can be shared or owned privately by a company.

If a short code is shared, certain keywords are set up to trigger the parsing activity of the computer system for the short code. The computer communication system that controls the short code is tasked with sending and parsing all the information for the short code. Shared short codes are easy and cheap to get, but can be risky or complicated depending on the types of text responses you expect to get, and how well the computer system is able to parse them.

Figure 6.1 *Short codes, such as the one shown here, are becoming more common in mobile marketing.*

Figure 6.2 *Another example of a short code used in advertising.*

Dedicated short codes are ideal, especially for big bands, because they allow you to control the branding and capture all the information that is sent to the short code. The disadvantage is that they can be expensive, and the process to acquire them can be time consuming and cumbersome. Common short codes are generally registered or leased, for a period of time, much like a domain name. The body that controls common short codes in the United States is called the CSC Registry and they have a website at www.USShortcodes.com. Once a short code is leased, you must send applications to each of the carriers in the region that your text messaging campaigns targeted, so that your campaign can be reviewed, provisioned and approved by the carrier. Your application must also pass review from the CTIA Monitoring Agent, who evaluates the campaigns adherence to the Consumer Best Practices.

Initially, SMS was used as a way for carriers to communicate with their subscribers. Later, SMS began to take off as a means of person-to-person communication. It offered a significant cost savings over traditional voice calling and allowed recipients to view and respond to the text message at their discretion. In North America, the first cross-carrier SMS marketing campaign was run by Labatt Brewing Company in 2002. Now, in 2009, it is estimated that more than 74% of mobile subscribers are active users of SMS, and more than 90% of the mobile marketing revenue comes from SMS messaging.

Coupon Delivery via Picture Messaging (MMS)

The late 1990s also saw the development of picture messaging, otherwise known as Multimedia Message Service (MMS). MMS is an extension of the SMS messaging standard but uses the WAP coding language to display multimedia content. Picture messages are sent in much the same way as text messages, but they can contain images, timed slideshows, audio, video, and text. The first group to launch an MMS campaign was a carrier out of Europe called Telenor, in 2002.

Picture message marketing has not been widely adopted in North America, partly because mobile carriers charge for both sending and receiving picture messages. The cost is usually 5 to 10 times higher than it would be for a text message, which creates a substantial disincentive for people to remain opted in to that kind of messaging.

The lack of mass adoption of this type of marketing could also be because no sufficient platform can efficiently send bulk MMS messages. Complications caused by discrepancies in the different networks' MMS messaging standards, and different phone-rendering capabilities make deploying a successful picture messaging campaign time-consuming and difficult.

As with email, concerns arise about unwanted SMS and MMS marketing, otherwise known as spam. This is more prolific in countries where carriers are allowed to sell the phone numbers of their subscribers to third-party advertisers. Many mobile carriers in the United States and Europe now police their own networks, to prevent SMS and MMS SPAM from reaching their subscribers. In December 2005, the Mobile Marketing Association (MMA) outlined Consumer Best Practices Guidelines, which included instructions for SMS marketers. This document is updated twice a year, and is considered the best set of guidelines available in the United States. Be sure to review these guidelines before launching any SMS or MMS marketing campaign. You can find the guidelines here: http://mmaglobal.com/bestpractices.pdf

Mobile spam is covered in more depth in Chapter 13, "Mobile Marketing Privacy, Spam, and Viruses."

Location-Based Couponing

Mobile coupons can also be delivered directly to your device when you respond to a location-based prompt that is part of a Bluetooth or WiFi broadcast, or is embedded in a billboard or display as a QR code or infrared beam. LBS is discussed later in this chapter.

Mobile Coupon Redemption

Mobile coupon redemption is another aspect of mobile couponing for which there has yet to be a consensus. The two basic methods of mobile coupon redemption are through the use of alphanumeric redemption codes and barcode scanners.

- **Alphanumeric codes**—Redemption codes can be used for both manufacturer and retailer coupons. In this scenario, a redemption code is sent to potential customers via SMS. The message should include information about the coupon and when it expires. When the recipient goes to redeem the coupon, he simply gives the code to the clerk at the register. If your company has an online presence, the recipient should also be able to redeem the coupon when shopping online. The difficulty with this method of redemption is mostly seen if manufacturers have not worked directly with their retailers to ensure consumers' ability to redeem the coupon at their registers.

- **Barcode scanners**—In Asia, many retailers are equipped with scanners that can read barcodes, known as QR codes, directly from a mobile handset. These are not prevalent in the United States, but that may change as mobile marketing becomes a more powerful force in the industry (see Figure 6.3). In this scenario, coupons are sent as a text message, with a link to the mobile coupon and barcode that can be scanned at the register. Alternately, coupons can be sent as an MMS message that includes the barcode directly in the message.

If you are a retailer and you can ensure that all your retail locations have the equipment required to scan barcodes off phones, then this can be a good strategy. However, if you are a manufacturer, ensuring quick redemption of these coupons becomes more difficult. Mobile marketers who are launching campaigns in a region where mobile barcode scanners are not ubiquitous should include an alphanumeric code with the barcode message, to ensure that recipients will be able to redeem the coupon.

UPC-A Barcode

Maxi Code

EZ Code

QR Code

Figure 6.3 *QR codes are more common outside the United States, but that could change soon. Photos courtesy of Maly LOLek, Darko, Ajenbo and Brdall, via Wikimedia Creative Commons License 3.0, a freely licensed media repository and Share Alike 2.0, also a Wikipedia freely licensed media repository.*

In either redemption scenario, you can choose to send the same message to everyone or you can choose to segment your message to learn more about your customers. In some cases, you might want to run an A/B test to see what offers recipients find more compelling. To do that, you write two different promotional messages that are each linked to different redemption codes. When coupons are redeemed, you can quickly and easily see which marketing message was more compelling and then use that information to guide future marketing messages.

If you have a loyalty program in place, you can also use information from your loyalty program to send the same message to different types of customers. The catch is that messages sent to different customer types contain different redemption codes. This allows you to track the individual segment's response to the same marketing message. If you segment your customers based on their average annual spending, gender, or zip code, and give each group a different redemption code, you can learn which groups are more responsive to your marketing message.

You can also segment messages to determine which method of delivery is most effective for your customer base by sending one group an alphanumeric promotion code and the other a link to a mobile Web coupon or a scannable bar code.

Digital Proximity and Location-Based Marketing

Obviously, one of the most valuable aspects of mobile marketing is that the phone is with its owner all the time. Many brick-and-mortar stores may have had a hard time using the traditional Internet to drive foot traffic, but location-based marketing turns the tables and gives them an incredible opportunity to get people into stores (evaluated in the industry as cost per pair of feet, or CPPoF). Mobile promotions reach potential customers when they are most likely to make a purchase. Location-based services (LBS, sometimes also called near LBS, or NLBS) are digital systems that broadcast digital messages to enabled devices within a specific radius or proximity. According to Robert McCourtney, from Metamend, the following advantages can be seen from location and proximity marketing (paraphrased here):

- **A captured target**—The consumer is already in or near your place of business. A customer is much more likely to come through your door if a competitor's store is a 20-minute drive away but your store happens to be right around the corner from where they are standing (and you have what they are looking for).

- **Increased impulse buying**—Real-time delivery of advertising can prompt benefits of immediate response—for example, "Come in within the next 30 minutes and receive 20% off your meal."

- **Development of one-to-one relationship marketing**—Consumer purchasing history can be examined, thereby enhancing future marketing messages.

- **Direct marketing spending effectiveness**—True targeting of promotional materials, meaning materials are delivered electronically and on demand, as required. There's no hard copy waste or excess printing inventory.

- **Psychological nurturing**—The consumer feels like a somebody, building brand recognition and loyalty.

- **Increased return on investment (ROI)**—Repeat or additional consumer purchases during a visit. Time-based incentives or promotions can be sent to increase the total value of the sale.

Proximity and Location-Based Marketing Technology

For retailers, marketers, and independent advertisers, proximity and location-based marketing efforts generally leverage one of five technologies described in detail in upcoming sections of this chapter—Bluetooth, WiFi, infrared (IR), near field communication (NFC), and ultra-wide band signals (UWB).

 Note

Location-based marketing can also be done in coordination with carriers. Mobile phone carriers can determine where their subscribers are based on GPS data from the phone, or based on the triangulation of radio signals sent to and from the phone. In this model, advertisers work directly with the carrier to determine what locations they want to target with location-based messages. The carrier then works with the advertiser to determine pricing, the duration of the campaign, and what the message will say. These types of campaigns generally use text or picture messaging, because the carrier has the ability to send their subscribers text messages, without the cost of the text message appearing on their subscribers' bills, which is very important to the subscribers.

Bluetooth

Bluetooth technology uses radio bands to transmit signals to Bluetooth-enabled devices, including mobile phones, handheld computers, and laptops. With this technology, a small server can be placed in any location and set to send out coupons, barcodes, applications, vCards, vCal, video, MP3, MP4, and text messages (also known as BlueCasting). It generally works in a circular 100m radius, but like all signals, it can be hindered by thick concrete walls or other obstacles. Bluetooth marketing is generally used to simultaneously target shoppers in a retail location, as well as passersby outside the retail location (see Figure 6.4).

Figure 6.4 *Small Bluetooth beacons can be placed just about anywhere—signs, posters, or kiosks, for example—and can broadcast coupons, barcodes, and more.*

Bluetooth broadcasting systems can also be set up in posters or worn by promoters, to encourage passersby to enable their Bluetooth devices and download promotional information about a product or event. Some brands are even placing Bluetooth broadcasting systems in bars and clubs, and even at the beach or at music festivals to engage the local audience with mobile media and promotions. When the server is set up, it can be programmed either to broadcast the same message throughout the day or to broadcast different messages at different times of day.

All Bluetooth devices have specific numbers associated with them that never change. When a Bluetooth-enabled handset enters the range of the server, the server captures that number and information about the handset. It then queries a database to ascertain what, if any, communications have been sent to that device previously. The server then sends back content that has been optimized for that particular handset or particular user. Specific protocols and dependencies can be programmed into the system to determine what communication should be sent, and different messages can automatically be sent based on those dependencies.

The European chapter of the Mobile Marketing Association (MMA) has set a list of Bluetooth marketing guidelines for the United States and Europe. These focus mostly on the opt-in process and how to ensure user privacy. The full set of guidelines is available here: http://bloo2.bluetooth-zone.info/files/Proximity-Marketing-Guidelines-V1.0_082808.pdf.

WiFi

WiFi technology basically broadcasts and receives a short-range radio signal to provide Internet access for Web-and WiFi-enabled devices. Companies can use WiFi marketing in a couple different ways to create brand awareness.

You can broadcast a signal to send a message to potential customers in a particular radius, as described earlier with Bluetooth marketing. You can also take a more passive approach and send marketing messages over the WiFi signal while your potential customers access the Internet on their mobile phones or laptops. The simplest of these methods involves including marketing messages in the name of your WiFi network so that when potential customers select your network from the list of available networks, they see your marketing message. This is especially valuable if you suspect that customers are coming to your establishment to take advantage of the WiFi but are not purchasing items or driving any revenue for your company.

CoffeeCompany, a Holland-based chain of coffee shops, used WiFi router names such as OrderAnotherCoffeeAlready, BuyAnotherCupYouCheapskate, BuyaLargeLatteGetBrownieForFree, or TodaysSpecialEspresso1.60Euro. Although they have not yet reported any statistics, they believe that it was a good way to ensure that patrons understood that the WiFi was really not free, and they were expected to buy something.

Another way to use WiFi for your marketing efforts is to create a sponsored WiFi system in which people who login are presented with an advertisement that they must watch before they are given full access to the Internet. The WiFi network operator can also set time limits on the use of the WiFi so that people who use the Internet are prompted to watch another advertisement after they have been online for a certain amount of time. This type of marketing is commonly used in airports and business parks, which have a captive audience of people who want to access the Web.

Radio Frequency Identification (RFID)

RFID technology allows items to be "tagged" to or tracked using radio waves. The tags are very small and require no batteries, so they are frequently used for product tracking and asset management. RFID chips can also be used to store and send information from static displays or posters to phones that are capable of reading an RFID signal. For marketing purposes, RFID is usually used with devices that send a radio frequency to the chip, activating it so that it may pass a message, much like in a Bluetooth transmission. The message can be a URL, phone number, email address or a promotion code.

Near Field Communication (NFC)

Near field communication relies on high-frequency messages to be sent and received from two enabled devices, each sending its own signal. Near field–enabled devices can be used like smart cards that are waved over a reader, but in a marketing scenario, the mobile device is waved over a poster or other off-line marketing material. This type of smart card technology is already widely used in cards that allow people to access locked buildings or garages, in many public transportation systems, and as a form of payment at some stores.

The main way mobile marketers are using this technology is by embedding chips into billboards and displays (see Figure 6.5). The range of NFC is much shorter than Bluetooth, reaching only about an inch and a half, so the person receiving the marketing message must swipe their phone over the sending technology to receive the message. NFC is already being used widely in Japan, where users can pay for goods by swiping their phones over a receiver at a register. Many anticipate that this technology will be widely used for mobile ticketing, mobile payment, personal identification and even used to turn a mobile phone into a building or garage access key.

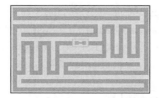

Figure 6.5 *An RFID tag used at Walmart. Image under the terms of the GNU Free Documentation License, Version 1.2.*

Ultra-Wide Band (UWB)

Ultra-wide band communication uses a large portion of the radio spectrum to transmit broadband communication at a short range, requiring very little radio energy. Ultra-wide band transmissions can share a variety of different narrow band radio signals without interfering with those transmissions. Its uses are very similar to those of Bluetooth technology, but it is less widely adopted.

InfraRed (IR)

Infrared is one of the oldest and most limited forms of broadcasting mobile messages. It was tested in the early 1990s but has limited range, reaching only about a foot from the broadcasting beacon. Some laptops and phones are equipped with infrared technology, but it has not been universally adopted by handset manufacturers. These limitations make infrared less desirable than other more universally accepted technologies available.

Creating Mobile Loyalty Programs

Whenever a potential customer interacts with your company via cellphone, you can track those interactions. To do a really great job with mobile promotion, it is vital to create a robust back-end preference center that can be tied to a loyalty program.

Mobile couponing can help you gain a lot of insight about your customers' preferences, and those preferences should drive future messaging. You can track which promotions are most effective at driving purchases from each of your customers, but you can also track what kind of phone they are using, what method of delivery they prefer, where they are redeeming the coupons, and how long they waited before redeeming the coupon.

With a robust preference center and loyalty program, you can ascertain which coupons drove sales for that customer and which ones did not. Then you can begin to replace coupons that have never driven sales from that customer with coupons that he or she has historically redeemed. If a customer always redeems her coupons at one particular store, you can send her notifications when that store is having a sale. If she always shops when a particular sale is going on, you can send her reminders that "the sale is going on now and will end soon," encouraging her to make it into the store more quickly.

The information in your preference center should be used to send messages that are customized to the recipients' redemption and purchase history. When your mobile couponing strategy is tied to specific users, the users' purchase history can be back-tracked. This kind of personalization will help you really understand your customers' needs and provide a higher level of service, which will improve the lifetime value of your customer base.

Case Studies

The following six case studies show how major brands have used mobile promotion and location based marketing to reach their target audience.

PSC "Sí" Political Initiative in Catalan, Spain

This was an ingenious and simple use of mobile marketing to bolster a political campaign within a region in Spain. The regional social-democratic party in Catalan, called the PSC, was forwarding an initiative that would give their government more autonomy from Spain. Before the referendum was voted on, the PSC hosted four political rallies where, among other things, they hosted a Bluetooth booth where party members could download videos, images, and ringtones to their mobile phones to help the cause. They could then share these downloads with others, creating a viral effect for the campaign. Whether because of the political beliefs of the voters or the mobile marketing, the initiative for more autonomy passed with 73.9% of the votes.

Whistler Ski Resort

In 2006, Whistler Ski Resort placed Bluetooth- and infrared-enabled posters throughout the London Tube to encourage London commuters to enter a sweepstakes to win a free ski trip to Whistler (see Figure 6.6). The posters did a great job of explaining how to take advantage of the offer using a Bluetooth- or IR-enabled mobile phone. After commuters opted in to receive messaging from the poster, they were sent an animated GIF telling them whether they had won the trip and encouraging them to visit the website. Although the program had some usability problems and probably was an immediate letdown for many participants, Whistler was an early adopter of location-based mobile marketing and did a good job getting visitors' attention and explaining how the technology should be used.

Figure 6.6 *Bluetooth-enabled posters in the London Tube for Whistler Ski Resort in Canada.*

Corona Beer

A company called HyperTag worked with Corona to help adjust the perception of the brand in Spain, to show that it was still "hip." Corona deployed a team of promoters to bars and clubs around the country, equipped with wearable Bluetooth transmitters that could send bar patrons cool, free branded images. They also were able to send reminders about the 5 p.m. happy hour ("It's Corona time!"). The effort helped shift the brand image, and the calendar reminder helped keep the brand top-of-mind when people were likely to be most receptive to the message.

CNN

In 2007, when CNN wanted to raise awareness for their mobile website, they created Bluetooth- and infrared-enabled posters to be distributed throughout the London City Airport and also the Barcelona 3GSM mobile phone trade fair. When passersby interacted with the poster, they were sent an SMS message that included a link to the mobile site. If passersby preferred, they were able to send a text message to a short code instead of using their Bluetooth technology to get the link sent to their phone. The effort was considered a success, driving much-needed international traffic to the mobile website and positioning CNN as a tech-savvy and mobiley engaged news service. This effort is also a good example of how companies should leverage multiple technologies and methods of digital communication to have the most effective reach with their marketing message.

Nike

In 2009, Nike used an MMS 2D bar-coding campaign to drive awareness for their sponsorship of the "Dew Tour," whose primary sponsor was the Mountain Dew soft drink. The target audience was extreme sports enthusiasts between the ages of 13 and 18, and Nike wanted to make attendees feel more connected with the athletes. To achieve that goal, event attendees were encouraged to take pictures of 2D barcodes and send them as an MMS to a short code that would respond by sending back videos and information about the athlete featured in the billboard or poster that hosted the 2D code. All the content was automatically optimized for the handset that had sent the MMS, which made it a very good user experience.

This strategy was similar to a QR coding strategy, but QR code readers are not common features of American mobile phones; instead, they processed the codes after they were sent in as an MMS. This method prevented attendees from having to download a QR code reader before interacting with the media. The campaign was so successful that Nike is looking at integrating similar initiatives into all aspects of the marketing mix in 2010.

Northwest Airlines

Northwest Airlines is the largest foreign airline in Japan. They wanted to reach out to their Japanese demographic to show them that they were tech-savvy and understood the Japanese culture, so they created a QR code campaign to collect email addresses of their passengers. Billboards with QR codes were positioned throughout urban Tokyo. The campaign did a lot to create the brand association that Northwest was looking for and also generated a lot of positive PR and buzz about the campaign. The mobile website visits were 35% above the target for the initiative, and the campaign was extended as a result.

7

Micro-Sites, Mobile Affiliate Marketing, and Web Directories

In some cases, the best mobile marketing you can do might not be on your main website or even your mobile website. As is true on the traditional Web, you can frequently take advantage of sites other than your own to promote your products or drive revenue for your company. This chapter focuses on how to use micro-sites, mobile affiliate marketing, and mobile Web directories to help drive revenue. These methods of monetization are quite new in the mobile realm but follow paths that are well worn on the traditional Web.

Mobile Micro-Sites

Micro-site is a term used on the traditional Web to describe websites that are created to achieve a very specific goal that represents only a small portion of the company's or brand's overall marketing goals. Frequently, websites that represent a large company or brand are not nimble enough to adjust to specific marketing initiatives or are not specific enough to rank well in search engines for very niche keyword searches. Instead of adjusting or adding to the main website, companies create micro-sites on separate websites.

Hotels and real estate agencies frequently use systems of micro-sites to target location-specific information and Web searches. The goal of these sites is to drive targeted traffic to specific micro-sites that provide very specific information related to the searchers interest. A good example is a site on the domain www.DenverHolidayInn.com. This site features information about all the Holiday Inns in Denver and allows visitors to book through the site, even though it is not actually the main Holiday Inn website. The main website might not rank as well for searches that include "Denver," because the main site is large and does not exclusively focus on Denver.

A good example of a system of mobile micro-sites is the City.Mobi company. They have created city guides for a majority of the large cities in the world. The brand is City.Mobi, but the sites are all hosted on their own city-specific domain, such as Chicago.mobi or London.mobi. The location-specific domain name and Web content ensure that the websites rank well in location-specific Web searches from mobile phones.

In the traditional Web, micro-sites have also commonly been used to create campaign-specific Web experiences. Instead of changing the main brand website to fit a campaign, they can create a different site to venture further away from traditional brand guidelines, be edgier, and offer a more custom experience. A prime example of this is the Subservient Chicken campaign that Burger King ran to promote new chicken sandwiches to 13- to 27–year-old men and women. The micro-site featured a man dressed as a chicken, wearing women's lingerie. TV and radio campaigns created awareness for the site, and the humorously odd content ensured that it was also quickly promoted on social networks and by news pundits.

The desire to centralize Web content and build up a primary site for search engine rankings has decreased the traditional online marketing communities reliance on micro-sites, but they can still be very valuable in the mobile world. Creating micro-sites that have a local focus and creating websites that have a controlled experience are both strategies that can be important in the mobile marketing world.

Campaign-specific micro-sites are actually quite common in the mobile world, because many of the mobile campaigns are much edgier than the brand would traditionally be. This tactic has worked quite well for many companies. A large part of the success with edgier campaigns can be attributed to the viral nature of the campaigns. Frequently, the edgier campaigns target a younger demographic that is more plugged in to social networking and more likely to spread a viral message. Mobile phones are particularly good at spreading viral messages quickly because they are always on hand and have more messaging options than traditional computers. Viral messages can be spread on social networks; by SMS, MMS, or chat; or with a phone call.

Axe Body Spray has done a good job using mobile micro-sites to drive campaign-specific initiatives. In 2009, they ran commercials and co-branded creative on MTV, Comedy Central, VH1, and the Spike networks, all promoting the "Axe Hair Crisis Relief" campaign. Commercials prompted viewers to text in so they could be sent links to the mobile micro-site. The micro-site was built around the idea that Axe hair products could prevent a "hair crisis" for men, who usually were unaware there was a "crisis" in the first place. The micro-site hosted funny videos of "hair interventions" and allowed visitors to download ringtones and wallpapers. It also featured various Axe products and explained how they could be used to help stave off a hair crisis. Visitors could also submit friends who they suspected were in crisis, or become part of a "Hair Crisis Solution" for their friends.

Mobile Affiliate Marketing

Affiliate marketing is a unique form of marketing in which other companies agree to help you sell your product or drive traffic to your website, in return for a portion of the profits from each sale they send (see Figure 7.1). Commissions can be paid based on clicks, sales, or leads/acquisitions. In some cases, affiliates are referred to as "partners" because they are acting in the best interest of both parties. If you are on a website and are interested to see if they have an affiliate marketing program, links to the programs are usually included in the footer at the bottom of the site.

Affiliate marketing follows this cycle:

1. A customer visits an affiliate website.

2. The affiliate website directs the customer to the brand/seller, where the actual transaction takes place.

3. The brand/seller compensates the affiliate with a portion of the profit.

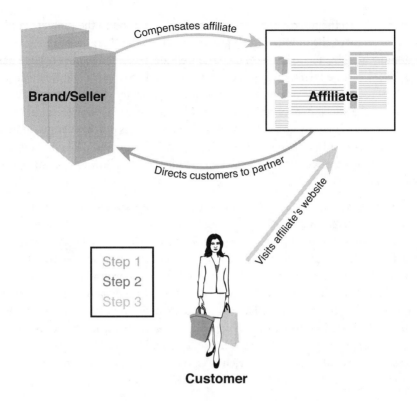

Figure 7.1 *Mobile affiliate marketing helps the buyer find the brand/seller and helps the affiliate and brand/seller earn money. It's a win-win-win. Public domain image.*

In the traditional model, affiliates create websites or sometimes micro-sites to help promote a brand or product for another company. Affiliates use traditional online marketing strategies to promote the website, such as SEO, PPC, email marketing, and online display advertising. Generally, because affiliates are not a direct agent of the brand, but instead are recommenders of the brand, they have license to be more aggressive with their marketing tactics.

One of the easiest ways to begin an affiliate program is to work with one of the major affiliate networks, such as Commission Junction or LinkShare. When you decide to work with an affiliate network you go in as either an advertiser or a publisher. Advertisers are the affiliates; they work to promote products and brands. Publishers or merchants are the companies with the products or websites that they want to promote. Publishers/merchants sign up with affiliate networks so that the network will help them find affiliates to market their goods or services.

As with the traditional Web, the original affiliate programs were launched by the adult industry and were quickly followed by the casino industry and then travel. In the traditional world, Amazon was the first major retailer to create a mainstream affiliate program. All the traditional affiliate programs should work on true Web-browsing phones that are capable of passing cookies, but since not all mobile phones are capable of passing cookies, it can be a risky proposition. If you believe that you may be passing a lot of affiliate traffic from visitors on mobile phones, it might be a good idea to set up an alternate form of tracking, such as passing a variable in the URL, to ensure that you are getting full credit for all of the mobile traffic. No major mobile-only retail affiliate programs have been developed or aggressively marketed yet but this will no doubt change as mobile tracking improves.

One of the benefits of being an affiliate is that you can use one website to drive traffic to multiple affiliate programs. For example, if your company/brand were a part of multiple travel affiliate programs, you could create city- or state-specific sites—or micro-sites—and link from those sites to a variety of different affiliate programs, making money on every click from your site and still providing value to the user.

Currently, most of the mobile affiliate marketing is to help promote mobile Web content, specifically ringtones, wallpapers, and games. These are an obvious fit for mobile marketing because they can be downloaded straight to the phone. Cellphone accessories such as clips and covers are also commonly marketed through mobile affiliate marketing, but these are more difficult to work with because the purchase must be made over the handset. If users find what they are looking for and then transfer to a traditional computer to make the final purchase, the affiliate tracking code is lost and the affiliate will not get its commission.

The most likely avenue for more mainstream affiliate marketing will be as a part of a mobile comparison-shopping or product engine such as Amazon or eBay. There's also a chance that mobile affiliate marketing will not take off beyond ringtones, games, adult, casino, and travel categories, but that remains to be seen.

In some cases, it might make sense for your company to start its own mobile affiliate program. An affiliate program is a good way to fill in the gaps in your existing marketing strategy and can be a boon for many companies. A mobile affiliate program creates the potential for an army of marketers working to promote your products, who are paid only when they successfully pass traffic or sales to your site (much like being paid on a 100% commission basis). The commissions you pay your affiliates will never cost as much as it might cost to hire employees to do the job that your affiliates have done for you.

An affiliate network can also help drive natural search traffic because it ensures that your competitors' websites are pushed lower in the search results by your affiliate websites that rank for your key terms and point back to your site for the final sale. The one thing you have to be careful about here is to make sure your affiliates are not doing a better job of ranking for top key terms than you are. If they are, you will be paying out more commission than necessary. Similarly, if you are bidding on brand-related terms in PPC, it might be a good idea to create a list of keywords that your affiliates are not allowed to bid on, because the increased competition will only make all the PPC clicks more expensive.

The most important element of creating a successful mobile affiliate program to promote mobile content is ensuring that tracking codes are set up properly so that each affiliate gets credit for all the sales and traffic it produces. Affiliate sales are generally tracked though unique affiliate codes that are created for each affiliate and passed in the URL as a parameter rather than in a cookie, because some mobile browsers have trouble with cookies. In some cases (this is becoming much more rare), mobile browsers have trouble passing parameters, so the tracking is lost, but this is generally a more mobile friendly method of tracking than using JavaScript or cookies.

The next problem is that some phones are better equipped for mobile e-commerce than others. If your affiliate program is paying out for click-throughs, but visitors are having trouble completing a transaction when they are on your website, the cost of the click-throughs will start to add up. When this happens, the return on investment (ROI) will be low or negative because no sales are being made.

The same is true of acquisition sites that are seeking only to collect email addresses or phone numbers so that people can be marketed to later (that is, the affiliate isn't selling a product or service, per se; the affiliate is simply collecting information for your company to use later for marketing purposes). If people have problems filling out the form on their mobile phones, the acquisition and the commission are both lost. If these two hurdles are affecting your mobile affiliate program, consider paying only for effective and complete conversions and don't include click-throughs as a commissioned conversion.

Mobile Web Portals

Because the mobile demographic is very interested in accessing information quickly and easily, mobile Web portals tend to be quite successful. A portal is simply an entry page that gives viewers immediate access to information and news without having to search for it or visit multiple websites. Portals bring in news, weather, and information from other sites, to aggregate it and make it easily accessible for their users.

Although creating mobile portals is not exclusively an act of marketing, it could be a good way to create and maintain relationships with your customers. If you have the right product, and have the resources to create and maintain a portal, it might be worth your time and effort to promote it in other channels to drive traffic. (If you are not interested in creating a portal, existing portals are always a good place to advertise.) Table 7.1 lists some of the top mobile portals.

Table 7.1	Top Mobile Web Portals
MSN	http://home.mobile.msn.com
Live Search	http://m.live.com
Yahoo!	http://new.m.mobile.com
AOL	http://iphone.aol.com, http://wap.aol.com
Dir.Mobi	http//dir.mobi
Mobinks	http://mobinks.com
SitiosWAP	http://english.sitioswap.com
Feed2Mobile	http://feed2mobile.kaywa.com
Mowser	http://mowser.com
FeedM8	http://feedm8.com
Winksite	http://winksite.com
ZeroRubbish.com	www.zerorubbish.com
In Your	http://inyour.mobi
M4u	http://m4u.mobi
Keytoss	http://m.Keytoss.com

Figures 7.2 and 7.2 show examples of Web portals for MSN and Yahoo!.

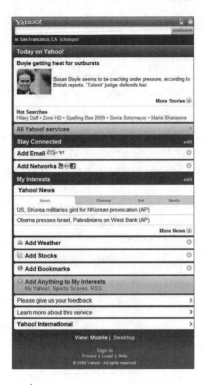

Figure 7.2   *Yahoo!'s portal.*

Figure 7.3   *MSN's portal.*

A lot of well-seasoned competitors operate in the mobile portal business, so one of the best opportunities for success is to create a portal for a niche whose needs are not being met. Many groups of users are interested in different types of news than the rest of the world. Some examples of niche portals include these:

- **SmartPhone and Pocket PC** (http://mobile.smartphonemag.com)— A portal dedicated to news and information about smart phones and pocket PCs.

- **Nickelodeon** (http://wap.nick.com)—A children's mobile portal, based on the children's TV network Nickelodeon.

- **FreeMob** (www.freomob.mobi/)—A fun mobile portal that pulls in jokes, quizzes, a txt spk dictionary, tarot cards, and horoscopes.

- **NetVibes2Go** (http://m.netvibes.com)—A personalized home page that allows you to customize the content that is pulled into your personal mobile portal page.

- **Optimum Online** (m.optimum.net)—A mobile version of a New York cable TV station website that pulls in national and New York–specific news and weather.

Mobile Directories

Many of these portals offer directories of mobile websites to help users navigate the mobile Web. If you think back to before search engines were as good as they are today, many people used directories to navigate the Web, much like you would use a phone book to find a local business. In a directory, different mobile websites are organized by categories and subcategories so that mobile users can find what that they are looking for quickly and easily.

Mobile directories are particularly valuable on the mobile Web if the sites that are listed have been editorially reviewed to ensure that they offer valuable content and will render correctly on mobile phones. Until mobile Web rendering improves, mobile directives can be used in place of search engines if users are having a hard time finding what they are seeking.

Mobile directories are also a good way to promote micro-sites, affiliate sites, and traditional mobile content. In addition to helping mobile viewers find your content, links from mobile directories can help create search engine relevance and improve rankings for your mobile content, as long as the anchor text on the link is keyword rich. Chapter 10, "Mobile Search Engine Optimization," covers this more deeply.

8

Mobile Applications

Smart phones come preinstalled with an operating system and a stock set of programs or applications. These applications usually include an email client, an address book, a calendar, a program for taking notes or saving text, a Web browser, and a couple simple games. When users need more than these preinstalled programs offer, they might need to add software to their phone. The multitude of small programs that can be installed after market on phones are grouped and called mobile applications, or apps for short.

Mobile applications have changed how we conceive of our mobile phones. They have moved the collective unconscious from believing that mobile phones are preloaded with all the software and functionality that we could ever need, to believing that mobile phones, like computers, will always need additional functionality to achieve our specific needs. Mobile applications can be developed and sold as independent revenue-generating programs, or they can be developed as marketing tools to help promote a specific brand, product, or service. The marketing power of mobile applications is mostly in the repeated exposure to the brand and brand message.

Although they've been made famous by Apple's App Store, downloadable mobile applications have been around since Palm and Treo launched the first PDA's and smart phones. The first mobile applications were almost universally aimed at improving personal productivity, with text-editing programs, calculators, alarms, reminders, and simple accounting programs. Now, thanks to the surge in demand for more capable smart phones, and third-party developers, the variety and quality of mobile applications has improved quite a bit.

Today users can choose from a vast array of apps to make their mobile phone more personal and to customize it to their needs. The largest segment of mobile applications is mobile games, which can be very powerful for marketing.

Mobile Game Applications

Good or bad, no one can deny that video games have made their mark on our society. Some of the first auxiliary programs that were added to mobile phones were simple games such as Brick Breaker and Mine Sweep. But as mobile phones have become more sophisticated, so have the mobile video games.

Until third-party applications became widely available, all the mobile games were preloaded on the phone within the operating system. Now, roughly one-third of the downloadable mobile applications available are games, and more are being developed every day. Although it is not universally true, most mobile games are downloaded as applications rather than preloaded on the phone or run live from the Web. Mobile games provide marketers a unique opportunity for branded game development, product placement, and game sponsorship.

Branded Game Development

The most obvious way to market using mobile games is to actually create a game for your company and your brand. The idea here is to extend your brand or brand experience to the mobile phone while providing entertainment. Branded games that are not engaging or are too overtly meant as advertisement will not be well received, but users will tolerate subtle marketing cues if the game is fun.

If you do decide to go this route, here are a few tips for developing a game application that will be popular and well received by your audience:

- Review other games available and make sure that your game has something significantly different and valuable over the competition.

- Find the balance between marketing and creating a fun gaming experience. The more heavily branded and simple your game is, the less you will be able to charge for it. If users can tell that your game is pushing a specific product or brand, they might be less willing to pay to download the application.

- Think of mobile gaming applications as a brand awareness and reinforcement campaign. The price you charge users to download your game should help cover some of the development costs, but it likely will not cover them all. Ideally, the return you get will be an overall lift in sales, as a result of the increased brand awareness.

- Always provide clear instructions and help options. Playing games on mobile phones might still be a new experience for many people, so they might need help.

- If you are developing a game application exclusively for the iPhone, try to have some aspect of the game work with the motion sensors known as accelerometers, but always provide a button alternative for users who prefer not to use the motion sensors. This will add to the interactivity of the game but also leave it opened to be adapted for other operating systems later.

- Consider creating a multiplayer mode that uses WiFi or Bluetooth to join multiple users in one game.

- Be conscious of the amount of memory the application will take up when it is downloaded to the phone. Users might be hesitant to download games that take up too much memory space on their phone.

- Consider providing upgrades or additional levels as separate downloads for users who have mastered the game.

- Follow the application promotion instructions offered later in the chapter and promote your mobile game everywhere you can.

Mobile Game Success Stories

Before launching a mobile game, take some cues from existing mobile games that have been well received:

- **FooPets**—A co-promotion for the movie *Marley & Me* and Purina Dog Food. The user is able to interact with Marley the puppy, petting, playing fetch, and feeding it. When the user chooses to feed Marley, a bag of Purina Dog Food passes in front of the screen.

- **Hell's Kitchen**—A cooking game that allows you to progressively unlock 35 different recipes, all while Gordon Ramsay watches and scores you. This downloadable app helps reinforce the Hell's Kitchen brand, increasing the viewership of the show, not to mention helping sell the PC and game console versions of the game.

- **Monopoly**—Allows the players to have a full board-game experience, including using Chance and Community Chest cards, chatting with other players, and saving and resuming games. This game is a top seller and has probably recouped the development costs on its own, but it also helps promote Monopoly and other Hasbro board games and mobile applications.

- **Mobile Guitar Hero III**—An application on the Verizon network that approximates the experience of the popular console game. Players press buttons on the phone in time with a song as it is playing, and are scored based on their accuracy and rhythm. This is another good example of brand awareness marketing that enables fans to take their favorite console game with them on their mobile phone and hopefully share it with friends. This effort also encourages more purchases of the console game and the mobile application.

- **Spin the Coke**—A simple branded game that allows users to re-create the adolescents' game Spin the Bottle. This is a great example of a heavily branded free game. It is very simple and likely took minimal development time. This game application is simply meant to provide short-term entertainment and amusement, unlike other complex multi-level games.

- **iBeer**—This is another simple branded game—or, more accurately, a visual gag meant for short-term entertainment. iBeer, owned by Coors Brewing Company, allows users to make their iPhone look like an actual glass of beer that they can tilt, sip, and shake; they can even pour the beer from one iPhone to another. Players can choose from a variety of different beers, but this mobile game is currently the topic of major litigation regarding the original owner and creator of the game (claims have been made by a U.K. company with an app called iPint), so the branding has been noticeably lifted.

- **Audi**—This game allows users to become virtual owner of the new Q5. Clearly promotional but undoubtedly fun, this game is the best of both worlds. The game allows users to customize their experience, even working with the camera to superimpose a picture of their ideal Audi Q5 in a picture of their own driveway. This type of interactivity creates a deep affinity between the user and the brand. It also has a viral bonus: Users can send photo compilations and race their Audi against a friend's Audi.

Product Placement

As Digital Video Recorders (DVRs) and subscription-based satellite radio have become more prevalent, traditional advertisers are turning more to product placement as a means of getting eyes on their product offerings. Although product placement is a much softer sell, it can be an effective way to use mobile marketing to keep your brand top-of-mind and to create or reinforce your brand image.

Historically, strategic product placement has been included in TV shows and movies. Advertisers pay for the right to have a product, logo, or advertisement featured in a movie or popular TV show. The best example of this is BMW's long-standing relationship with James Bond films. The elaborately equipped cars that Agent 007 drives in his films are always BMWs, and BMW pays for that privilege. As video games grow in importance and trade off with people's consumption of other media, product placement has spread into this channel as well.

When done correctly, product placement in mobile game applications can be a win-win-win situation for the user, the game publisher, and the advertiser.

- For the user, the product placement creates more realism in the game.
- For the game publisher, it increases the margin on the game.
- For the marketer, there is an increase in brand awareness and affinity.

Again, the immediacy and interactivity of the mobile channel is key to this type of promotion. Within mobile gaming product placement is the opportunity for clickable product placement and linking, otherwise known as plinking. As an example, if a user is playing a driving game, he might pass a billboard that you have sponsored in the game. If the user is interested in finding out more about your product, he can click on the billboard to find out more information. Similarly, a user playing a "single-man-shooter" game might pass a storefront that you have sponsored in the game. If the user wants to find out more, he can simply click on the storefront.

 Caution

Before you begin marketing in this channel, you must research and understand both the game you will be placing your product in and the audience that the game will attract. It is crucial that your product and message be as targeted and relevant as possible. If you don't approach this avenue with caution, you run the risk of a negative branding effect because some users might resent your marketing message being a part of their gaming experience.

Game Sponsorship

The final option for mobile marketing in video game applications is through game sponsorship. In this model, a product or brand pays for the right to run short advertisements or promotions before or after the game is played. These short ads are called pre-roll or post-roll promotions, and advertisers can choose to sponsor entire games or share sponsorship with other advertisers. These advertisements can be still or animated, depending on the game, and usually last between 10 and 30 seconds. Mobile games or applications with sponsorship are usually offered as a free download because the game-development costs are subsidized by the advertising.

The allure of mobile game sponsorship is the massive targeting capability and the interactivity and immediacy of the mobile channel. If gamers are interested or want to find out more information about your product, they can click on the ad to visit your website, register for emails, or purchase the product without having to go to the computer. This type of immediate interactivity is simply not available on more traditional gaming consoles.

Most gamers will understand that the advertisements they see before and after playing a game are a necessary evil to endure because they drive down the price they have to pay to download the game. That being said, they are usually prepared to ignore your advertisement, unless it is particularly engaging, funny, or compelling. Instead of playing it safe, this is an opportunity to be outrageous or a bit flamboyant to get players' attention and overcome the "banner blindness." Pay attention to the game's target demographics, and create something that will catch their eyes. Mobile display advertising companies such as AdMob, GreyStripe, and AdWhirl offer services that embed rotating advertisements within mobile applications, including mobile games.

Mobile Utility Applications

Mobile applications are by no means limited to games. You can create many types of applications to help promote your brand. In many cases, providing a valuable service can do more to engender trust and brand affiliation for your brand than providing entertainment. Here are some examples of highly valuable and regularly downloaded utility applications:

- **Phone utilities**—Flashlights, carpenter levels, additional security and memory, phone usage statistics, password keepers, unit conversion charts, and so on

- **Educational**—World maps, foreign languages, poetry, books, math tutorials, flash cards, graphing calculators, periodic tables, chemistry calculators, dictionaries, thesaurus, and so on

- **Financial**—Stock reports and tickers, banking and personal finance, budgeting, bill reminders, mortgage calculators, and so on

- **News and entertainment**—TV and print newsfeeds, celebrity gossip, sports scores, game highlights, and so on

- **Weather**—Current condition, alerts, weather maps, moon phases, allergy and ozone reports, and so on

- **Business productivity**—Checklists, spreadsheet programs, PDF reader, voice recording, expense tracking, remote meetings, time tracking, and so on

- **Navigation and travel**—Road and traffic maps; flight, bus, and subway delays; currency exchange; alternate route finders; and so on

- **Shopping**—eBay, Amazon, comparison-shopping tools, grocery lists, and so on

- **Multimedia**—Music, white noise, photography tools, photo-editing programs, radio, musical instruments, and so on

- **Lifestyle**—Snow reports, golf cards, recopies, drink mixing, nutritional facts, gym assistants, calorie counters, and so on

- **Social networking**—Facebook and MySpace applications, Twitter feeds, social shopping tools, and so on

Where Do You Get Apps?

Apple's App Store has been touted as the place to go to get mobile applications, but it is not the only place you can download or purchase an app. Applications downloaded from Apple's App Store are usable only on devices running the iPhone operating system, but mobile apps are available for a variety of different mobile operating systems. Google and Windows Mobile both offer apps that are tied to their operating systems—Android and Windows Mobile, respectively. Figure 8.1 shows the Windows Mobile Marketplace. Applications can also be developed for other mobile operating systems, including BlackBerry OS, Java, Mobile Linux, Palm and Palm Pre OS, Qualcomm BREW, and Symbian OS.

Figure 8.1 *The Windows Mobile Marketplace offers many mobile applications.*

There's also a growing list of mobile app vendors such as Handango, Pocketland, and MobiHand. Users can find mobile app aggregators that gather different databases of mobile applications and allow them to search from one portal, such as iMobile.us and VilleMobile.com.

Google offers Android Market, where users can upload applications and comment on other applications. Eric Chu, Android Program Manager, says:

Similar to YouTube, content can debut in the marketplace after only three simple steps: register as a merchant, upload and describe your content, and publish it. We also intend to provide developers with a useful dashboard and analytics to help drive their business and ultimately improve their offerings.

This could be marketing gold for some companies as they try to establish what applications their audience really finds engaging.

The Windows Mobile Catalog also allows users to search for and download apps for smart phones that are running Windows Mobile. Other than the Windows Mobile Catalog, more than 18,000 Windows Mobile applications are spread all over the Web with no central repository or store. Luckily, Microsoft is taking cues from Google and Apple, and plans to launch its own app store, called Skymarket, with the launch of Windows Mobile 7.

Do I Need My Own App?

With the success of the App Store, a rush of companies has been clamoring to create mobile applications. Mobile apps can be a good way to grow a client base, spread brand awareness, create goodwill with existing clients, and monetize the mobile channel. However, not every company with a mobile presence needs a mobile application.

Developing mobile applications can be quite an undertaking. Different versions of the application must be created for each mobile operating system it will be marketed to, and each mobile app store has different requirements for submission and upkeep of the application. If you are considering developing a mobile application, it is imperative that you plan where and how the app will be marketed and have a good understanding of how you will recoup your development costs.

Developing an App

If you decide there's a good business case for developing your own mobile application, you must first consider the demographic for which you are developing an application. Do this before you decide where and how your application should be marketed, and even what the application will do.

The iPhone is broad reaching, targeting higher-end consumers quite well. In the long run, however, Android phones might be more appealing to the more tech-savvy power users. Consumer-based applications are generally being developed for

Apple and Android phones, but enterprise applications have focused on Windows Mobile, BlackBerry, and Palm devices. How heavily the iPhone and Android phones will play in the enterprise market remains to be seen, but this is an important distinction to make when developing a mobile application.

Your developer should use a software development kit (SDK) from the mobile operating system in which you want to deploy the application. The two newest and most-viewed app catalogs are on the iPhone and Android platforms. Researchers in Motion (RIM), creators of the BlackBerry, have also launched an SDK to drive third-party development for their application store, called the Application Center (see Figure 8.2). Windows Mobile also offers SDKs for each of the operating systems they have released, but they will likely promote the SDK for Windows Mobile 7 to dovetail with the launch of Skymarket.

Although more users have iPhones, it is generally easier to develop for the Android platform and it's usually easier to publish apps for the Android. The iPhone SDK is more comprehensive, but the Android SDK allows developers to leverage all the native functionality of the Android operating system. This is a key difference if you are interested in using capabilities such as VoIP or P2P file sharing, which might be blocked by the iPhone SDK or not permitted in the App Store.

Figure 8.2 *The Application Center is one location where you can find apps for your BlackBerry.*

Since games are not a primary focus for the Palm Pre, the SDK for developing games and other applications is not very sophisticated, and has left a lot of developers wishing for more. The availability to render high-quality graphics in games and use of the accelerometers are both much more limited in the Palm Pre than in the other mobile application development platforms.

Google tends to be easiest to work with during the application development process. Google is more responsive to queries and requests regarding the SDK, and offers clear communication regarding the publishing and launch of your application. In contrast, Apple does not provide clear criteria for approving or rejecting apps that are submitted, and is not generally as responsive to questions about the

SDK, the approval process, or the applications launch, unless you are very well-known brand.

In terms of payment, mobile application stores work on a percentage of revenue model. Some apps are free, but many cost $1–$15. The various application stores market your applications directly to the consumers and split the resulting revenues with the company or developer who submitted the application. Both Google and Apple return 70% of the revenue to the developers, while RIM promises to return 80% upon the launch of its application store.

You also should consider an app store's return policy when you are trying to decide which of the mobile platforms for which you want to develop. In some cases, as is the case with the AppStore, if a customer returns an application, they are credited 100% of the cost of the application. The app store then charges back 100% of the cost to the developer, but the AppStore will still keep the 30% commission from the original sale, leaving the developer at a loss.

Promoting Your App

In most cases, it's not enough to just create an app—you must promote it, too. All the mobile applications stores are flooded with new applications every day. Many of these apps offer the same or similar functionality to applications already available. You can do much to improve your chances of being noticed in the crowd of competing applications, but you must appeal to both the user and the App Store search engine.

Make It Viral

The simplest method of mobile application promotion is to leverage the friends and acquaintances of the people who download your application. You should always include a function within your app that allows people to recommend it to their friends.

Another great way to build a viral element within your application is to create some benefit to interaction with others as part of the application. If your application is a game, you would obviously allow people who download the game to play against their friends. If the application is for something other than entertainment, integrating a viral element is more difficult. Consider how group interaction would add to the experience through things such as voting, picture sharing, or status updates. If none of those are an option, you can try to integrate your application with other existing networks and applications, such as Twitter, Facebook, or LinkedIn.

Facebook, in particular, offers something called Facebook Connect that allows application developers to loop Facebook into the initial development of the application. It allows people who download your application to port their personal information from Facebook. The information that can be imported includes basic information, a profile picture, a friends list, groups, and photos. This is useful for people who don't want to enter or upload all that information twice, and it helps make the application more prominent and viral in Facebook.

Do Something New

In most cases, this goes without saying, but something that is creative and new always gets more attention than something that has already been done. If you are just creating a new Blackjack game, it will be hard to create any buzz or draw crowds away from Blackjack applications they have already downloaded. If you do something that has never been done, there is a much higher chance that it will get written about, downloaded, and passed on.

It can be difficult to think of something new to do, but the first place to start is existing applications. Keep your eye on the top applications lists provided by some app stores, to get an idea of what people are really downloading.

If you have some idea of what type of application you would like to build, but you don't know how to make it new and exciting, start by reviewing the competition. Once you have a good idea of what is available, evaluate the strengths and weaknesses of each competing application. Try to figure out key elements that could make the application more functional, more interactive, or more fun. If you are building an iPhone application, think about how you can leverage the accelerometers and Bluetooth to make the application more useful or even more amusing.

If you are still at a loss for how you will improve on the applications that are already out there, begin looking at the top applications in a totally different category. If you are creating a business application, look at games; if you are creating a search application, look at business tools; and so on. This will help open your mind so that you can think more creatively about your project. Can you incorporate images, audio recordings, or GPS? Think about why the top applications that you are looking at are so popular, and then think about your project in similar terms.

Get Rated and Reviewed in the Store

Reviews within the application stores are important for two reasons. First, they can obviously help convince people who are considering downloading the application. Second, they play a role in how well you rank in the application search feature that the stores provide. The application stores have a vested interest in presenting the most successful and liked applications before the others. Those app stores will always rank the top applications above the applications that are not reviewed.

No one wants to be the first to review a product, so the best way to get reviews is to initiate the process yourself. Have people you know try the application, and encourage them to submit honest reviews to the application store. Once the first couple of reviews are in place, people will be less hesitant to submit their own reviews. Also, if the existing reviews are overwhelmingly good, detractors will think twice before submitting negative reviews.

Have a Good Name

Again, this may sound obvious, but many application developers go wrong simply by getting too creative or abstract with their application names and logos. Describe your application in as clear and compelling terms as possible.

Always include the keyword that you want to rank for in the title of your game. For instance, a dancing application called The Right Foot Forward might sound snappy and compelling, but doesn't include the word *dance.* Instead, you might call the application iBallroom Dance and use "The Right Foot Forward" as part of your tag line or other marketing copy.

Bryson Meunier, Associate Director of SEO at Resolution Media, gives a great description of the importance of your application name in his article, "How to SEO for Apple's App Store" (the article also references the image shown in Figure 8.3).

> Users entering the keyword "fun" in the app store search box will find a tip calculator listed prominently among the other apps that are apparently fun. Is this because the tip calculator is inherently more fun than Bejeweled 2, Catcha Mouse, or the other popular game apps that are listed below it? It's more likely that the tip calculator is listed because it included the keyword "fun" in the name of the app. If developers think their application is also fun, they can alert the search engine to this fact by placing the keyword in the name of the app, and help themselves appear higher in the search results for informational queries.

Have a Good Logo or Icon

When creating the logo that will be added to the user's phone, be sure that it is well designed, aesthetically appealing, and not too cluttered. It should be a good representation of what the application does, without crowding too many thoughts or ideas onto the small icon. Again, it is important to find out what the top applications in the category look like. Although it is not advisable to copy any of the competitions' logos, you can get ideas from the imagery and layout they have chosen.

Figure 8.3 *Using the right name for your app can make it appear more frequently in user searches.*

Write a Compelling Description

As with application names and reviews, descriptions are valuable because they can help drive downloads once visitors find your application. However, descriptions also can help searchers find your application in the first place, by making it appear better to the application store search results.

Think about your description as a TV commercial or value statement for your application. Use language that highlights what makes your application different and valuable to your target market. Use bulleted lists, headings, and text formatting to make your description easy to read. As with most Web copy, it is also a good idea to write in brief, direct sentences instead of complex sentences. This makes your descriptions easier for people to scan. Avoid using pronouns such as *it* or *we* because those don't help create relevance with the search engines. Instead, replace them with specific descriptive phrases such as "this dance tutorial" or "the iBallroom Dance development team."

It's also a good idea to mention popular or related applications in the description of your application. This help readers connect with your application and understand what it does. Mentioning other popular or related apps also can provide some additional exposure if you rank well for the name of the popular and related application names, too. You can also include a keyword in the "Name of the Developer" section on your website. To do this without appearing manipulative or spammy, you can just add a title with the name, so it might read "Cindy Krum, Dance Application Development."

Price It Right

The most commonly searched single term at app stores is "free," obviously because people don't want to pay for applications when they might be able to get a similar application for free. Figure 8.4 shows iPhone apps and the prices paid (or not paid) by what percentage of the buyers. Even if you can't offer your entire application for free, it is a good idea to offer a lite version of the application for free. Despite having limited functionality, the lite version should do enough so that users are understand how the application works and are enticed to download the paid version of the application later.

iPhone App Distribution by Price

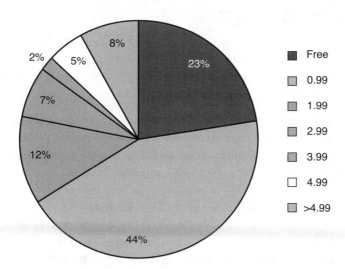

Source: 148Apps.biz

Figure 8.4 *As you can see, 67% of iPhone app buyers spent a dollar or less on purchased apps.*

Including the word *free* or *lite* in the title should do a lot to improve the number of downloads right away. This is also a good way to be listed twice within a search result, because both the full version and the lite or free version of the application will rank. A dual ranking is valuable because it pushes competing applications farther down the search results page, making them harder to find.

Promote the Application on Your Website

Make sure that you mention your application on the home page of your website. If possible, include a page or a subdomain dedicated to promoting the application. Include links to marketplaces and other locations where the application can be downloaded, or allow the application to be downloaded directly from your site.

Again, use compelling text and screen shots that will help readers understand the value that your application will provide and help those pages rank well in search engines such as Google and Yahoo!. This is your chance to really use the search engines to create awareness for you application. If you can get the listing in the App Store and a listing on your website to both rank in Google search results, you will be doing a lot to drive traffic to your application, while also decreasing the traffic to competing applications. All the traditional search engine optimization strategies will help the promotional page on your site rank in search engines, so include the name of the application and top keywords in the title tag on the page and throughout the text description on the page.

Promote It with the Bloggers

A very effective but frequently overlooked method of driving lots of traffic to your application is to reach out to the blogging community. You should reach out to at least two groups of bloggers—the application bloggers, who review and discuss applications, and the bloggers in your business niche.

- **Application bloggers**—Application bloggers love applications but are frequently flooded with requests to review their applications. Be creative in your approach so that you will get noticed amid all the other requests. In some cases, it is a good idea to contact bloggers with a "sneak preview" or "free trial" before the application is available online. If the application is already available for download, provide a link and an offer code so that they can download the application for free. Some great resources for finding application bloggers are the iPhoneApplicationsList, Apple iPhoneSchool, and WhatsoniPhone.

  It is crucial that you do as much footwork as you can for the bloggers, to make their review almost write itself. Include great screen shots of the application in all its various states, offer a brief company history, give a link to your website, and provide a clear description of game play and rules. Because bloggers are probably not very familiar with your industry, you might need to give a deeper explanation of the value your application provides people within your industry. Be sure to avoid industry jargon or references that outsiders might not understand.

- **Bloggers within your business niche**—Your strategy when reaching out to bloggers within the niche that your application serves is much the same, but your message can be more targeted. If you are creating a business application, reach out to known business bloggers. If you are creating a cooking application, learn who the top cooking bloggers are, and so on. Focus on blogs that get a lot of traffic—traffic from people you think would be interested in your application. If similar applications are available, you can also search for people who have already blogged about the competing applications, and contact them to write a follow-up post about your application. However, be sure to highlight what makes your app different and better.

When contacting bloggers, regardless of what camp they fit into, include as much contact information as possible, in case the blogger has questions or needs a quote from you for the post. This obviously includes your Web address, email address, and phone number, but if you have them, it might also be a good idea to include instant messenger and/or Twitter screen names.

Promote Your App via Mailing Lists and Twitter Followers

It's also a great idea to promote the application within email lists and to your Twitter followers, because popularity is such an important factor in the natural rankings of the application store search engines. Any traffic that you can send to the App Store listing should have a positive impact on your applications search rankings.

Promote the Application in Pay-Per-Click and Display Advertising

If it makes business sense, you can also promote your application by paying for traffic in pay-per-click (PPC) and display advertising. Include compelling images and text in your advertisements, with a call to action such as "download today" or "play now," to create a sense of urgency and to improve your conversion rate. There are also application exchange programs—such as the one offered by Admob called the iPhone Download Exchange. This app allows you to trade ad-space on your application for adspace on another developer's applications. This helps both developers get their ads in front of more potential buyers.

Submit Your Application

Plenty of application directories and lists exist, so make sure the application is listed with links to where people can download it. These lists and directories are frequently updated, so make sure you keep a list of all the websites that are linking to your application, and check back periodically to ensure that the listing is still there. In some cases, lists and forums allow readers to rate or comment on your application, so monitor that, too. Again, never leave a listing without a rating or review, and don't rely on others to start the conversation about your application. As soon as you are listed, submit an unbiased review of your application, or have someone you know who has downloaded the application rate and review it on the site.

What If You Don't Want to Develop an App?

In many cases, companies don't have to create their own application to benefit from the popularity of the technology. You can also become a part of mobile search applications simply by being listed in the results. Mobile search applications are downloaded to the phone just like other applications, and they allow users to search certain industries or certain types of information to find what they are looking for without searching the Web-at-large.

If your company fits neatly into a specific vertical, such as travel or dining, it may be more cost-effective for you to identify the top mobile search applications for your industry, and do what it takes to ensure that you are well listed and ranked in those mobile applications, instead of developing your own application. Table 8.1 lists some of the top mobile search applications. Figure 8.5 shows a few interestesting iPhone apps.

Table 8.1   Top Mobile Applications by Vertical

Local Dining	Recipes	Friends
Urban Spoon	AllRecipies.com	Facebook
Open Table	BigOven	MySpace
MetroMix	iFoodAssistant	WPMobile
		Loopt
Local Business	**Real Estate**	WhosHere
Around Me	Trulia	
Yelp	For Sale by Owner	**Products**
YPMobile		eBay
Slifter	**Videos**	Amazon
	Truveo	Near By Me Now
Jobs	YouTube	Is it Me
Job Compass		
iJobs	**Images**	
Now Hiring	JuiceCaster	
	PhotoBucket	
	Flickr	
	Picas	

EverNote   Shezam   Urban Spoon

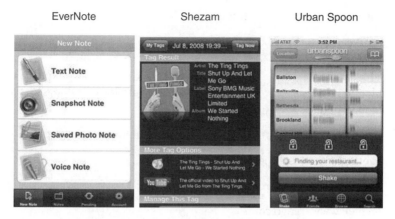

Figure 8.5 *Find a wide variety of apps at the Apple Apps Store.*

Mobile Application Development Companies

Following is a partial list of mobile application development companies.

- **Air2Web**—www.air2Web.com

- **Gateway Mobitech Research & Development**—
  www.gatewaytechnolabs.com/

- **Macronimous.com**— www.macronimous.com/

- **Plazmic Inc.**— www.plazmic.com

- **Endeavour**— www.techendeavour.com/

- **ValueLabs**— www.valuelabs.com

- **724 Solutions**— www.724solutions.com

Mobile Application Bloggers and Communities

Following is a partial list of application bloggers and communities where you can
learn more about applications for mobile devices.

- iPhone Application List: http://iphoneapplicationlist.com

- iPhone AppPreview: www.iphoneappreviews.net

- AppleiPhoneStore: www.appleiphoneschool.com

- WhatsOniPhone: www.whatsoniphone.com

- iUseThis: http://iphone.iusethis.com

- ViewPoints: www.viewpoints.com

- AppVee: www.appvee.com

- AppStoreApps: www.appstoreapps.com

- Mobile Phones and Mobile Games: www.blogcatalog.com/blogs/mobile-phones-and-mobile-games

- CNet: www.cnet.com/topic/mobile-application.html

- SpotLight: www.spotlightm.com/

- ReviewStream: www.reviewstream.com

- Frengo: www.frengo.com/

Mobile Application Aggregators, Directories, and Stores

- America Online Mobile Applications: www.Mobile1.AOL.com

- Google Mobile Applications: www.Google.com/mobile

- Yahoo! Go Mobile Multi-Application: www.Mobile.Yahoo.com/go

- The App Store: www.apple.com/iphone/appstore

- Windows Mobile Catalog: www.microsoft.com/windowsmobile/catalog/cataloghome.aspx

- Android Market: www.android.com/market/

- BlackBerry App World: www.BlackBerry.com/AppWorld

- Palm Software Store: http://software.palm.com

- Handango: www.handango.com

- PocketGear: www.pocketgear.com

- Jamba/Jamster: www.jamster.com/

- FlyCast: www.flycast.fm

- MobiHand: www.mobihand.com/

- Electronic Arts: www.ea.com/

- Motricity: www.motricity.com/

- iMobile.us: http://imobile.us/

- VilleMobile: www.villemobile.com/

Mobile Website Development

As with any Web development, mobile website development is an ever-changing art. As the technologies improve, new coding languages are developed, and new coding standards are set, developers must adjust their skill set. In the mobile world, the changes can happen at a much more rapid pace and frequently are a bit disjointed. It can be hard to say what kind of technologies, software and standards will stick and which ones won't. What you will see is that there are a variety of possible solutions you can choose from, based on the requirements of your particular project requirements, budget and objectives.

Note

If you are building or rearchitecting a website to make it more mobile friendly, it is crucial that you read this chapter along with Chapter 10, "Mobile Search Engine Optimization." Development and SEO work hand in hand to create top mobile search engine rankings, and it is much easier and more efficient to build SEO into the initial design than to try to fit it in later.

The support of HTML5 standards is sure to have a dramatic effect on the mobile world, but it is still hard to tell when and how. The standards have not been fully ratified or endorsed yet, but they will be revolutionary in the way website s are developed, and some important industry groups are already embracing them.

HTML5 standards will change how the Web works, especially in terms of plug-ins such as Adobe Flash, Adobe Reader, and Microsoft Silverlight. HTML5 includes semantic replacements such as <nav>, <article>, <section>, <aside>, and <footer> that will make mobile rendering more intuitive and clear for the browsers. Also, specifications such as <audio> and <video> have been added to standardize the coding calls for specific media types. Some inline styling attributes such as <font>, <frameset>, and <center> have been eliminated, putting further emphasis on the style sheet presentation. HTML5 standards also provide a geolocation API that can be used to programmatically determine the location of the user.

The platform that has embraced HTML5 standards the most is a popular open source layout engine called Webkit. Webkit was first developed by Apple and is now used in the iPhone operating system, Symbian operating system (Nokia), Google's Android operating system, and the Palm Pre. This chapter does not focus on HTML5 because it is not yet mainstream, but it helps demystify some of the other more basic requirements for mobile coding and website development.

Although it is quite exciting, the full adoption of HTML5 is still too far in the future to make it an ideal coding language now. Instead, this chapter focuses more on XHTML and XHTML-MP, which are the most current and broadly accepted mobile programming languages today. This chapter also references CSS and WCSS—two methods of controlling the style and design of the content on your mobile website.

Mobile Web and WAP

In the United States, carriers first began offering mobile Internet access in the mid-1990s, but it not until the later 1990s did the first real mobile marketing campaigns began to take form. The Internet that was available on mobile phones was mostly limited to Wireless Action Protocol (WAP) sites on carrier decks. WAP was developed and released in 1998, and it allowed mobile phones that had WAP browsers to view simplified versions of websites. Separate websites had to be developed in Wireless Mark-Up Language (WML) to be viewed by the WAP browsers. At the time, most mobile phones displayed information only in black-and-white and could not render complex images.

Development of WAP sites was difficult because there were no good, mainstream WAP authoring tools to help content creators develop their WAP content. Later versions of WAP were developed in 2002 to allow XHTML rendering of more complex websites, which improved the user experience quite a bit.

U.S.-based carriers began creating branded "WAP decks," which were essentially a limited version of the mobile Internet that customers could access from their mobile WAP browsers. These decks were designed much like portals and used to sell downloadable mobile content, such as ringtones, wallpapers, and simple games such as Brick-Breaker and Mine Sweep.

Carriers took a "walled garden" approach that prevented users from accessing the Web-at-large, which is otherwise known as going "off-deck." There was more opportunity to sell to their customers if the customers stayed "on-deck" viewing only the monetized content. In some cases, carriers even disabled the address bar in the mobile browser to prevent their visitors from going off-deck. Many mobile carriers who allowed subscribers to go "off-deck" filtered access to the Web-at-large, to make navigation of the mobile Web more difficult and further encourage users to stay on their WAP deck.

With the introduction of WAP2.0, users of the mobile Web began to expect their phone to do more than render simplified WAP versions of their websites. They wanted color, images, and interactivity. Now coding languages have evolved further, and most mobile browsers can render sites that are built to a strict XHTML standard. In addition to coding sites in XHTML, top Web designers build in elements with "progressive enhancement" or "selective degradation" that will offer sophisticated Web content when displayed on a traditional computer, but provide visitors on less capable Web rendering devices with less sophisticated content, as the more sophisticated content silently and seamlessly fails. This is described in more detail later in the chapter.

dotMobi Domains

dotMobi, or .mobi, is a top-level domain that was created to indicate that a website was developed specifically for mobile access. dotMobi domain names were first made available for purchase in 1996. They were originally designed to help distinguish mobile websites from traditional websites. Although notable companies such as Microsoft, Google, Nokia, Samsung, and Vodaphone originally backed the dotMobi domain extension, it was also criticized for violating the notion of device independence.

Device independence is the idea that the Web should always work, regardless of what type of device is accessing it. The theory is that the device and the browser should adapt to the Web content rather than forcing Webmasters to create content that is specifically designed for a certain set of devices. Tim Berners-Lee, who is credited with inventing the World Wide Web and the HTTP protocol, has always been staunchly against the dotMobi domain extension. In an article he wrote called "New Top Level Domains .mobi and .xxx Considered Harmful," Berners-Lee expressed the following concerns:

> Dividing the Web into information destined for different devices, or different classes of user, or different classes of information, breaks the Web in a fundamental way.

> This domain will have a drastically detrimental effect on the Web. By partitioning the HTTP information space into parts designed for access from mobile access and parts designed (presumably) not for such access, an essential property of the Web is destroyed.

In my opinion, he is quite right. The idea of creating device-specific domains could easily become a slippery slope where new domain extensions and standards are developed each time a new Web-enabled device is developed. This would be an absolute nightmare for developers and consumers alike.

Effectively Organizing and Architecting a Mobile Site

One very important aspect of mobile website strategy is the architecture of the mobile site. In this case, "architecture" simply refers to where and how the pages of the site will be organized and stored on the Internet. There are three basic mobile site architecture options to choose from:

- A separate mobile site, on a different domain than the main site
- A mobile subdomain or subdirectory on the main site
- Mobile-traditional hybrid pages on your main site

The architecture option that you choose will affect your ability to control the mobile user experience, the content that you are providing to your mobile users, and your site's ability to rank in search engines. The following sections outline the pros and cons of each of the three options. Different architecture options and configurations will be appropriate, depending on other elements and requirements of the project.

Separate Mobile Site

Separate mobile sites are hosted on a different domain than your main site and work completely independent of your main site. Frequently, marketers choose to put their separate mobile sites on dotMobi domains or shortened versions of their main domain. For example, the mobile version of BusinessWeek.com is hosted on BusinessWeek.mobi, but if the domain were available, *BusinessWeek* could have also opted to host its mobile site on a shortened version of the domain, such as BW.com or BW.mobi. The goal of this strategy is simply to save users from having to type a longer domain on small phone keypads.

Separate mobile sites can be good when they are used in tandem with offline marketing channels that drive mobile traffic to the domain, or if they set up agreements with carriers to promote the mobile site on-deck. Relying on users to find your mobile content on a new mobile-specific site can be challenging if you are not promoting it through other channels. New mobile sites do not benefit from any of the traffic, links, or rankings from the primary website. New mobile sites must build up rankings in mobile search engines, and they must compete with other mobile and traditional sites that are already in good favor with the search engines.

One of the main arguments against having a separate mobile site is that they can be confusing to users. Many users will have a hard time remembering one domain, but a separate mobile site forces them to remember two domain names, and possibly even two sets of Web content and navigation. Creating a separate mobile site also doubles the amount of website maintenance you have to do. When important updates are made to the main site, they must be made to the mobile site, too. In general, the cost of creating and maintaining a separate mobile website tends to be higher than other architecture options. It is also important to note that as mobile browsers improve, other architecture options will fall more into favor because the need for separate mobile websites will fade.

Mobile Subdomain or Subdirectory

Many popular websites choose to put a mobile version of their site in a subdomain or subdirectory on their primary domain. This prevents users from having to remember a new domain and allows the mobile pages to benefit from the traffic, links, history, and keyword rankings that the main site has with search engines. This is beneficial because it means that the mobile website does not have to start from scratch and can begin attracting traffic from mobile search engines much faster.

Mobile subdomains and subdirectories are relatively easy to create, and the content on the mobile pages can be easily tailored to fit smaller mobile screens. There is no consensus in the mobile SEO community on whether a subdomain or subdirectory is more desirable, and this is discussed more later. Other than SEO value, little difference exists between mobile subdomains and mobile subdirectories, except for their expression in the URL.

You can essentially copy your site and put it in the subdomain or subdirectory, and then start formatting the content for the smaller screens of mobile phones. You can name the subdomain or subdirectory any way you like, but the most common mobile designations are mobile, m, mobi, wap, and mob.

Subdomains

Subdomains are subsections of your website that are represented in the URL with the name of the subdirectory, then a dot (.), and then the full domain name. For example, www.Ruters.com has its mobile site on a subdirectory called `mobile`, so the URL to access the mobile content is www.mobile.Reuters.com. All mobile content on the site is hosted in the mobile subdomain. Many SEOs believe that mobile subdomains are likely preferred over mobile subdirectories in search results because they are a more intuitive break or differentiation in the site.

Subdirectories

Subdirectories are sometimes called folders or subfolders. They operate in much the same way subdomains do, but they are represented differently in the URL. The BizJournals.com website has a mobile subdirectory called `mobile`, so the URL for the mobile content is www.BizJournals.com/mobile. All the mobile content on the site is hosted in the `mobile` subdirectory. Many SEOs believe that mobile subdirectories are better than subdomains because they allow more of the search engine value that is given to the domain to pass down to the content in the subfolder.

One of the benefits of this approach is the capability to tailor content that eliminates unnecessary components and controls the mobile user experience. In many cases, you might want to eliminate elements from the traditional site that would take a long time to download on a mobile phone or might create rendering problems. You can also simplify the page layout by organizing everything in one column with well-marked headings.

The main drawback of this approach is that creates a duplicate content risk with the search engines, which is discussed more in Chapter 10. The other substantial disadvantage to this strategy is the duplication of overhead and effort required to maintain the site. Each time a change is made to the traditional website, it likely has to be made again on the mobile site; with sites that have rapidly changing Web content, this can be quite cumbersome.

Mobile/Traditional Hybrid Pages

A less-known but very logical option for many website s is to use multiple Cascading Style Sheets (CSS) to make all the existing pages on your existing site work on mobile phones, too. Cascading Style Sheets are the rendering instructions that control how the content of your site is displayed. When a page is displayed, the browsers pull the style sheet to see how the page should be laid out and what fonts and colors to use when rendering it. (This differs from older HTML coding standards, where font attributes were included in-line with the code.)

Style sheets can be internal, meaning that the code is actually part of each page, or external, meaning that the code that controls the page is housed in a separate file on the server. External style sheets are text documents that control how every page (or just a group of pages) on the site renders. This makes it easy to update your entire site simply by updating a single CSS file. Style sheets are also great for mobile because they enable you to streamline the code that the phone has to interpret to render the page. This minimizes the time it takes your page to render on a mobile handset. Also, because the style sheet has to be downloaded only once, subsequent pages on the site will download to the phone even quicker. Originally, not all mobile phones supported CSS, but now most phones that honor WAP2.0 or above have at least some support for CSS.

If your traditional website is cleanly coded (XHTML is preferable) and style sheets have been employed to control the rendering of the site, you can simply create a new "handheld" style sheet that will direct how the content of your existing site is rendered when it is on a mobile phone. All you have to do is add a link to the mobile style sheet in each page, after the link to the traditional style sheet (as shown in the following example). Mobile browsers will automatically pull the handheld style sheet if it is available.

```
<link rel="stylesheet" type="text/css" media="screen"
href="screen.css"/>
<link rel="stylesheet" type="text/css" media="handheld" href="hand-
held.css"/>
```

In some cases, this can be a great way to save time and money on mobile site development, and it is actually an elegant solution. It enables you to leverage all the existing links and search engine rankings of your existing site in mobile search, and it prevents you from having to make updates in two places whenever your site needs to be updated. This option is also ideal because it eliminates the risk of duplicate content being indexed in the search engines, which, again, is discussed more in

Chapter 10. (Mobile style sheets should also be used on mobile-specific pages that are hosted on subdomains or subdirectories, but they don't benefit as much from the search engine rankings of the primary pages.)

You can even use the "display=none" attribute in your style sheets to have things show on the mobile site and not the traditional site, or vice versa. This can be a bit tricky if you are not skilled in CSS, but overall it is a very simple solution. The biggest caveat is that hybrid pages are not a great option for sites that have a lot of images or things like Flash that would bog down a mobile browser. In most cases, you want to eliminate those large elements from the mobile rendering. Remember that even if the style sheet is used to make these items not display, they still have to be downloaded, which drastically slows the load time of your mobile page.

In some cases, browsers might have a hard time pulling the appropriate external style sheet. This is especially true of Mobile Internet Explorer, which is known for pulling the traditional "screen" style sheet instead, and also true of the NetFront browser, found on PlayStation, which renders only style sheets that are embedded in the page. The following code, courtesy of Johann Burkahrd at JohannaBurkard.de, embeds a style sheet for the handheld media type (for NetFront/PlayStation) and hides the screen style sheet from IEMobile and NetFront (see http://johannburkard.de/blog/www/mobile/Linking-CSS-for-handheld-devices-revisited.html):

```
<link rel="stylesheet" type="text/css"
    href="handheld.css" media="handheld"/>


<script type="text/javascript">
if (/(NetFront¦PlayStation)/i.test(navigator.userAgent))
    document.write(unescape('%3C') +
    'link rel="stylesheet" href="handheld.css"\/' + unescape('%3E'));
if (/(hiptop¦IEMobile¦Smartphone¦Windows CE¦NetFront¦PlayStation¦Opera Mini)/i
    .test(navigator.userAgent))
    document.write(unescape('%3C%21--'));
</script>


<style type="text/css">
@import URL("handheld.css") handheld
</style>


<link rel="stylesheet" type="text/css"
    href="screen.css" media="screen,tv,projection,print"/>


<!-- -->
```

HTTP Header Review

The HTTP headers on a website help clarify the characteristics of data that is being sent or received from the Web. A variety of headers that can be included in a Web page, but the following headers are more relevant for mobile development than others.

User Agent Profiles (UAProf)

User agent profiles are stored in an XML document on a server called the profile repository, which frequently is maintained by the device manufacturer. The UAProf is stored in the header of the mobile phone and is received by the website when the first request is sent. The header contains a link to the server and sends back information from the server about the screen size and other important elements on the phone. This enables the phone manufacturer to update the user agent profile information so that it can be updated independent of the websites or handsets.

User-Agent Header

The User-Agent header is stored on the phone and the mobile browser your Web patron is using. Your website can request and check this header to determine what type of content should be served. This is discussed more in "Directing Traffic with User Agent Detection," later in this chapter, but it should also be mentioned here.

Checking this header is especially important if you have pages or content that has been created for specific user agents, or if you are serving content dynamically based on user agent detection and device specifications. One of the main difficulties of User-Agent headers is that the format of the header is different among phones and phone manufacturers. Because this can be confusing and time-consuming, lists of mobile user agents are available online. They can also usually be accessed directly from the phone manufacturer's website. Wikipedia has a good list of the popular user agents available at http://en.wikipedia.org/wiki/List_of_user_agents_for_mobile_phones.

Cache-Control

The Cache-Control header is used to specify whether the elements of the page should be casced by the phone or the server. When working with mobile devices, it is important to minimize the amount of content that mobile phones must download, whenever possible. Allowing servers to cache the style sheet, logo, or template images will prevent the user from having to download them independently each time, which minimizes the bandwidth necessary to view the website. When it is necessary, the Cache-Control headers can also prevent the reuse of content that has been adapted for one device but should not be used on others, or prevent caching all together. The following directives can also be useful for mobile content.

"Cache-Control: public" Allows content to be cached and shared among different devices

"Cache-Control: private" Allows cached content to be reused, but only by the originally requesting device

"Cache-Control: no-cache" Prevents all caching of the website on the phone and the server

Content-Type

The Content-Type HTTP response header describes various aspects of the content that is being sent, including the character set, encoding, and MIME type. For most mobile content, the content type header looks like this:

```
Content-Type: text/xhtml; charset=utf-8
```

The first aspect of the Content-Type header is the Multipurpose Internet Mail Extensions (MIME) type. A MIME type is a media designation included in the header of a Web page that tells the mobile browser how to interpret the code that it is sending, and it is the value returned in the Content-Type request. MIME types also help the mobile browser determine when a file is supposed to be launched in the browser and when it should be launched as an application or in a separate program.

The MIME designation always includes a main type and a subtype, which are separated by a forward slash; thus, the MIME type for an image might be image/GIF. Eight primary MIME types exist: application, audio, image, message, model, multipart, text, and video. Table 9.1 shows some of the more common mobile MIME types (excluding some media MIME types, which are covered later).

Table 9.1   Common Mobile MIME Types

MIME Type	File Extension	Remark
application/java-archive	Binary	Java archive
application/java-archive	.jar	Java archive
application/mtf	.mtf	Motorola theme
application/vnd.alcatel.animation	.ani	Alcatel animation (converted animated GIF file)
application/vnd.alcatel.colorpalette	.pco	Alcatel image (256-color picture)

MIME Type	File Extension	Remark
application/vnd.alcatel.picture	.pic	Alcatel icon
application/vnd.alcatel.seq	.seq	Alcatel polytone (converted MIDI file)
application/vnd.alcatel.vox	.vox	Alcatel sound format (converted WAV file)
application/vnd.eri.thm	.thm	Sony Ericsson theme
application/vnd.mophun.application	.mpn	Sony Ericsson mophun game file; this file runs only on a mophun runtime environment
application/vnd.nokia.gamedata	.nqd	Nokia game data
application/vnd.Nokie.ringing-tone	.rng	Nokia ringtone
application/vnd.nok-s40theme	.nth	Nokia theme
application/vnd.rn-realmedia	.rm	RealMedia video format
application/vnd.siemens-mp.skin	.scs	Siemens color scheme; compressed file containing several files
application/vnd.siemens-mp.theme	.sdt	Siemens theme file; compressed file containing several files
application/vnd.symbian.install	.sis	Symbian installation
application/vnd.symbian.install	.sis	Symbian installer
application/vnd.wap.mms-message	.mms	Binary MMS in MMS Encapsulation Protocol format
application/vnd.wap.xhtml+xml	.xhtml	XHTML-MP markup
application/xhtml+xml	.xhtml	XHTML-MP markup
application/x-nokiagamedata	.ngd	Nokia game data
application/x-pmd	.pmd	Polyphonic ringtone format
application/x-smaf	.mmf	Samsung truetone format
audio/adpcm	.adp	LG truetone format
audio/midi	.mid	MIDI audio format (ringtones)
audio/midi	.midi	MIDI audio format (ringtones)
audio/vnd.qcelp	.qcp	QCELP audio file
audio/x-aac	.aac	Nokia audio format
image/gif	.gif	GIF format
image/jpeg	.jpeg	JPEG format

Table 9.1 Continued

MIME Type	File Extension	Remark
image/jpg	.jpg	JPG format
image/png	.png	PNG format
image/vnd.nok-3dscreensaver	.n3a	Nokia screensaver
image/vnd.nok-oplogo-color	.nol	Nokia operator logo (GIF image)
image/vnd.wap.wbmp	.wbmp	WAP content: WAP bitmap image
image/vnd.wap.wbmp	.wbmp	Wireless bitmap Image
image/x-bmp	.bmp	BMP image
text/css	.css	CSS1, CSS2, and wireless CSS
text/html	.html	HTML
text/vnd.sun.j2me.app-descriptor	.jad	J2ME content: Java descriptor file
text/vnd.wap.wml	.wml	WML markup
text/vnd.wap.wmlscript	.wmls	WML Script
text/x-co-desc	.cod	Nokia Content Object Description file
text/x-emelody	.emy	Sony Ericsson eMelody sound format
text/x-imelody	.imy	iMelody, a feature-rich ringtone format
text/x-vCalendar	.vcs	vCalendar, a format for electronic calendaring and scheduling
text/x-vCard	.vcf	Exchanging information about people and resources
video/avi	.avi	AVI video format
video/mpeg	.mpeg	MPEG video format
x-epoc/x-sisx-app	.sisx	Symbian installer
x-nokia-widget	.wgz	Nokia Widget Archive

Most Web servers do not come preconfigured to support mobile MIME types, although this is becoming more common. If you are serving mobile content, it is a good idea to check your servers and manually add any mobile MIME types that are not already present and recognized by the Web server.

In some cases, devices can accept multiple file types but still have a preference, usually because the device has a more complete and comprehensive capability to execute a specific file type. You might be able to use a combination of User-Agent headers, accept headers, and a User-Agent profile (UAProf.) to provide the preferred type of content based on the handset that is accessing the site.

The second part of the Content-Type header is the character set, or charset. The character set you choose can impact the bandwidth necessary to transmit a page, because some characters require more memory than others. If your website is written primarily in Latin-based characters and languages, such as English, French, and German, you should be using UTF-8. If your website is written in non-Latin characters, such as Chinese, Japanese, or Hebrew, UTF-16 is ideal.

Content-Disposition

This header enables you to specify that a file should not be displayed automatically, but instead should open outside the mobile browser and prompt a File Download dialog box whenever accepted MIME types are requested. This is particularly helpful when your Web page allows visitors to download applications, games, images, ringtones, wallpapers, or other types of non-Web content.

Mobile Code Review

The most important thing you can do ensure the success of your mobile website is to code it correctly. The code affects how quickly the pages download, how they look on different mobile handsets, and what features are available and working in the mobile environment.

If you are starting from scratch or from a premade template, you should strive to create an XHTML-compliant code base. XHTML has the most rigid set of HTML coding standards and, thus, is best for ensuring that your website will work well across the broadest number of mobile handsets and browsers. XHTML requires text alternatives to all nontext elements, which is ideal for mobile, in case the phone downloads some portion of the Web page incorrectly.

Before style sheets were developed, Webmasters used "tables," much like a spreadsheet or a grid in Excel, to organize a Web page. The code of the Web page included specifications about the table width, row height, and other attributes of the grid. The actual grid was never visible by the Web visitors, but it did help the Web designer control the layout of the page.

When developing or adapting a page for mobile, tables are not desirable. Many phones can render a simple table-based layout, but the table specifications embedded in the page create a lot of extra code that can slow the download of the page. In more complicated pages, table-based layouts can include tables within tables, or "nested" tables. Nested tables are known to cause more problems for mobile viewing, either rendering incorrectly or not rendering at all.

One of the overarching rules in mobile development is to always provide text alternatives for any nontext content. This includes images, videos, audio files, scripts, and objects. Every type of content has its own alternatives when the files cannot be downloaded, but you should always at least include alternative text (Alt text) to describe the content. Ideally, all mobile pages will still be useful if rendered exclusively in text, with no images or scripts.

JavaScript

JavaScript is a coding language used on the traditional Web to enhance the traditional HTML user interface and make a more dynamic Web experience. On the traditional Web, it is frequently used to control navigation, drop-down menus, form submissions, and pop-up windows, but it can create problems when displaying on many mobile browsers.

The primary concern should always be navigation. When JavaScript navigation is displayed on a mobile browser that is not equipped to display it, either the navigation will display without rollover characteristics that enable you to see drop-down menus, or it will display in full, as a long list of navigational options. This will force your main content lower on the mobile screen, in some cases, making it hard or impossible for users to know when they have successfully loaded a new page because all the unique content is below the bottom of the mobile screen.

If your JavaScript navigation is displaying in full, consider moving your main navigation to the bottom of the page when it is displayed on a mobile phone, and replace it with a short list of access keys, jump links, or bookmarks at the top of the page (as shown in Figure 9.1). These jump links can help people quickly move to the main content, the main navigation, and the other important elements on the page without pushing the unique content too low on the page or requiring the user to scroll. This gives visitors a preview of the content on the page and helps them find what they are looking for quickly and easily.

Figure 9.2 shows an example of good versus bad mobile content layout.

Figure 9.1 *Mobile jump links enable users to quickly navigate your mobile site.*

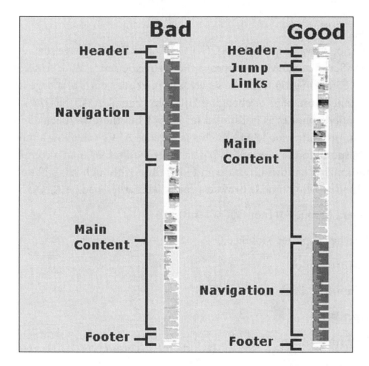

Figure 9.2 *Good mobile design vs. bad mobile design.*

Another application of JavaScript is to create hover effects within navigation and images. Hover effects are represented in JavaScript as mouseover and mouseout. These can be problematic because most mobile phones, including the iPhone, do not offer the capability to hover over any particular object on the screen, because the phones do not have mice to hover with. Even when there is mouse capability function on the phone, the hover JavaScript will likely not execute. (On a similar note, the :hover pseudoclass in CSS doesn't work on iPhones, either.)

JavaScript can also be used to create pop-up windows, which are problematic on the traditional Web and even more so on the mobile Web because many mobile browsers can handle only one window or tab at a time. Many of the new mobile browsers are blocking pop-up windows by default, and the JavaScript that calls for pop-up windows can actually cause some mobile phones to crash; this should be avoided.

In the past two years, mobile browsers have come a long way in their rendering of JavaScript. Most true Web browsing phones can now handle basic, well-coded JavaScript, but more complex or sloppily coded scripts are still a problem. On the iPhone, JavaScript is limited to five seconds of execution time.

AJAX

Asynchronous JavaScript and XML (AJAX) is a coding language that essentially mixes JavaScript and XML to improve the Web experience. With AJAX, a website can receive information from the server and re-render parts of a page without reloading the entire page or changing URLs. In general, AJAX has the same problems on mobile phones as traditional JavaScript, but there has been a movement recently to promote mobile AJAX. This is because AJAX can allow a mobile Web page to respond to the user with a partial page load rather than a complete page load, minimizing bandwidth usage and load time. Although it is still not mainstream, the following mobile browsers can render at least some AJAX:

- Opera Mobile 8.0 (not Opera Mini)
- Internet Explorer Mobile 5.0
- S60 3rd edition
- Minimo
- OpenWave
- NetFront 3.4
- Safari Mobile

When using JavaScript or AJAX on a mobile Web page, it is important to program with graceful degradation in mind. Graceful degradation is a design principle that ensures that browsers are presented only with content that they are able to render correctly; thus, less sophisticated browsers can render a page one way, and more sophisticated browsers can render the same page another way. Because there are so many different mobile browsers, and they all handle scripting languages a bit differently, this is very important. This principle is covered in more detail in "Directing Traffic with User Agent Detection," later in this chapter.

Forms

Web forms can be programmed in a variety of languages, including JavaScript, AJAX, C#, ASP, and ASP.NET. In the mobile world, forms can cause problems, either because the form labels don't line up correctly with the form entry boxes or because the JavaScript in the Submit function simply doesn't work. The only way to know for sure that your form will work on mobile phones is to actually test it. Although this problem has no universal solution, a couple best practices are associated with mobile forms.

- First, include links for users to email or text-message themselves a link to the form so that they can complete it later. This is helpful when the form is not working or if the user simply doesn't want to type all the information on the mobile phone. If possible, include a phone number that viewers can click on to call and submit their information over the phone rather than through a Web form. This is especially useful if users have questions or need special assistance, and it loops in the full functionality of the phone.

- You can use a variety of methods to allow visitors to enter information on a form. As on a traditional computer, they can be radio buttons, check boxes, text boxes, drop-down menus, or even calendar widgets. The main concern is that the form must be quick and easy to use and also intuitive.

- When designing a form, be sure to use an asterisk (*) to designate when fields are required, and eliminate as many optional fields as possible. Use radio buttons and check boxes as much as you can, to prevent your users from having to type too much on the phone keypad.

- If you are using a drop-down menu, the HTML <SELECT> element, a unique feature on the iPhone, turns the menu into a dial that can be flicked up or down when it is displayed on the iPhone, as shown in Figure 9.3.

Figure 9.3 *An example of the iPhone menu dial that displays when the <SELECT> element is included.*

- If you have to request a narrative or sentence response from your users, be careful with large response fields that would normally have a scroll bar in them, because these will not work on the iPhone. The iPhone never uses scroll bars, even along the right side of the page, like most browsers, so it will not include the scroll bar in your text field and the viewer will not be able to see the contents of the text response. Technically, iPhone users can use a two-finger method of scrolling within the box, but without a visual cue to indicate that this is possible, it creates a serious usability concern. Form fields such as this one tend to have a fixed height and width, so first adjust the height designation and then test on the iPhone to see if it will address the problem. If that doesn't work, you might have to break the questions into multiple questions or eliminate it.

Each of your questions should be labeled, and the input fields should be directly below or next to the label. You can also include input prompts within the text boxes, to remind the user what type of information you are requesting or to give more instructions about the response, as shown in Figure 9.4. In some cases, when users are typing their information into a phone, the values will be all text or all numbers. Many phones use the same buttons to control numbers and letters, so the user might be forced to use an Alt or Shift key repeatedly to complete the field.

Figure 9.4 *An example of form input instructions. "Google Custom Search" is the input instruction for this form.*

- You can also use WAP Input Format or WCSS. Table 9.2 shows a variety of property values, called the input masks.

Table 9.2   WAP Input Format Property Values

Format Characters	Usage
A	Lowercase letters or characters
A	Uppercase letters or characters
N	Numbers and number characters
N	Number characters
X	Any lowercase letter, number, or symbol
X	Any uppercase letter, number, or symbol
M	Sets the default entry value to lower case
M	Sets the default entry value to upper case

- When applied in the code, <input type="text" style="-wap-input-format: "N""/> forces a number, and <input type="text" style="-wap-input-format: "m""/> forces letters.

  When setting the WAP input property, you can specify the order of the inputs and the number of a particular type of input. For instance, -wap-input-format: "NN" tells the form that it can accept two number characters in a row, but wap-input-format: "2N" tells the form that it can accept no more than two number characters in the field. If you would like to automatically capitalize the first letter of a form field, such as for a person's name or a street name, you could use wap-input-format: "A*a" which would make the first letter that is input a capital letter but will allow any number of lowercase letters after it.

- When creating mobile forms, it is best to authenticate the information as the user types. This makes it easier for users to update the fields as they go, rather than having to go back through the form later, to identify and update form fields with errors. It is also important to be as flexible as possible with mobile form inputs. This includes accepting information in a variety of different formats. For instance, a form should be able to accept the types of phone number formatting shown in Table 9.3. It should do so without showing an error and should also display the information correctly on the mobile phone and parse the information correctly for the database on the back end. Similar standards should be followed with credit card numbers, serial numbers, and any other entries that could be entered in a variety of different ways.

Table 9.3   Acceptable Phone Number Formatting for Web Forms

123-456-7891	1-123-456-7891	1(123)456.7891
123.456.7891	1 123-456-7891	+1(123)456.7891
123 456 7891	+1-123-456-7891	1.123.456.7891
1234567891	+1 123-456-7891	+1.123.456.7891
(123) 456 781	+1(123)456-7891	11234567891
(123) 456-7891	+1(123)-456-7891	

- As browsers get more sophisticated, they might also incorporate autofill features. These will be quite handy when they are integrated into mobile browsing and will make it more likely that mobile visitors will be willing to complete your forms. Currently, most autofill programs recognize the field names shown in Table 9.4.

Table 9.4   Recognizable Field Names

email	phone
first-name	street
firstname	city
last-name	country
lastname	state (used for county outside US)
full-name	postalcode
birthday	zip
company	Ecom_ReceiptTo_Postal_Name_First
jobtitle	Ecom_ReceiptTo_Postal_Name_Last

- Also consider using autocomplete features whenever possible. Autocomplete is similar to autofill, but it works on a field-by-field basis and uses the first couple values that the user inputs to anticipate what the user is intending to type and provide suggestions that they can select instead of having to finish typing the word on their own. Most mobile browsers offer an autocomplete in their address bar, but you can also do this in form fields.

- Finally, when working with online forms, submitting to a secure server can also cause problems. Some information, such as credit card numbers, should be passed only over a secure server, but this should be avoided whenever possible in the mobile world. For more information about accepting payments over a mobile phone, refer to Chapter 12, "Mobile E-Commerce."

Flash and Video

Flash and video are becoming much more common on mobile phones, but they still can be quite tricky. Traditional Flash does not work on most mobile phones, but a streamlined mobile version, called Flash Light, is supported by phones from the manufacturers shown in Table 9.5.

Table 9.5   Flash Light Capable Phones

Fujitsu	Motorola	Samsung	Siemens
Hitachi	NEC	Sanyo	Sony
Kyocera	Nokia	Sendo	Ericsson
LG	Panasonic	Sharp	Toshiba
Mitsubishi			

Many of these handsets are available primarily in Japan, but it is expected that Flash Light will become much more prominent in the rest of the world as well. For a full list of phones that can display Flash Light, visit www.adobe.com/mobile/supported_devices/handsets.html. Flash Light files are similar to traditional Flash, except that they have lower picture and audio quality. The next iteration, Flash Light 3.1, is available on Windows Mobile phones, the Nokia S60, and the Palm Pre, but not the iPhone.

Clearly, the iPhone will some day support some type of animation, but it is expected to be an iPhone-specific version of the Flash player that will be more compatible with the entire iPhone framework. If the technology is not developed quickly enough, HTML5 also will support the embedding of different animations and video, which might make Flash unnecessary.

Silverlight

Silverlight is another browser-based media player add-in that Microsoft developed to rival Flash. Silverlight is available on Windows Mobile phones, as well as the Nokia S60 and the iPhone. The allure of Silverlight comes from the promise that the same video can be used on traditional and mobile browsers, but can be adapted on-the-fly to fit the size and file requirements of the phone it is sent to.

Silverlight is a .NET-based platform that enables developers to add interactivity to their videos, much like a Flash file. It lets you zoom into videos with amazing clarity and also supports multitouch commands, as with the pinching and pulling on the iPhone. (The MIME type for Silverlight is `xaml`.)

YouTube

YouTube is another video resource that can be useful on mobile phones. It accepts the following file formats: avi, .mpg, .wmv, and .mov. For videos to be available in YouTube on the iPhone, however, they must be converted to the H.264 compression format. For mobile, the safest file format is MPEG4 and MP4 (QuickTime) AVI, H.264/AVC, 3GP, and 3GPP.

As mentioned earlier in the chapter, it is important to designate common MIME types in your page files, but you must also do that for your rich media content. Figure 9.5 shows a list of the rich media MIME types that are accepted by the iPhone.

MIME Type	Description	Extensions
audio/3gpp	3GPP media	3gp, 3gpp
audio/3gpp2	3GPP2 media	3g2, 3gp2
audio/aiff audio/x-aiff	AIFF audio	aiff, aif, aifc, cdda
audio/amr	AMR audio	amr
audio/mp3 audio/mpeg3 audio/x-mp3 audio/x-mpeg3	MP3 audio	mp3, swa
audio/mp4	MPEG-4 media	mp4
audio/mpeg audio/x-mpeg	MPEG audio	mpeg, mpg, mp3, swa
audio/wav audio/x-wav	WAVE audio	wav,bwf
audio/x-m4a	AAC audio	m4a
audio/x-m4b	AAC audio book	m4b
audio/x-m4p	AAC audio (protected)	m4p
video/3gpp	3GPP media	3gp, 3gpp
video/3gpp2	3GPP2 media	3g2, 3gp2
video/mp4	MPEG-4 media	mp4
video/quicktime	QuickTime Movie	mov,qt,mqv
video/x-m4v	Video	m4v

Figure 9.5 *Media Mime Types accepted on the iPhone.*

Frames

Web developers use frames to bind content from two different pages into a new page. Two basic types of frames exist: HTML frames, otherwise known as framesets and included frames, or i-frames. Framesets have fallen out of vogue because of their negative impact on the user experience and search engine indexing; as mentioned earlier, they will not be accepted in HTML5. They generally enable you to scroll within a certain portion of the page without scrolling the entire page. If you are working with a website that uses HTML frames to display content, there is a good chance that only the main content on the page will display on a mobile phone, and any of the additional HTML frames that are being pulled in will not be displayed. As mentioned earlier, the iPhone never includes scroll bars, so HTML frames won't work on the iPhone.

Included frames, or i-frames, are still quite common in traditional Web-based coding and are more likely to render correctly, but they can still cause problems with mobile rendering. In many cases, if the browser on the phone doesn't support i-frames, the included element will simply not show. iPhones and Windows Mobile devices currently support i-frames, but many BlackBerries, Motorolas, and Nokias do not.

Everything You Need to Know About Transcoding

Transcoding is the process of updating the code of a traditional Web page on-the-fly, before it is rendered, to adapt the code to display better on a mobile phone. Transcoding utilities can be standalone or can be included as part of a mobile search engine experience after a user clicks from a listing in the mobile search results page.

A variety of different transcoding platforms exist, and they all work a bit differently. They can do various things, including the following:

- Resizing text and images that fit better on smaller mobile screens

- Breaking one page into multiple smaller pages that are easier for the mobile browser to download (pagination)

- Reformatting JavaScript navigation to improve its mobile usability

- Simplifying site color schemes and designs

- Stripping out some CSS styling

In some cases, companies can host transcoding software on their servers to use on their website whenever it is accessed from a mobile device. Transcoding services also can adapt and tweak the code of a company's website, shepherd the entire process, and then add the newly created files to the Web server, to be displayed when the site is accessed by a mobile phone. In other cases, the users can access a transcoding utility from their mobile phone and enter the URLs for pages that they would like to be transcoded one at a time. In most cases, though, transcoding is done by search engines, after a mobile search result is clicked.

Transcoding can be good if you don't have time to update your website for mobile viewers, but it can also be bad if the transcoding engine doesn't do a good job updating the site. When a user arrives on a transcoded page, it is not actually a page hosted on the website, but it is a temporary page, hosted by the transcoding utility. In some cases, pagination will happen at inopportune or illogical places on the page, images will not scale correctly, or problems will arise with page navigation. This causes problems for site tracking and analytics programs, and it also frequently prevents any activity that requires a secure server. To preview how your website might look when it is transcoded by Google, visit http://yeswap.com/gtran.html.

If you want to prevent transcoding, the best way to is to present mobile pages to the search engines so that their crawlers perceive no need to transcode the page and place a no-transform directive in your cache control header. You can also submit a mobile site map to the various search engines, and this should prevent the pages included in the mobile sitemap from being transcoded. That works in most cases but if it doesn't, the next step is to include a link in the header to the mobile version of the page. The link should look like this:

```
<link rel="alternate" media="handheld" href="http://www.yourmobile-
site.com/" />
```

Replace `http://www.yourmobilesite.com/` with the location of the mobile page, whether it is on a subdomain, subdirectory, or separate domain.

Hosted Mobile Development Solutions

Depending on your content, it might make sense to use a hosted mobile website instead of actually updating your code base or changing your Web server settings. Having a hosted mobile Website is very similar to having transcoding software on your server, except that the transcoding software is part of a Web service hosted away from your primary site. A service like this usually places it on a domain that the transcoding service hosts, hence the designation "hosted mobile solution." Sometimes these services are also called mobile site builders.

Much like other transcoding options, hosted mobile websites are smaller, simplified versions of your existing website. Many services claim to "mobilize" your website, and the prices are usually reasonable, based on the number of pages, the number of monthly page views, and additional add-on services.

If you are using a service such as this, and your mobile website is hosted on a subdomain, away from your main domain, it is important to understand that the mobile website will not get any SEO benefit from your main domain because it is on a different domain. The good news is that the hosted mobile site might benefit from the historical value of the hosting company's domain, although because the other websites on that domain are likely about different topics, it might lack any search engine relevance.

If you want to use a hosted mobile solution but also want the mobile website to appear as if it is on your primary website's domain, the only way to do that is to change the DNS host in the records of the hosted mobile service provider's domain. The DNS, or Domain Name System, associates IP addresses of websites with domain names, much like a phone book.

Two of the newer and more comprehensive hosted mobile solutions are Mobify.me and MoFusePremium. Their service enables you to graphically organize the content of your website, create and update a handheld CSS, and preview the mobile site on an iPhone, Razr, BlackBerry, and Nokia phone simulators.

Directing Traffic with User Agent Detection

User agent detection is a means of adapting what type of content is served based on what type of device or "user agent" is accessing the website. This is the most effective means of selective degradation, mentioned earlier in the chapter. With user agent detection, a Webmaster can either hone the information served on a particular page based on the device that is accessing it, or redirect the user to a totally different URL that has been crafted specifically for that user agent.

In many cases, the most important user agent detection happens on the home page of your traditional website, but the functions should be included in all the pages throughout the website. The site should be set up to identify when a mobile user agent has reached the page and should send users directly to content that is optimized for a mobile experience. One of the quickest ways to make this update to your existing website is to add the scripts to your page templates so that, as new pages are added, the script is already included.

Mobile browser-detection code generators are available on the Web to help with this process. My favorite is DetectMobileBrowsers.mobi because it is simple to use. It enables you to specify how you want to treat iPhone, Android, Opera Mini, BlackBerry, PalmOS, and Windows Mobile device with an online form; then it generates the specific set of code that you requested. In each case, you can choose to treat the phone like a mobile device or like a traditional computer, or to send it to a specific URL.

The capability to send users to a specific URL is especially nice if you have multiple mobile websites set up for different types of browsers—for instance, if you have a set of mobile content for older text-based mobile browsers and a separate set of content for newer, more sophisticated mobile browsers. This particular code generator is also nice because it includes code that automatically sends any mobile device that is not specifically addressed in the redirect scheme to a specific page; it redirects all traditional user agents back to the traditional Web page, and all mobile user agents to the mobile version of the page. The capability to substitute content on the same page without changing URLs is also good for SEO because it avoids duplicate content issues.

More comprehensive instructions on DetectMobileBrowsers.mobi specify where and how the code must be added, and detail some server settings that you might need to change to make the settings run correctly in HTML pages. (If you use this utility, note that the code does not come free; you are expected to pay $50 for any commercial Website that uses the code.)

User agent detection is a term that was carried over from the traditional Web world, and it is a reference to detecting specific "devices." In the mobile world, there are so many possible devices that mobile handsets (user agents) are frequently grouped by the mobile browser that they run. Thus, mobile user agent detection is often a combination of "user agent" detection and "browser" detection.

When it comes to user agent detection and redirection, usability studies have shown that users on the iPhone and the Android phone still prefer a mobile experience, despite the fact that their phones are capable of rendering entire traditional Web pages. The left-to-right scrolling and zooming required is still too cumbersome, so redirecting to a mobile-specific or iPhone-specific page is still desirable.

XML and RSS Mobile Websites

If you are working with a website that is primarily text based, such as a blog or a news website, one of the quickest ways to create a mobile version of your website is to use the RSS, ATOM, or XML feeds that might already in place. Feeds for each page can be ported directly to pages on a mobile subdomain or subdirectory. Service companies also can provide this expertise and further optimize the mobile experience. Because these feeds are text based, they output to mobile quite well, and very simple style sheets and graphics can be used to update the look of the feed.

How to Adjust for Mobile Screen Size

One of the most obvious changes you must make to a website when you are preparing it to be displayed on a mobile device is to update the resolution of the page to fit the screen. As with many other aspects of the mobile world, there is no standard screen size—and there will probably never be. Screen resolution is variable based on the type of phone and manufacturer.

According to Phillip Nagele of Mobile Zeitgeist, 96% of all phones have a screen size aspect ratio of between 3:4 and 4:3, which can make your life a bit easier. With a similar aspect ratio, content will scale in a similar way to fit different screens that have the same aspect ratio, even if they are a different size.

The main concern when developing mobile websites in terms of screen size is width. Some phones do allow right-to-left scrolling, but all mobile browsers are meant to scroll up and down. One of the best ways to easily accommodate a variety of screen widths is to use relative positioning and percents instead of absolute positioning and absolute pixel widths. This will allow your content to stretch and shrink to fit whatever screen it is being displayed on.

Now, as mobile phones become more interactive, some phones can be viewed in either landscape or portrait mode, reinforcing the point that your website should be flexible in the way it displays so that it can stretch and shrink to accommodate the screen, whether it is being displayed in landscape or portrait mode. If you are designing a page specifically for the iPhone, you can also use the following code to specify the screen width when the phone is held in landscape or portrait view:

```
<!--[if !IE]>-->
<link media="only screen and (max-device-width: 480px)"
  rel="stylesheet" type="text/css" href="iphone.css"/>
<!--<![endif]
@media only screen and (max-device-width: 480px) {
  .navigation { display: none;  } }
<meta name="viewport" content="width=480; initial-scale=0.6666;
maximum-scale=1.0;
minimum-scale=0.6666" />
```

Screen size is always measured as "width × height," so 320×480 is the size of the screen when it is displayed in portrait mode, and 480×320 is the size of the screen when it is displayed in landscape mode. The most common mobile screen size is 320×480. Figure 9.6 shows how different screen sizes and resolutions compare.

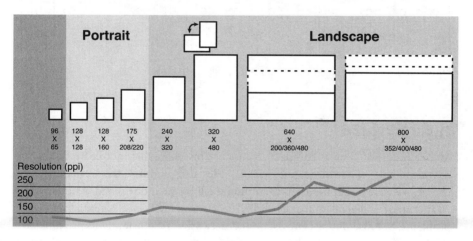

Figure 9.6 *Mobile screen resolution comparison.*

As phones have become more capable, screen sizes have gotten bigger and can accommodate more functionality. Figure 9.8 shows the change in the number of phones with different screen resolutions over time. As you can see, the 240×320 screen resolution has superseded the other popular screen resolutions and continues to grow. In many cases, handset manufacturers will come out with two different models of a phone: one with a smaller screen and a premium offering with a bigger screen. The other two popular screen sizes represented in Figure 9.7 include both the standard and the premium screen sizes, with the 176×208/160 and the 128×128/220.

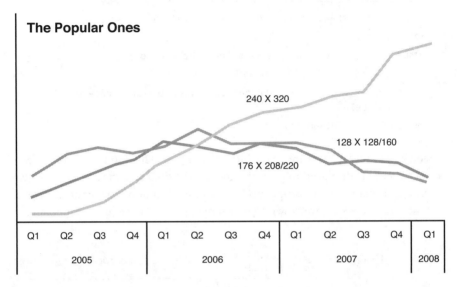

The Popular Ones

240 X 320

128 X 128/160

176 X 208/220

| Q1 | Q2 | Q3 | Q4 | Q1 | Q2 | Q3 | Q4 | Q1 | Q2 | Q3 | Q4 | Q1 |

2005   2006   2007   2008

Figure 9.7 *Mobile screen resolution popularity over time.*

Page File Size

Mobile files should be as compact as possible, to ensure that mobile browsers can download and render them quickly. Small files also minimize the amount of charges viewers might incur on their phone bill for each download. As mentioned, clean, simple code is the most desirable and creates the fewest potential rendering problems. Because phones, browsers, and networks are constantly improving, no hard-and-fast rule governs the file size or page weight, other than "as small as possible."

Based on the growing availability of smart phones and the residual prominence of older, less capable phones, you should keep mobile pages between 20KB and 35KB apiece. A page that is just over 20KB will take about 1 second to download over WiFi, 2 seconds to download over a 3G network, and about 7 seconds to download over GPRS.

Many methods to limit the page size have been included in previous sections of this chapter. If your mobile pages are still too large for optimal mobile rendering, the next step might be to create a pagination scheme and break the content into multiple pages. If your website is small, you can do this by hand, but if you are working with a bigger, more dynamic website, you should investigate different software and server scripts that can add pagination automatically. If you believe that landing on the second page of an article or blog post is not a good user experience, you can use the robots.txt file or the meta "NO INDEX" tag to block these pages from being included in search results.

What to Expect with Your Images

In the design process, it is important to consider how images will appear if the mobile browser misaligns them or rearranges them to fit on the smaller screen. This is quite common and can make it difficult for users to understand the message being conveyed. The best way to prevent this problem is to ensure that each image can stand on its own, without needing another image file directly adjacent to it in order to convey meaning. This way, if images are rearranged or misaligned, their message is still conveyed effectively. This is especially important if text is included in the images, because the message conveyed in the text could be totally lost when images are misaligned.

The following are some tips for using images in your mobile site:

- In general, do not rely on images for architectural or structural means in the design of your website. Especially avoid using image spacers, image maps, and background images. A reasonable chance exists that they will not be rendered where they were intended, so they will not provide any benefit and could cause confusion.

- The file size of your images is more important on mobile devices than it is on traditional computers because mobile phones have slower connection speeds and lower processing power. Compress all images as much as possible, to prevent them from slowing the load time or being blocked by proxies. Images that are a higher resolution than the screen is capable of displaying might be blocked or might hit the upper limit enforced by the carrier proxy, so always be sure to test higher-resolution images on different phones and different carrier networks.

- If you are creating pages or content that is adapted for a specific phone or screen resolution, it is important to code each image with a specific height and width, to maintain the phone-specific design you have created. In any other instance, it is important to code images with relative positioning and sizing so that they can stretch and shrink to adapt to different screen sizes and orientations.

- One of the simplest ways to limit the file size of your images is to keep them physically small in the design. Instead of having one or two large images, consider five or six medium and small images. The smaller the image file sizes are, the less likely they will be blocked by proxies or will slow the load time of the email. For the best user experience, page file size (including dependents) should be 50–100KB, so ideally, each image should be between 10KB and 20KB. If you are targeting more sophisticated phones, the images can be larger, but the iPhone does not support .GIFs, .PNGs, or .TIFFs over 8MB, or .JPGs over 128MB.

- Using image maps on your pages can also cause problems in mobile rendering. Image maps are graphics where multiple areas on the image have been programmed with links. Unfortunately, when images are rescaled to fit on a mobile phone, the corresponding map of hotspots might not be rescaled at the same rate or in the same way, so there is a risk that the images and links will not match up when rendered on the phone. If you use image maps on your website, it is crucial to provide alternative methods of navigation on the mobile rendering of your site.

- This is discussed more in Chapter 10, but it is also important to include top keywords in your image filenames and Alt attributes. This will help the search engines understand the relevance of the images, and thus help them rank the page for the appropriate search queries.

Adapting Fonts for Mobile Viewing

The fonts that are rendered when you are viewing Web pages are actually stored on the computer or mobile handset that you are using to access the Web. For that reason, it is important to design your mobile Web pages in fonts that are generally available on mobile phones. This will prevent the phone browser from displaying your website in a default font, which could throw off the look and feel of your website.

In general, the most common fonts, on both the traditional Web and the mobile Web, are Arial, Times New Roman, Courier, Helvetica, and Verdana. In addition to those, if you are targeting just the iPhone, it supports the following fonts: American Typewriter, Arial, Arial Rounded MT Bold, Courier, Courier New, Georgia, Helvetica, Helvetica New, Marker Felt, Times New Roman, Trebuchet MS, Verdana, and Zapfino.

In your style sheet, you can designate one or two specific fonts that you want your website rendered in, and then end the instructions with a generic font family name, such as Sans Serif, Serif, or Monospace. The following code instructs the page to render first in Arial, if it is available; then in Helvetica, if Arial is not available; and then, if neither is available, to render in whatever sans-serif font is available:

```
p {font-family: Arial, Helvetica, sans-serif}
```

The size a font is rendered on a mobile phone is also particularly important. If text is rendered incorrectly, it can take up too much space or not be readable. You must use relative sizing instead of absolute pixel sizes. This ensures that the font adapts to fit the phone it is being displayed on.

The font-size attribute that can be used in style sheets, with simple designations such as small, medium, and large. You can also set font sizes as percents (between 1 and 100), or you can use what are known as HTML font intervals (between 1 and 7, with 1 representing the smallest font available on the phone and 7 representing the largest font on the phone). For instance, the HTML font interval for a medium-size font would be expressed in the style sheet as {font-size=4}.

10

Mobile Search Engine Optimization

Internet access and Web search have changed the mobile marketing landscape. They are changing the way we think of mobile devices as a whole, making many things that were previously hard to access now instantly available.

Many of us have a hard time even remembering what we did or how we accessed the information we needed before the Internet. When computers were all (or mostly all) hooked up to the Internet, it improved their utility exponentially, and the same is true of mobile phones. Mobile phones provide infinitely more value when they are Web enabled. We will soon become accustomed to even more instant access to the endless wealth of knowledge that the Internet provides, to the point that some day we might not remember why we found mobile phones so useful when they just made calls.

Searching on mobile phones is still not as good of an experience as searching on a traditional computer, but mobile searchers are motivated searchers. A mobile search is a clear indication of intent. People search on mobile phones because they need information immediately, and they cannot wait until they get back to their computers to find it. The good news for us as marketers is that the information people tend to search for usually informs an immediate purchase decision, meaning they are ready to spend money, and they need to know where to spend it.

Interestingly, when the mobile Web becomes faster and less clunky (and it will) marketers might have a more difficult time separating those searchers who are most likely to make a purchase from those who are merely surfing. The current mobile Web is slow and clunky and because of that, motivated purchasers are easier to spot. What happens when everyone with a smart phone can surf just for fun? How will the marketer sort the wheat from the chaff? Just food for thought...

Mobile search is one of the most useful utilities a mobile phone provides. Most activity on the traditional Internet begins with a search, and the same is true on the mobile phone. In both traditional and mobile computing, many people set a search engine to their home page. Searching is the way people find what they need. If you have a mobile website, it is critical that it rank well in mobile search engines.

Mobile search engine optimization (mSEO) is a very new tactic for improving the reach and impact that your company's website can have on a mobile phone. The strategies and tactics change rapidly as the mobile search algorithms change and as the mobile handset technology improves. A large portion of mobile SEO is actually architectural, as covered in Chapter 9, "Mobile Website

Development." With sound website architecture in place, mobile SEO becomes much easier. If the architecture is less than ideal, the effort to optimize a website becomes harder.

Many different mobile search engines exist, but in most cases, the top mobile search engines in any country are the same as the top traditional search engines in that country. In the United States, these are Google, Yahoo!, and MSN/Bing. For mobile marketing, we must understand mSEO.

How Do Mobile Search Engines Work?

Currently, the biggest difference between traditional search engine bots and mobile search engine bots is that the mobile bots evaluate your site as if it was being displayed on a mobile device. If the bots determine that your site will perform well on mobile devices, it will be ranked well in mobile search results. If they determine that your site will not perform well, it will probably not rank well in mobile search engines. Furthermore, mobile search engines can detect what type of mobile device you are searching from and, in some cases, rank sites according to how well those sites will perform on that specific device. If the site will perform well on the device, it has a better chance of ranking well in the search results shown on that device. This is just one of the factors that can affect your rankings. It makes sense, because the search engines do not want to rank sites that searchers will not be able to view on their particular mobile phone.

Traditional search engines and mobile search engines are very similar. Both have programs that called bots, spiders, or metacrawlers that are sent out to read and categorize the information available on the Internet. They categorize websites and Web pages so that they can be ranked in search results, based on their relationship to a searcher's query. In simple terms, the closer the relationship between the content on your site and the search query, the higher your website should rank.

Traditional search engines and mobile search engines both look at a variety of things to determine how websites should rank in search results. They store the information that their bots or crawlers find when they are crawling the Web in an index, much as books are indexed in a library. Every website in the search engine index has the potential to rank for a search query, but websites that are not in the search engine index will never rank for a search performed in that search engine.

The three major search engines have multiple indexes, which supplement the information in the main index. These additional indexes are used to categorize specific types of search results, such as local results, images, videos, and mobile results. When someone performs a search, the search engines use a complicated math equation, called an algorithm, to evaluate the information stored in the indexes. The algorithm mathematically compares different websites that are relevant to the search query, to determine how they will be ranked in search results. In many instances, the search results on both a traditional computer and a mobile phone consist of listings from the main index, as well as the top-ranking websites from the other indexes.

One of the most important points to understand about mobile search engines is that they frequently pull their results from both the traditional and the mobile search engine indexes. The mobile search engines provide mobile results whenever they can, but mobile pages must still compete against their traditional counterparts to rank well in most mobile searches. On smart phones this is true unless users click on the mobile link from the search page, which takes them to a set of mobile-only search results, in which no traditional results will compete. Most people assume that when they are searching from a mobile search engine, they will only be given mobile results, but that is not the case.

Even when a company has a specific mobile offering on its website, the traditional home page can outrank the mobile home page in mobile search. This is apparent with simple searches performed on a mobile phone (a BlackBerry Curve, in this case) for "coffee" and "weather." Both Starbucks and AccuWeather have mobile pages on their site (mobile.Starbucks.com and AccuWeather.com/m) and both are in the mobile index, but the traditional ".com" results are the ones listed in search results. Only when users click the mobile link from the search screen (meaning they are searching only the mobile index) do the mobile versions of the site rank in the results.

Basic Mobile SEO Best Practices

For the most part, mobile SEO is similar to traditional SEO. This chapter simply highlights the most important SEO strategies and how they are different when optimizing for mobile search results.

When search engine crawlers are on your website, they are evaluating on-site SEO factors, such as the text on the page, the site architecture, and the code that makes the site work. When Web crawlers are off your site, they also index things that are related to your website, including other websites linking to your website, editorial mentions of your website, and the popularity and success of your website in existing search results. Both mobile and traditional search engines look at on- and off-site ranking factors to determine how a website or a page should rank in search results.

On-site SEO Factors

The general rule of thumb is that you should include keywords wherever possible on your site without hurting the user experience or appearing overoptimized. It is important not to overdo it, so your best bet is to pick three different keyword phrases to target per page. Jill Whalen, CEO of High Rankings, suggests that one of the best ways to determine whether your website is overoptimized or spammy is to read it out loud. If it doesn't sound appropriate when it is read out loud, it is probably overoptimized.

Limiting the number of keyword phrases you target on a page is a good idea for a couple reasons:

- If you try to target too many keyword phrases on one page, it will begin to look overoptimized or spammy.

- If you use too many keywords, there is a good chance that the search engines will not be able to focus on any one of the keywords that you are targeting.

In addition to having visible text on your site describing your offerings, search engines determine your rankings based partially on the placement of keywords in the HTML code:

- **Title tag** (`<title>`)—The title tag displays as the blue link in search engine results pages and, thus, should describe what the page is about. In Google, it can be 67 characters long, including spaces, and should include the top three keyword phrases for the page. Anything after 67 characters is truncated, and the title appears in search results with an ellipses (…) where it was cut off (see Figure 10.1). In MSN Mobile and MSN Live Search Mobile, which both now redirect to m.Bing.com, only about 55 characters are displayed. Yahoo! Mobile, which in the United States is located at us.m.Yahoo.com, displays as many as 60 characters. (Because they are quite near to each other, the best bet is to optimize with Google in mind, as that's where the bulk of mobile search traffic comes from.) Ideally, each page on the website will have a different title tag. Instead of simply listing the keywords in this tag, it is important to form a complete and compelling thought so that people will want to click on the link from the search results. Including the word "mobile" in your title tag should encourage mobile clicks and make it more obvious to the search engines that the page is intended for mobile viewing.

Figure 10.1   *This is a description tag of a Wikipedia search entry (as shown by Google) that has been truncated because it is more than 156 characters long.*

- **Keyword metatag** (<META NAME="Keywords" CONTENT=)—The keyword metatag is used to list keywords for which the page is relevant. At one time, search engines used the keyword metatag to help in rankings, but it was abused so much that it has almost all its value. Despite that, it is still a best practice to include it, so I recommend including only the top three keywords for each page in the tag. This way, if you ever wonder what keyword phrases you were targeting on a page, you can simply check the keyword metatag. This metatag should never be more than 200 characters long, including spaces.

- **Description metatag** (<META NAME="DESCRIPTION" CONTENT=)—The description metatag is pulled into the search results pages under the title tag. Although the content of the meta description tag does not have a direct affect on search engine rankings, it has a secondary effect because it helps create a high click-through rate on your search listing. The content of the description metatag also decreases the number of people who get to your site and immediately leave, otherwise known as the bounce rate. Click-through rate and bounce rate are both very important parts of the search engine algorithm.

  The description metatag should be no more than 156 characters, including spaces. It should be treated like ad copy and should include value propositions and a call to action. Again, including the word "mobile" toward the beginning of the tag helps searchers understand that your website is meant for mobile viewing, which will improve your click-through rate.

- **Heading tags** (<H1><H2><H3> etc.)—These tags help prioritize different text content on the website. Use them for headings and subheadings on the page. Search engines consider the H1 tag to be most important, and the value decreases though the H6 tag. Most SEOs concern themselves only with heading tags 1–3.

  It is a best practice to only have one H1 tag per page. Feel free to use the H2 and H3 tags more liberally, as long as they highlight important, optimized text on the page. Never include more H1 tags on the page than there are H2 tags, or more H2 tags than there are H3 tags, and so on down the line. Including keywords in all the heading tags is a good idea. The length of a heading tag should never be longer than the length of a normal heading or subheading that would appear in the text on a page.

- **Alt tags** (`alt=`)—Alt text, alternative text, and alt attributes are used to describe images. In some cases, images might not appear when a website is viewed on a mobile phone; when they are missing, the alt text is displayed instead. These tags should be short but should be keyword-optimized and descriptive of the picture they are meant to represent.

- **Text link** (`A href=`)—Link text, or anchor text, is the part of a text link that is clickable, and it is usually indicated by text that is underlined and in blue. The anchor text of a text link passes search engine value to the page that it links to. This counts for links to pages within your website, as well as links to pages on other websites. When keywords are included in the anchor text of a link, they create relevance for the page they are pointing to for the particular phrase in the anchor text.

  Be careful to avoid making anchor text from irrelevant phrases such as "more info" and "click here." Doing so wastes your opportunity to create search engine value for another page.

In many instances, your search engine results will improve more dramatically when you include the same keyword phrases or their variations in more than one of these locations—for instance, in the title tag, alt tags, and heading tags. There appears to be a multiplier effect, whereby adding a keyword phrase to one element is a 1x improvement on rankings. Adding the same keyword phase to two elements could have a 3x or 4x improvement on rankings. Consider an example of how a Las Vegas hotel could include top keywords in multiple tags without appearing overoptimized:

- Title Tag: "Las Vegas Hotel and Casino: Cheap Rooms Just off the Strip"

- H1 Tag: "Las Vegas Strip Hotel & Casino"

- H2 Tag: "Cheap Hotel Rooms in Las Vegas"

- Alt Tag: "Luxury Hotel Room, Las Vegas, NV"

- Text link anchor text: "Las Vegas Hotel Room"

When you include different variations of the top three keywords phrases for the page in your visible page copy and all the HTML tags listed above, that page will be poised to rank well in both mobile and traditional search results.

It is also important to use keywords in the structural elements of the website, such as the domain name, filenames (including image names), and directory names or subdomain names. Search engines use the structure of your website and the paths or URLs of the pages to help them understand how sites should rank in search results. For example, a search engine would probably rank www.fishing.com/fishing-gear/hooks better than www.fishing.com/shop/index.cfc?submit=1&istartrow=1 for searches on "fishing equipment" because it can readily understand that "hooks" are a subset of "fishing gear."

For mobile rankings, it is important to use conventional mobile designations in your file structure. If the mobile aspect of your website is on a mobile subdomain, the subdomain should be called `m.` or `mobile`. If the mobile aspect of your website is on a subdirectory, it should be called `/m` or `/mobile`. These are the most common designations, and the search engines understand them as mobile designations. Chapter 9 discusses mobile subdomains and subdirectories more.

Offsite SEO Ranking Factors

In addition to including keywords in the text on your website, it is important to have links from other relevant websites pointing to your website, ideally with optimized anchor text. Remember, anchor text is the part of a text link that is clickable, and it is usually indicated by text that is underlined and in blue. In general, the more links you can drive from other websites to your website (from either traditional or mobile websites,) the better you will perform in search results. Because many mobile search results pages include traditional pages, this tactic is still relevant. It is especially true if the links are from sites that have a mobile designation in the file structure, have content that is somehow related to your content, or are considered authorities in their industry.

Links from images on other websites can also be valuable, although they are generally considered less valuable than text links. The best way to ensure that an image link from another website passes value to your website is to ensure that the image has a keyword-optimized alt tag and is surrounded by keyword-rich content. Images on your website that link to other pages on the site can also pass SEO value if the image filename and alt text use the top keywords for the page you are linking to.

The higher the quality and relevance of the site that is linking to you the more value it will give you in search results. Links from websites that have nothing to do with your website, or from websites that get minimal Web traffic or have low search engine rankings will pass minimal value. Whenever you can, encourage links from high quality sites that have content that is related to your product or service. The best way to encourage links such as that is to have good mobile content and a good mobile user experience. Other than that, you can encourage links by publicizing your mobile content in press releases, news articles, blogs and offline media.

One word of caution: Search engines do not like it when companies pay for links or acquire links in a deceptive way. The best way to get high-quality links is to offer a high-quality product or service and promote it to people who are willing to write about it and link to the site. Purchasing links from link brokers can actually hurt your rankings. If you are interested in what the search engines—and, specifically, Google—believe is deceptive link acquisition, review the Google Webmaster Guidelines at www.google.com/support/webmasters.

In What Searches Do I Want My Mobile Site to Rank?

When talking about search, it is important to understand what types of mobile search engine queries are most valuable. In SEO, search queries are described as keywords or keyword phrases. As you determine the keywords you should target with your mobile site, it is important to think like a potential customer and avoid jargon that your customers might not know. This sounds simple, but it can be harder than you think. A thought leader in the Internet marketing space, Frederick Markini, gives the following example:

> A well known lending institution had taken it upon themselves to opti-
> mize their site for all different searches related to lending: personal
> lending, commercial lending, subprime lending, lending rate, residential
> lending, etc. They were proud of their work, and began to rank well for
> searches related to lending, but they were still disappointed with the
> traffic and conversions that their site they were getting.

> What went wrong? They were not thinking like a potential customer.
> Potential customers were not searching for "lending." Potential cus-
> tomers wanted to "borrow" and were searching for terms related to
> "borrowing."

While bots can understand code and layout, they have little appreciation for aesthetics. Search engine bots evaluate only what they can read, so your best bet to rank well in both mobile and traditional search engines is with text. You must determine what phrases people might type into a search engine when they are look-ing for the product or service that you offer. Again, Markini illustrates the point quite well (paraphrased here):

> A well known candle company that sold scented jar candles also
> worked to improve their search engine rankings. The candles they sold
> were called "house warmers," playing on the idea that a nicely-scented

home would create a feeling of "warmth." Since the candles were described on the site as "house warmers" rather than "jar candles," the traffic to their website suffered.

The search engine had no idea that the company was actually selling "scented candles" or "jar candles" because it was not written on the site. It only knew that they sold "house warmers," and while the idea of creating warmth in a home may have been appealing, it is not what they were searching for; they were searching for "scented candles" or "jar candles." Adjusting their product names and descriptions helped increase the Web traffic dramatically.

The differences between a mobile keyword strategy and a traditional keyword strategy are slight. Some reports show that mobile searchers use longer keyword searches, and others show the opposite. In general, mobile keywords are action oriented and are more likely to include verbs, as in "find dry cleaner" or "download ringtone." They also are frequently location specific, such as when the searcher is looking for a retail outlet or destination. Including verbs and location information, such as your neighborhood and zip code, near your other keywords will improve your visibility in mobile search engines. In some cases, branded searches can be more common in the mobile world, since mobile is used less for researching a product and more for immediate action, such as "find McDonalds Denver."

Targeting Long-Tail Keyword Phrases

When choosing your top keywords, be sure to think in terms of phrases instead of single keywords. Searchers have become savvy enough to understand that broad, one-word searches, such as "pizza," will rarely yield the desired result except in a map-based search. Optimizing for keyword combinations or phrases is more realistic and enables you to narrow the number of companies that you are competing against for search engine rankings.

The Long Tail theory, popularized and described by Chris Anderson in the book *The Long Tail: Why the Future of Business Is Selling Less of More* (2006), can be applied to the keyword selection for your website. The model basically shows that in a market with a high freedom of choice, such as the Internet, 80% of your website traffic will come from very specific and descriptive "long-tail" terms, whereas only 20% will come from short, generic "head" or "short-tail" terms.

With this in mind, it is generally best to target two or three word phrases in your SEO. A good example of this strategy is a store that sells golf clubs in Miami. Instead of targeting "golf," this company should target keyword phrases such as "Miami golf shop," "golf store Miami," "Miami golf clubs," and so on. The natural benefit of targeting two- and three-word phrases is that when you start to rank and get traffic for the longer keyword phrases such as "golf store miami," you will also begin to rank better for shorter versions of the keyword phrases, such as "golf store," "golf shop," and "Miami golf."

In some cases, you might run into problems with words that have multiple meanings, such as "Miami golf club" or even "Miami golf clubs"; people could be searching for these terms when they are looking for a golf course but are not interested in finding a retail outlet for golf clubs. This might seem problematic, but it is actually a great opportunity for the retailer to garner more mobile Web traffic and gain visibility to their targeted audience. By creating a resource page on their site that lists the locations of golf courses, or "miami golf clubs," they can actually create search engine relevance for the keywords they are targeting, potentially get links from other websites that appreciate the resource, drive sales and awareness for their actual product offering, and help build creditability with their clientele.

It is a good idea to optimize for more specific keywords on pages that offer more specific information. "Miami golf shop" might be a good keyword for the home page of the store, but when specific products are offered online, those pages should be optimized with different variations of the product name and description—for example, "Nike Unitized Tiempo," "Nike 34 putter," and "stainless steel putter."

Mobile Keyword Research

Tools are available to help you choose the best keywords for your site and discover new keywords based on historical searches that have been performed in the search engines. Some of these tools are free, and some have a small one-time cost or an ongoing subscription fee associated with them.

The best tool available for mobile keyword research is part of Google AdWords, Google's advertising platform. It is a bit difficult to access, but it is free and high quality, so it is worth the struggle.

1.   The first thing that you must do is log into a Google account. If you don't have an account with Google, you can create an account with Google AdWords simply by signing up at http://adwords.google.com. If you have an existing Gmail or AdWords account, you can just use that.

2.   When you are logged into Google, simply click My Account in the upper-right corner of the Google home page; on the next page, click AdWords.

3.   If you already have a campaign set up in AdWords, you can go directly to a page that enables you to add new AdGroups. If you don't have a PPC campaign set up, you must create a mock campaign to access the keyword tool.

4. To set up a mock account, first go to the Home screen in AdWords, locate Active Campaigns, and, in the drop-down, choose Keyword Targeted (as shown in Figure 10.2).

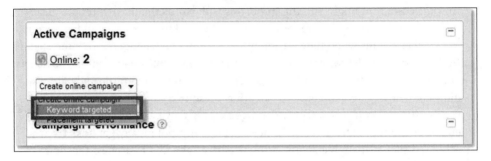

Figure 10.2 *Choosing a keyword targeted campaign.*

5. This takes you to the page where you establish the Campaign Settings. Although this has nothing to do with mobile SEO or keyword selection, you must do this to access the tool. In your mock campaign, you can choose any settings you want, but take my advice and set the Daily Budget to $0.01, just to ensure that the campaign doesn't accidentally go live and start costing you money.

6. Click Save and Continue at the bottom of the page, and on the next page you can create AdGroups.

7. Click the Create New AdGroup button. It should take you to a page where you can set up rules for that particular AdGroup. Again, this is just a mock campaign, so any settings will do, but keep the budgets at $0.01.

8. You will need to write mock ad copy and put your domain name in the Display and Destination URL fields. Then be sure to put at least one keyword in the list. The one I added for this example is "poker." When you are done, click Save AdGroup.

9. When the AdGroup is set up, you are taken to a page showing a graph and some information about the mock campaign. Click the Ads tab. (Although this tab is visible earlier in the process, it is not clickable until a campaign is set up.)

10. From the next page, click the New Ad drop-down and select Mobile Ad (see Figure 10.3).

Figure 10.3   *Select Mobile Ad.*

11. Next, AdWords takes you to a page that is meant for developing a key-
     word list. Under the AdGroups heading, click Mock Campaign. New
     options appear on the right site of the screen. In the text above the
     white box, click Keyword Tool, as shown in Figure 10.4). (Yes, I know
     this is a lot of work—you're almost done!)

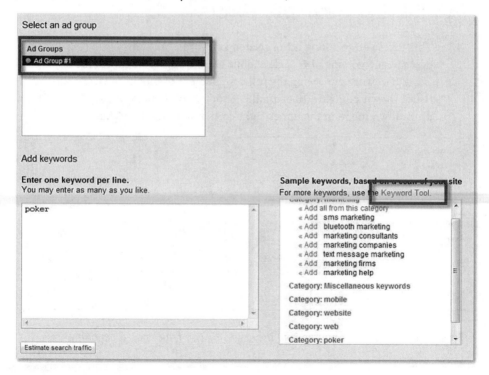

Figure 10.4   *Starting the Keyword Tool.*

12. Now, you move to a page that looks exactly like the traditional Google AdWords Keyword Tool, except for one small modification: the sentence that reads "Results Are Tailored to Mobile Searches" (see Figure 10.5)." After you land on the Mobile Keyword Tool Start page, enter one keyword or phrase per line in the box on the right side of the page, and then select Get Keyword Ideas.

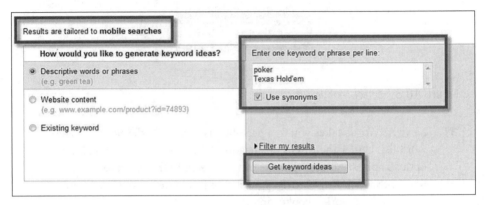

Figure 10.5 *This is where you add your keywords.*

13. This takes you to a long list of related keywords and statistics that describe the volume of Google Mobile searches associated with the keyword. If you are not seeing the full complement of mobile keyword statistics shown in Figure 10.6, use the Choose Columns to Display drop-down menu in the upper-right corner and pick Show All.

Keywords (mobile devices)	Estimated Ad Position	Estimated Avg. CPC	Advertiser Competition	Local Search Volume: June	Global Monthly Search Volume	Search Volume Trends (Jul 2008 - Jun 2009)	Highest Volume Occurred In	Match Type:
								Broad
Keywords related to term(s) entered - sorted by relevance								
poker	not shown	-		201,000	20,400,000		Apr	Add
texas holdem	not shown	-		12,100	673,000		Jan	Add
holdem poker	not shown	-		880	90,500		Jun	Add
poker tips	not shown	-		390	33,100		Jan	Add
poker	not shown	-		91	12,100		Aug	Add

Calculate estimates using a different maximum CPC bid: US Dollars (USD $) 0.01 Recalculate

Choose columns to display: Show/hide columns

Figure 10.6 *Here you can see how the keywords you have chosen perform.*

14. You can now see a number of keywords that might be related to your product or service. In terms of mobile SEO, you will also see Local Search Volume and Global Monthly Search Volume, as well as the Search Volume Trends and the month with the highest search volume. The other columns are relevant only if you are setting up a paid advertising campaign in AdWords, which is covered in Chapter 5, "Mobile Advertising." Your goal is to choose relevant keyword terms that have a high search volume.

15. To create a list, simply click the Add button next to the keywords you want to add. After you have developed a comprehensive list in the right column, you can click Export to export the list in a variety of different file types, including Excel and CSV files. If you think you might have missed a segment of keywords, simply click the Back button and add a word that you think will trigger that segment of keywords; then click Get Keyword Ideas again.

Everyone in the mobile community is hoping Google will make this Keyword Tool publicly available without an AdWords account so we don't have to go through the hassle of setting up a mock account, but that has yet to happen. The good news is that when you have the mock campaign set up, you can use it again and again, so you have to go through the hassle only once.

Other mobile keyword research tools are available, but although they are generally much easier to access, they are less robust and possibly even less accurate. After the Google Mobile Keyword Tool, the next best option for mobile keyword research is to use the Keyword Suggest tools from the various search engines on your mobile phone. These are accessed by performing searches in your mobile browser.

Whenever you use your phone to do a search on Google or Yahoo!, as you begin to type in a query, you will see a drop-down menu of similar searches. These are meant to allow users to select one of the options instead of having to finish typing their search term, but they are also helpful to mobile marketers looking to develop a keyword list because the lists order the keywords by query volume.

Add high-volume queries that relate to your product or service. If you are using Google and prefer to do keyword research from your traditional computer, you can go to http://google.com/m/html/search.html to get the same results.

You can also access Related Searches from both Google and Yahoo! mobile to build your SEO keyword list. Related Searches will not always appear, but if you are searching for something that is slightly obscure, the search engines will include alternative query ideas or Related Searches at the bottom of the mobile search results page. You can do this on a mobile phone or from the mobile search portal accessed from your traditional computer. Figure 10.7 shows an example using YahooOneSearch on the iPhone.

Figure 10.7 *Yahoo! Keyword Suggest utility for example searches on "String Theory."'*

To show how it works, I did a search in Google Mobile for my name, "cindy krum," and it did not return any Related Searches at the bottom of the page. This is because the search was quite straight-forward and there were no related topics that it assumed I might have missed.

Alternately, I did a search for "string theory," which is much more complicated and has the potential to return results on a number of related topics. For this search, Google returned the traditional results with the following Related Searches listed at the bottom of the page: string theory simplified, string theory video, m theory, chaos theory, theory of superconductivity, dark matter, time travel, and black holes (see Figure 10.8). Google has determined that all these searches are related to my search for "string theory" and, thus, could be valuable keywords for a site about string theory.

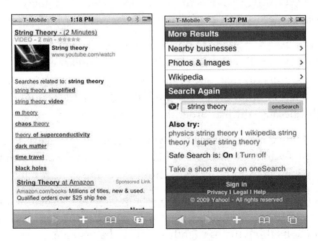

Figure 10.8 *Recommended searches on "string theory" from Google and Yahoo!.*

If you have a limited product set or category, as with the "Miami golf clubs" example, you can start with a list of about 50 keyword phrases. If you have a much larger product offering or many locations or departments, as with a Walmart department store, you might need to develop multiple keyword lists for each category of products you offer on the site.

Find Out How You Rank on Your Top Keywords

After you have developed a list of keywords that you want to rank for, it is important to know how well you already rank for them in search results. It is a good idea to set a benchmark and routinely record how your website is performing in mobile search engines. If you already have a website, the first thing you might do is go to your phone and perform searches to see where your website ranks on the first page. This will give you a good basic idea of how your website is performing in mobile search results. However, it is not comprehensive or 100% representative because the search engines, especially Google, are adjusting results based on several factors, as described in the following sections.

Phone Specifications

Search engines can detect the handset when the search is sent, and as mentioned previously, the search engines adapt mobile search results based on the phone that is doing the searching. They do this to ensure that the websites that are ranked well in the search results will be usable on the phone that is doing the searching. Although it is unclear how heavily this factors into the mobile search algorithm, it is definitely a factor. That means that doing searches from different phones could yield different results, so research on just one handset might not be entirely representative of how your website is ranking in all mobile searches.

Personalization

Search engines (especially Google) can also use your previous search behavior to modify the search results presented to you. If you are logged into a Google account on your phone and have clicked on one search listing quite frequently, it will move to the top of search results when you are personally searching for it; similarly, if you have never clicked on a result that ranks quite well, it will move lower in the results. This customization means that other searchers might receive different search results whenever they are logged in to perform a search. On the traditional Web, Google has even made this a more active process, including buttons so that you can promote websites higher in results, demote results to move them lower in the results, or totally delete results from your result set.

This ability to customize search results means that there are even more potential variations in how your website will rank in other people's search results. If you are doing your own mobile searching to find out how your website ranks, it is important to log out of your Google account, to ensure that your frequent visits to your website are not impacting the rankings Google is showing you. Right now, not many people are signing into their Google account from their phone, but this could change soon. When Google allows you to associate a mobile phone number with your Google account or other search applications, you might be functionally logged in all the time.

Localization

Google also adjusts search results based on the location of the searcher, so someone searching in New York will get different results than someone searching in LA; more dramatically, someone searching in Houston might get different results than someone searching in Denver, even if they are both searching from Google.com. This means that, again, just because you are ranking well in one place does not necessarily mean that you are ranking well in another place. Currently, your location must be manually input into all browser-based search engines, but as more mobile phones incorporate location detection, based on cell towers, WiFi, or GPS, this information likely will become more deeply integrated into mobile search results. This change could happen quite quickly, but currently the mobile search algorithm is no more specific about location than the traditional algorithm, and it actually might not respond to it at all unless the location is manually input. The only exception arises when you are doing a map-based search from Google Maps, in which case, it plots your current location and orders results based on relevance and proximity, and when you are using the Google iPhone application, which automatically detects your location.

Tracking Mobile SEO and Keyword Rankings

When you are working with a traditional website, you can use a variety of tools to find out how your website is ranking in various search engines. Although these tools have no way of accounting for the problems with personalization or localization, they are a quick way to see how your website is performing in traditional search results over time. Because none of those tools currently report on mobile search engine rankings, you have to do searches by hand or rely on your analytics to see what keywords are driving the most traffic.

The main disadvantage to using analytics instead of actual search results to measure the effectiveness of your SEO efforts is that analytics show you only how you are doing on keywords that are performing well, because they records information only after someone clicks from a search result to your website. If a keyword is ranking but no one is clicking on it, analytics won't ever tell you that. Similarly, if you are not ranking at all on an important keyword, analytics won't specifically bring that to your attention.

When doing keyword reporting for a traditional website, one tool available, called Enquisite Optimizer, can help eliminate some of the questions present with other keyword-reporting platforms. Enquisite Optimizer reports on all the different ranking positions and physical locations a keyword is in when it was clicked from a search result; although it can't tell you whether the person was logged into a Google account, it can tell you where that person located when performing the search. The Enquisite team is currently working to add the capability to segment the results by mobile browser or user agent, so in the future, we might be able to understand, based on the mobile browser, how keywords are ranking in different places and on different mobile browsers using this tool.

Until the new mobile features are available on Enquisite Optimizer, you can use other analytics programs, such as Google Analytics, to see how much traffic each of your top keywords is generating from mobile devices. In Google Analytics, you can segment traffic to include only organic searches or only iPhone searches so that it will show you what keywords are driving traffic in organic searches from iPhones.

If you are working with other phones, you can use the browser/operating system segmentation options in Google Analytics to drill down to find out how your keywords are performing on specific phones. You can also create Advanced Segments in Google Analytics to group all mobile searches together or set up individual segments for different mobile browsers, operating systems, and screen resolutions, and then easily move among the results for specific handsets. This is covered in more detail in Chapter 3, "Mobile Targeting and Tracking."

If your segments are set up correctly, you can then gather information about what keywords are driving traffic from specific phones and ascertain from that how well your website is ranking in searches performed on the various phones. If your website is not exclusively mobile, the best way to really understand this information is to aggregate all the mobile information and look at the mobile results as a whole.

If you have a Google Webmaster Tools account, you can also go there to find out what terms Google has determined are relevant for your site, what terms are driving the most impressions for your site, and what terms are generating the highest click-through from search results. Chapter 9 also covers Google Webmaster Tools.

When you have determined how you will evaluate keyword performance, it is important to routinely generate a report for how your website is performing and track changes in the rankings or traffic associated with your top keywords. If your website is targeting both traditional and mobile computers, you will want to record the performance on both.

Whenever you make a change to the website, it is important to track how it affects your keyword rankings in the search engines. If you are using the same website for both mobile and traditional traffic, you should track how both results are affected. If you are making major changes to the website, you will need to report on your keyword rankings daily, but if you are making less significant changes to the website, you can report on keyword fluctuations weekly. If the site does not change much, it might even be okay to run keyword reports monthly, if you are not very concerned about search engine traffic.

Advanced Mobile SEO Best Practices

The differences between mobile and traditional SEO strategies and tactics all stem from the fact that different crawlers are indexing and evaluating your website as if it was being displayed on a mobile phone. It is essentially the same model, with slightly different parts and different algorithms determining how the website will be ranked. That being said, some more advanced SEO strategies are specific to mobile search engine optimization.

Search engines index the Web page by page, but they also evaluate the power and historical value of a domain name or website as a whole. A domain name that has been around for a long time, ranks well, and gets consistent traffic is considered more valuable than a new domain that has little history, few rankings, or little traffic. Each page on a website is judged independently, but pages on a more established domain will generally perform better than the same page on a less established domain.

Because the search engines index the Web based on individual pages or URLs, you must have only one URL for each unique page on the website. Some websites get into trouble when multiple versions of one page are indexed in the search engine, either because the servers are set up incorrectly or because multiple URLs are being dynamically generated and used to represent just one page.

Having multiple indexable URLs that represent only one page of content is a problem we call duplicate content, or DUST (which stands for duplicate URL, same text). This is a problem for traditional and mobile search engines because it crowds their indexes. Generally, the search engines will pick only one of the duplicate results to rank in search results. The best practice is to ensure a 1:1 ratio between the number of URLs that will resolve in a browser and the number of pages you would like to rank in search results.

In some instances, server settings or ModRewrite programs can be used to eliminate extra versions of a page that renders in a browser address bar. A good example is htt://mysite.com and http://www.mysite.com. These addresses both bring up the same page, but could confuse the search engines, because one page has two addresses. In this situation, you would want to see which of the addresses ranks better in search engines, and redirect or automatically re-write the other one to appear as the primary or 'canonical' one.

Alternately, a canonical meta tag can be included on the secondary page, indicating the primary or canonical page there. That tag looks like this: <link rel="canonical" href=http://www.mysite.com/> and it explains that, in this case, the primary or canonical version of the page is the one with the 'www,' and this tag would be placed on the page that doesn't have the 'www' included in the url.

In the mobile world, things can get more complex, because some websites may have on page for the traditional rendering of the website, and another page for the mobile rendering of the website. They may even have one version of the traditional rendering of the website, and multiple versions of the mobile rendering of the website. In that case, you may need to use a mobile robots.txt, to explain to the search engine robots which content they should be crawling and indexing.

Mobile Robots.txt

When compared to their traditional counterparts, mobile websites are frequently at a disadvantage for search engine ranking. Even without taking duplicate content issues into account, traditional websites have more history, links, and traffic recorded within the search engines. If you have mobile-specific pages on a mobile subdomain or subdirectory, the mobile pages of the site generally have less history and traffic, and fewer links credited to the pages than the corresponding traditional pages do. Thus, frequently the traditional pages of the site outrank the mobile pages of the site, even in mobile search.

This is obviously one of the more complex aspects of ranking that the search engines must face, but until they get better at understanding when to rank the traditional pages and when to rank the mobile pages, we can use a robots.txt file to give them instructions. A robots.txt file is stored in the root directory of your website, and it is used to control how the metacrawlers, otherwise known as robots or just bots, index and evaluate your site. Because there are both mobile and traditional bots evaluating the Web, you can tell the traditional bots to index one set of pages and tell the mobile bots to index a different set of pages. For mobile pages hosted on a subdirectory, a robots.txt file prevents the traditional bots from indexing the mobile content and prevents the mobile bots from indexing the traditional content.

If you have separate mobile pages on a subdomain, you need two robots.txt files: one for the main domain and one for the subdomain.

Creating and maintaining appropriate robots.txt files can be quite complicated, and if these files are coded incorrectly, they can severely impact your rankings. It is best to have someone who understands this doing work on your `robots.txt` file. It is also always a good idea to run your `robots.txt` file through Google's Webmaster Tools Robots.txt Checker to ensure that it is working the way it should. (See www.google.com/support/webmasters/bin/answer.py?answer=35237.)

Mobile Site Map

In addition to submitting a traditional site map to the search engines, you should submit a mobile site map that lists all pages on your site that should be listed as mobile friendly in the index.

Site maps are another tool for ensuring that your site is indexed correctly and for avoiding duplicate content. Generate site maps for both your mobile and traditional Web content, and submit them both through Google Webmaster tools. Mobile site maps are very similar to traditional site maps. The main differences are in the configuration files that must be created with the site map if you are using Google's site map generator. You can use a website called SiteMaps.org to generate a traditional site map that can be submitted to all the major engines, but for a mobile site map, it is best to use Google site map generator.

To see an example of a mobile site map, visit www.google.com/mobilesitemap.xml.

A separate config file is needed for each markup language, and you should generate site maps for each config file separately. When you are finished, you should have a different site map for each of the coding languages your mobile site is written in and named separately.

When pages serve multiple markup languages, they should be included in multiple site maps. This process can be quite complex, so sometimes it is best to leave this part of the project to the technicians or the IT team. They can use filters to specify which URLs to include and exclude for each markup language. (For more information about creating the configuration file, visit https://www.google.com/webmasters/tools/docs/en/sitemap-generator.html.)

You should upload your mobile site map to the highest-level directory that you want the mobile search engines to crawl; in many cases, this is in the `/m` directory. If your mobile content is hosted on a subdomain, upload the mobile site map there. After the site maps are uploaded to the root directory, you can use Google Webmaster Tools to submit them directly to Google. You can submit mobile site maps within the primary site's Webmaster Tools account, or you can set up separate Webmaster Tools accounts for each subdirectory or subdomain.

In any instance, you should also link from the `robots.txt` file to both the mobile and traditional site maps. Google will direct you through a process to verify that the site is yours. After the site is verified in Google Webmaster Tools and you have uploaded a site map, you can check the Diagnostics section of the dashboard to see if the mobile metacrawler has detected any errors.

Mobile Search Engine Submissions

Mobile search engines are always looking for more mobile content to index and rank in mobile search results, so they have established submission pages where you can submit your website to be included in their search results. Search engine submission used to be a powerful strategy in traditional SEO efforts, but it has become less effective because so many webmasters and SEOs attempted to 'game' the system by getting their websites listed or linked multiple times in the directories. Luckily, it is still useful for mobile SEO because the mobile search engines are still looking for valuable mobile-friendly content to index and rank.

Submitting your website on a mobile search engine page is much less sophisticated than submitting a mobile site map, and it does not ensure that your site will be added, but it can still be a valuable strategy for improving mobile search engine rankings quickly or encouraging mobile Web crawlers to visit your site more frequently.

Mobile Directory Submission

Directories are utility websites designed to help people find websites that are relevant to specific topics. They are organized in much the same way that a Yellow Pages book might be organized, dividing things by categories and subcategories. Within each category and subcategory are links to websites with more information on the topic. Submitting to directories has also lost much of its impact on traditional results, but it can still be a good way to drive mobile traffic and search engine rankings.

Listings in top mobile directories help drive mobile traffic to the mobile website, and improve the mobile search engines' capability to index your website and understand what your website is about. They can also provide a good source of optimized mobile links, which should make your website appear more relevant to the search engines. A list of mobile directories and their submission pages is included at the end of this chapter.

Leveraging Universal and Blended Mobile Search Results

The top three search engines for both mobile and traditional Web content are Google, Yahoo!, and MSN. These three search engines all have a primary index, where they keep records of most of the content on the Web, but they also have other indexes for special types of content, such as business listings, images, videos, and news. In both mobile and traditional searches, the search engines will mix information from their other indexes with the traditional listings. In the SEO community, these are called blended results because they blend results for a variety of different indexes.

Blended results are actually quite common in mobile search because the search engines are trying to minimize the number of clicks it takes a searcher to get to the information needed. They try to anticipate what type of result the searcher is looking for. For example, when someone searches for "California Pizza Kitchen," the search engines will probably think they are looking for a specific restaurant location and return results from the local index with addresses and phone numbers before providing traditional links to Web pages.

Similarly, if you search for a movie title that is currently in the theaters, the search engines will direct you to listings for local theaters and the show times for the movie you searched for, before providing you traditional website links. The blended elements can appear at the top of the page, or mixed in with other results lower on the page. They might also include links to movie reviews, and YouTube clips of the movie trailer, but can also include images, news articles, or product listings.

Different tactics are used for ranking well in the blended results. Universal search results are pulled into traditional search results pages based on their rank and relevance in the specific index, such as Google News or Yahoo! Images. If you rank well in those searches, it is much more likely that your content—images, videos, local listings, news, or anything else—will be pulled in the blended results from traditional or mobile search.

Universal search results are included in mobile search results at a different rate, based on the handset that submits the query. Although optimizing your website for universal search results and mobile universal search results adds to the work you have to do to optimize your website for mobile and blended searches, there are clear benefits. Blended results are usually much more visual than traditional search results, and they include things such as star rankings and video or image previews. These are eminently more clickable than a traditional Web listing in a search result. It is also generally easier to rank well for specific keywords in the specific indexes because fewer websites are competing there.

Ranking well in blended search results can be a particularly appealing strategy because fewer websites are competing for rankings in the type-specific indexes than in the overall Web index. The following example illustrates this point quite well.

If you were marketing the movie *Ice Age 3,* if you do a search for "Ice Age," you would see the number of possible Google results for the various indexes as follows:

Google Web Results: 92,500,000 results

Google Images: 16,100,000 results

Google Video: 27,300

Google News: 10,185 results

Google Movie Listings: 40 results

Top-ranking items from each of these indexes showed on the first page of search results for the search term "Ice Age," despite the comparatively low threshold of competition in the different indexes. They were top results from the various indexes, pulled into the first page of Web-at-large search results. Ranking well in universal results is a bit like cutting in line; when you are ranked well in the smaller index, you are automatically put into the top listings in the big index. Many articles and tutorials have been written about ranking well in blended search results on the traditional Web, and for now, those tactics are basically the same for the mobile Web. A brief overview of important strategies is included below that cover local results, business listings as well as news, image and video results.

Local Results and Business Listings

Submit all your physical locations to the local directory for each of the top search engines, as well as online business directories such as SuperPages and MapQuest. Local search results are ranked based on traditional ranking factors, as well as their proximity to the searcher's location or, in some cases, the city center. As geolocation factors become more closely integrated with mobile search, the actual area code of the phone doing the searching might even be integrated when other methods of geolocation are unavailable. Local results are also heavily weighted on the star rankings, so be sure that all your local business listings have reviews and comments from satisfied customers.

Include as much information as you can when you are submitting your business to the various search engines and directories. Pictures, testimonials, hours of operation, and other details will all make it more likely that you will get a customer from a particular listing, and all are quite relevant to a mobile audience. Business citations, listings, and links from other online and mobile directories also do a lot to improve how your local results and business listings rank in mobile search engines.

You can do other things on your own website to encourage the search engine bots to automatically add your site to their local index.

- Have phone numbers and physical addresses listed on your website in text that is viewable to the crawler.

- You can also use microformats called HCards to help you include your location data in a format that is universally understood by all search engines.

- Include as much information as you can in your HCard, and don't forget to include your geographic coordinates (latitude and longitude). These will be important as the GPS becomes more closely integrated into mobile search.

Figure 10.9 shows example search results for the same term in three popular search engines.

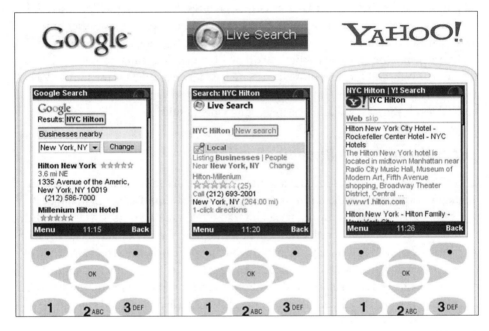

Figure 10.9   *Example search results for "NYC Hilton" in Google, MSN Live Search, and Yahoo! One Search.*

News Results

If your website frequently distributes news articles or press releases, it is important to be ranked in News search results. The first step is to request that your Web content be included in the search engines' News index. All the major search engines accept XML feeds or News site map to help them discover and rank news stories quickly, so developing one of these and submitting it to the search engines is quite important.

After you have requested inclusion and submitted the feed, you must think about the content being submitted. To rank well for searches in Google News, the articles and press releases you are submitting must include relevant keywords, just as in a page on your site. Always include the top keywords that you would like articles to rank for in the title, headings, and subheadings of the articles or press releases you are submitting.

News results are also ranked based on aggregate editorial interest, or the idea that articles should be ordered based partially on the number of people who will be interested in a story. A local story that is picked up by a couple news wires will generally not be ranked as well as an internationally relevant story that is picked up and sent out via a large number of wires. Similarly, search engines also attempt to determine the original source of an article based on the citations or links back to the original, otherwise known as citation or attribution rank.

Image Results

All the top search engines also have indexes for cataloging images from the Web. To rank well in these search results, use alternative text, otherwise known as alt tags, in the HTML of the page to describe all your images. Include the top keywords for the page in the alt tags and the text content that surrounds the image. You should also use top keywords when you are naming your files. For instance, instead of naming the image of a fish tank as `tank.jpg`, you should name it `fish-tank-5x2.jpg`. This tactic will help ensure that the search engines understand what the image represents and help them index the site appropriately.

Video Results

If you have videos on your website, it is important to get them ranking in video search engines, including YouTube and Google Video. Submitting your videos and using a video site map will help the search engines find and index the videos on your website more efficiently. These video file types can be included in your Google Video Site Map:

- `.mpg`
- `mpeg`
- `.mp4`
- `.mov`

- `.wmv`
- `.asf`
- `.avi`
- `.ra`

- `.ram`
- `.rm`
- `.flv`

The most common mobile video formats are 3pg and mp4. Flash (`.flv`) video files frequently will not work, so try to save your videos as `.mp4` or `.3pg` if you want them to rank well in mobile results.

Most video-editing software suites allow the author of a video to embed information about the video in the file properties. This information includes titles, descriptions, and sometimes even keywords. The search engines can access these directly from the video file when they are crawling and indexing it. Just as when you are optimizing a Web page, you should also include your top keywords in the video file properties itself before it is submitted to the search engines in a video site map.

You can use the video site map to include or add descriptions and other metadata for each of your videos that you are submitting so that the search engines have an easier time understanding what the videos are about. They also enable you to link to a thumbnail image of the video that will show in the search results. If you don't provide your own thumbnail images, the engine will generate its own thumbnails, and they might not be as compelling or interesting as you would hope when they show up in search results.

Application Search

Downloadable applications are becoming much more popular and, in some instances, are replacing mobile search engines. Search applications allow users to submit a query just like in a mobile search engine, but they usually focus on a specific type of product or service and provide some added value over the results in a traditional search engine. Table 10.1 shows some examples of top mobile search applications.

If there are mobile search applications related to your industry, product, or service, it is important for your website or company listing to rank well in searches within those mobile applications. Frequently, top mobile search applications have promotional websites where you can get insight into how the application receives and ranks the results it provides. In some cases, the owner of the application will have created a unique index, such as the SuperPages mobile application or the Flickr mobile application. In other cases, such as UrbanSpoon, the results are a combination of search data from Yelp, Yahoo!, and the site submission on their own website.

When you have determined how to get into the search application result, it is important to determine what makes some results rank higher or lower than other results. Because applications are meant to be interactive and personal, rankings are frequently highly weighted on user ratings and reviews, as well as popularity. Each time you make a change to your mobile website or even a mobile landing page, check whether and how it has affected your rankings in the mobile search applications for your niche.

Table 10.1   Top Mobile Search Applications

Local Dining:	Recipes:	Friend:
Urban Spoon	AllRecipies.com	Facebook
Open Table	BigOven	MySpace
MetroMix	iFoodAssistant	WPMobile
Local Business:	**Real Estate:**	Loopt
Around Me	Trulia	WhosHere
Yelp	For Sale by Owner	**Products:**
YPMobile	**Videos:**	eBay
Slifter	Truveo	Amazon
Jobs:	YouTube	Near By Me Now
Job Compass	**Images:**	Is it Me
iJobs	JuiceCaster	
Now Hiring	PhotoBucket	
	Flickr	
	Picas	

Alternative Input Search

Search on mobile phones is unique because users are not limited to typing their query into a text-input field to perform a search. Mobile phones have more options for inputting a search, such as voice, image, and SMS messaging. More alternative search applications for phones are being developed every day, but some of the top alternative-query-input mobile search applications are listed here:

- **RedLazer**—A one-dimensional bar-code reader that uses the camera in a phone to scan a bar code and return price comparison search results.

- **Shazam**—Application that listens to a song that is playing and searches a database of songs based on the audio. After probable song matches are identified, they are presented in search results with reviews and the opportunity to purchase the song.

- **Goog411**—Application that listens to you say a query on a phone call and sends you a text with a link to your search results.

- **Google Voice Search**—Application that Takes voice queries directly from an iPhone and submits them over the Web to return live Web results to the iPhone within the application.

- **SnapTell**—An image-recognition search application for CDs, DVDs, and video games. Users search by submitting a picture of the cover of a CD, DVD, or video game. Search results are presented to the user with descriptions, ratings, reviews, links for price comparison, and links to buy the item online.

- **EverNote**—Image, voice, and text recognition search that enables you to search your own database of files on your phone, whether they are images you have saved, voice recordings you have made, or text you have entered.

These types of search applications rank results in a variety of different ways. As a marketer, you should determine whether alternative input search engines address your target market and work with the search applications to understand how the results are ranked or prioritized. In any instance, search query results are pulled from an index, or multiple indexes, and the results are ranked based on a variety of factors—some that you can control and others that you can't. In many cases, the index that the search application uses might be supplemented with other indexes or search engines, so you might be able to rank well in the alternative input search engine by ranking well in the search engine being used to supplement application results.

11

Integrating Mobile Marketing with On- and Offline Marketing

Although mobile marketing is powerful, it is not meant to stand alone. The goal of mobile marketing is generally not to engage the user exclusively on the mobile device, but to continually engage the user and keep your brand top-of-mind when they are out, living their lives. This kind of active and frequent engagement is also known as participatory marketing. When mobile marketing is integrated into your on- and offline marketing campaigns, it can become participatory and be fully utilized to create a deep and lasting bond. Integrating mobile marketing into both on- and offline marketing campaigns also helps create long-term value in the customer relationship.

Mobile marketing closes the gap between on- and offline marketing. Studies have shown that most people have to be exposed to a brand or brand name at least eight times before they are cognitively aware of it, and another two times before it actually enters their consideration set when they are making a purchase decision. In the United States it is also speculated that more than 50% of major offline purchases are researched on the Internet first, so appearing on the mobile phone when people are in stores comparing products can be very important.

The right mobile marketing can create a bridge between your customers online and offline experience (online for the research phase and offline for the actual purchase). The lag time between research and the actual purchase decision can be long and usually is directly related to the cost of the item being purchased. The brand awareness created by an integrated participatory marketing campaign can be a key influencer to keep the purchase decision and the brand in the consideration set. This chapter covers how you can integrate mobile marketing with your existing on- and offline campaigns to create a truly participatory marketing campaign.

Unified Messaging with Varied Communication

Before you begin planning how you will integrate your mobile marketing effort with your other existing marketing strategies, it is important to create a theme that will develop a unified feel for all your marketing channels. This should go above and beyond just adhering to your existing branding standards: You must have a theme, slogan, or promotion to tie everything together. If your brand already has something like that in place, there's no need to make major adjustments to incorporate mobile marketing—you can just use your mobile marketing as an extension of what you already have. On the other hand, if your on- and offline marketing is not well synced, you should work to create a more unified feel. Your mobile marketing campaign will lose value if participants get confused or don't see the connection between the on- and offline communication.

The simplest way to give your marketing campaign a more unified feel is to use similar imagery across all the different marketing channels. Although the imagery can be the same across the different venues, it is better to include a variety of different images that have the same look, feel, subject, and tone. Additionally, it is important to have a similar call to action, hook, or slogan that reminds viewers of your other marketing message that they have seen before. For companies such as Nike, this could be quite easy, using something like "Just Do It—Turn On Your Bluetooth," or "Just Do It—Text In to Win!" Other companies might have to be a bit more creative.

It is important to create a cohesive, well-themed campaign, but it is also important to add value through all the different interactions that are possible with the campaign. The basic messaging should be the same, but the specific communication should relate directly to the channel that is delivering it. Be sure to somehow add value to each of the different types of communication that are available, not only by promoting your content, but by giving consumers something extra. This can come in the form of a tip of the day or an additional discount simply for engaging with your marketing material. Above all, the different points of communication should come together to tell a cohesive brand story.

Integrating Mobile with Offline Marketing

The most distinct advantage to mobile marketing is that the mobile phone goes with your customers wherever they are. It is a constant connection between you and your target market. Mobile marketing is uniquely able to build out traditional offline advertising with a mobile prompt that is immediately actionable, trackable, and measurable.

The integration opportunities can be divided into three different groups—print media, broadcast media, and offline display. Previous chapters covered many of these strategies, so I will focus here on how to make the different media work together. Some strategies, such as mobile email optimization, mobile video, and mobile social networking, are new, so they are covered at a deeper level in this chapter.

Integrating with Print Media

One of the biggest and cheapest mobile integration opportunities is with print. This can be as simple as encouraging viewers to visit your website on a mobile phone or to text a code to participate in a survey or contest or to receive information.

Integrating print marketing with mobile marketing can be achieved with the following assets:

- Newspapers
- Magazines
- Catalogs
- Flyers
- Letterhead
- Tickets
- Handouts
- Bills
- Shipping inserts
- Warranty papers
- Menus
- Envelopes

- Greeting cards
- Receipts
- Account statements
- Instructions
- Business cards
- Brochures
- Cups
- Plates
- Napkins
- Investor information
- Product packaging

One of the best ways to integrate mobile marketing is to work with existing print campaigns in newspapers, magazines, and catalogs. In these, you can include a mobile call to action that is related to the advertisement, instructions for downloading mobile coupons so that customers don't have to clip one from the paper, or promotional text that advertises the benefits of your mobile campaign and explains how to interact with existing location-based advertisements.

Companies can also incorporate mobile marketing into their billing and direct-mail marketing. They can allow recipients to sign up for mobile alerts when their bill is due or their account status has changed. If they ship products to customers, they can also allow them to text in to get the status of their shipment, or encourage them to opt in for special deals or discounts related to what they purchased.

Another way to incorporate mobile marketing is to include mobile calls to action or QR codes into your product packaging or temporary service items, such as paper plates, cups, and napkins. In Japan, McDonald's has done a great job, incorporating QR codes on their Happy Meals and burger wrappers (see Figure 11.1).

Other paper assets, such as letterhead , envelopes, flyers, and business cards, can be used to send people to your mobile website or encourage them to text a short code to get a vCard with important contact information or to get a vCal of your company's events (see Figures 11.2 and 11.3).

Figure 11.1 *QR codes used on McDonald's Happy Meals (left) and burger wrappers in Japan. Photos courtesy of mobile.kaywa.com.*

Figure 11.2 *A QR Code used in Ralph Lauren Print Ad. Photo courtesy of mobile.kaywa.com.*

Figure 11.3 *A QR Code used in a conference handbook. Photo courtesy of mobile.kaywa.com.*

Integrating with Broadcast Media

Whenever you are using a broadcast medium, you have the opportunity to loop a mobile marketing call to action into the campaign. Encourage people to communicate with a short code, through SMS; download an application; or simply visit your mobile site. The most common broadcast media include the following:

- TV
- IP TV
- Streaming TV
- Radio

- Digital and HD radio
- Digital signage
- Movies
- Television and cinema trailers

TV

With the advent of Digital Video Recorders (DVRs), many people are fast-forwarding though commercials, so it is important to find other ways to reach them when they are watching TV. When you loop TV into your participatory marketing campaign, you can make up for the ever-diminishing viewership of TV commercial advertising.

Integrating Twitter feeds during news programs and talk shows is a simple way to loop in mobile communication. The History Channel was one of the first U.S. stations to do a good job of integrating mobile calls to action during programming. During many of their TV shows, a small banner appears on the screen, encouraging viewers to text in a short code to get an alert whenever a new episode of the current show is about to air (see Figure 11.4). You can also promote TV shows with offline Bluetooth display advertising, as they did for *Man vs. Wild,* to help improve viewership.

Figure 11.4 *The History Channel provides short codes that viewers can text so that they receive notices when new episodes of a favored show will air. Photos courtesy of mobile.kaywa.com.*

American Idol was the first U.S. TV show to launch a mainstream text-messaging campaign, in which they allowed viewers to call or text in their votes to help determine which contestants would move on to the next round. Similarly, the show *Deal or No Deal* created a game that ran before every commercial, in which viewers could guess which one of six suitcases was holding $1,000,000; if they guessed correctly, they were entered into a contest to win the money.

Radio

If you are marketing for a radio station, you can encourage listeners to text in questions and comments about the show or have listeners text in song requests. You can also allow them to sign up to receive text alerts to find out when their favorite show or song is about to play, or send them information about concerts or events that the radio station will be sponsoring. You can also send listeners a link to your show where they can get a downloadable mobile music-streaming application to play your show. You could also provide links to where listeners can download the songs played on your show. Alternately, you can work with show sponsors to include a mobile couponing element with their advertising package, and send listeners mobile coupons, discounts, or promotions from show sponsors during the spot. In the United States, National Public Radio (NPR) does a great job integrating this kind of marketing into their programming.

If you are a mobile marketer who is interested in leveraging existing radio advertising campaigns, you can integrate a mobile call to action into your commercials. Encourage people to text in to get a discount, or have them send a mobile picture of them enjoying your product, to enter a contest. You can also use a radio commercial to promote any highly visible location-based marketing and explain how users can interact with it when they are nearby. Marketers can advertise existing mobile applications that your company has created to help improve the number of downloads and spread brand awareness.

Location-Based Broadcasts

Location-based broadcasts include digital signage, Bluetooth, WiFi, near field, and Infrared broadcasts. These technologies can be used to send marketing messages to users based on their physical location. Bluetooth beacons and WiFi routers can be used to broadcast marketing messages to people when they enter the range of the beacon. These are usually used to drive foot traffic into a brick-and-mortar store. Frequently, the message includes a coupon or promotion to incentivize a specific call to action. Mobile service providers can also leverage location information from GPS and cell tower triangulation to send targeted, location-specific messages alerts to subscribers, based on their location. In some countries, this type of communication is also being used to send regional safety and weather alerts. Chapter 6, "Mobile Promotion and Location-Based Marketing," covers location-based marketing more thoroughly.

Companies such as McDonald's are also testing location-based mobile marketing at the point of purchase by creating what they call the SMS Lounge. This German test presented a call to action at the point of purchase for the visitor to sign up and receive an instant coupon. Subsequently, visitors were offered the opportunity to opt in to future coupons sent via text message. Since its launch in July 2007, more than 10,000 participants have used this McDonald's service, and the brand has achieved response rates of up to 29%.

Integrating mobile marketing with location-based marketing is especially powerful because it can reach people both when they are short on time and need answers quickly, and when they have time to fill and need quick entertainment. You can use location-based marketing to interact with your demographic in a number of ways. The simplest method is to integrate a mobile call to action in billboards, banners, posters, and other outdoor advertising channels. You can take this integration to the next level by offering interactive SMS prompts, or even including QR codes or Bluetooth beacons on your advertisement. By promoting a specific mobile offering that is relevant to people in a particular location, you engage your audience and give them information that is uniquely valuable to them at that moment in time.

Figures 11.5 through 11.7 are good examples of how QR codes can be integrated into billboards and outdoor advertising. Figure 11.5 shows an ad for a Mini Cooper, Figure 11.6 shows a large billboard for a Swiss bank Zurcher Kantonalbank and finally Figure 11.7 features an image of Father Maurice Tournay, a Swiss missionary. In each of these ads, QR codes are included so that passersby can use their mobile phones to get more information on the topic. Information passed by QR codes from stationary advertising can be uniform, or can be tailored to the specific location of the advertisement. For instance, the Mini Cooper ad could give the viewer more information about the Mini Cooper, or it could give them directions from the billboard to the nearest dealership.

Similar to QR codes, image-recognition software, such as one created by Mobot, can be used to prompt mobile downloads. In this scenario, a company submits its print and display advertising to be scanned by a back-end database. That image is stored, and whenever someone takes a picture of the billboard and sends it in, the image-recognition software queries the database, to determine what advertisement it is; the database then sends a response to the phone, much like a QR code would.

The mobile marketing channel needs support from other media to be successful, so it is crucial to integrate it with your on- and offline marketing efforts. Appropriate integration will ensure that you are reaching your target audience effectively and efficiently, when they are most likely to interact with your marketing message.

Figure 11.5 *QR code used in a billboard for the Mini Cooper.*

Figure 11.6 *QR code integration in a billboard for Zurcher Kantonalbank.*

Figure 11.7 *QR code integration in a lighted bus stop billboard for Maurice Tornay.*

Integrating Mobile with Online Marketing

Integrating a mobile marketing campaign with an online marketing campaign is frequently overlooked but often quite simple. In most cases, it simply means promoting your mobile content on your traditional site. If you think about it, the people visiting your traditional website are possibly the most targeted audience to which you have access. Because they are visiting your website from a traditional computer, you already know that they are interested in whatever product or service you have to offer, and their propensity to consume content on your mobile site is much higher. Additionally, many consumers will turn to the Web to find out more information about your mobile offerings, if they missed a short code or are unclear about the offer. Your mobile marketing campaign needs to take into account:

- Websites
- Micro-sites
- Web directories
- Mobile advertising
- Mobile PPC
- Mobile SEO

- Mobile applications
- Podcasts
- Online video
- Mobile social networks
- Email

When you are integrating online mobile marketing with your existing website, you must ensure that your mobile offering won't do any harm to your traditional Web offering. If you are changing existing pages or their style sheets, you should track the effect of those changes on your search engine rankings, traffic, click-through, and conversion rates on the site. If you are duplicating your website and placing it on a mobile subdomain or subdirectory, or on a separate top-level domain, then monitoring search engine rankings and Web traffic is even more important because you might be presenting duplicate content to the search engines. For more information about the impact of duplicate content and how to prevent it, read Chapter 10, "Mobile Search Engine Optimization."

Mobile Websites, Micro-Sites, and Web Directories

One of the most important parts of an integrated, participatory mobile marketing campaign is to ensure that no part of your marketing effort stands alone. Your website is a great way to bring things together because it allows you to not only promote the same things that are being promoted in other channels, but also promote and explain the uses and benefits of the mobile interaction. Any marketing collateral that is being displayed in other locations online or offline should also be included on your website. This includes, but is not limited to, offline display advertising, radio commercials, location-based campaigns, and video. Downloads that are sent via QR codes or mobile downloads should also be available on your website.

The best way to inform customers that you have a mobile-friendly website is to include information about it on the home page of your traditional site. It can just be a small banner or informative button encouraging visitors to also visit your website on their mobile phone. If the content you offer on the mobile site is different than the content you offer on your traditional site, it is also a good idea to tell people what type of information they can get on the mobile site and explain the benefits.

If you have a particularly long URL or you think users might see value in viewing those particular pages on their mobile phone, include a feature that allows users to send a text message to their phone (or a friend's phone), with a link to the page. This is also a good idea if you offer customizable information such as driving directions or recipes. This allows users to view the information when they need it, without printing it. This is a great way to keep users engaged while they are not at their computer, and also a great way to collect phone numbers for subsequent SMS marketing campaigns. Of course, before you use the phone numbers the user will have to opt-in to your marketing messages, but this is discussed more in other sections of the book.

You should also use your website or campaign-specific micro-sites to link to other instances of your brand online. If you have social network profiles, mobile social network profiles, podcasts, videos, or downloadable apps, they should all be promoted and linked from the website. Encourage website visitors to opt in not only to email alerts, but also to mobile alerts and text messages from your website. Any product or service that you are providing in the mobile world should also be available on your traditional website. Providing good images of your mobile campaign will also enable bloggers and journalists to create more compelling posts about your offering because they will be able to use the high-quality images that you provide instead of having to search for good images, create their own images, or leave images out altogether.

If you have both a mobile and a traditional website offering, it is important to let viewers move between the two sites easily. This usually involves including a button or link at the top of all pages, allowing viewers to specify what type of device they are viewing their website on. If you have content or information that you think viewers might want to access on their mobile phone, include a "Send to My Phone" form that texts them a link to the page they're on.

Mobile SEO

Whether you have a mobile-specific website or mobile micro-sites, or are using your existing website to reach your mobile audience, it is important that your search campaigns be representative of the integrated campaign you're running. Although you should always do a good job of targeting your top keywords and brand name, it is also great to incorporate specific elements of your integrated campaign into your SEO campaign.

If you have created specific pages to host mobile downloads from other media, always include the tagline or hook for the campaign in places search engine spiders will see—title lines, heading tags, and Alt tags on images. This will help people who are searching for more information about the campaign or who want Web access to things they've seen on other on- or offline media.

When you are optimizing pages to promote your mobile campaign, don't forget to include the media name in the keywords. For instance, if you are running a TV commercial to promote a downloadable mobile insurance application, be sure to include the words "TV commercial" on that page when you are optimizing the page. Similarly, if you have a series of Bluetooth-enabled posters in the London Tube stations, include the words "London Tube" and "Bluetooth posters" in your SEO copy.

Learn more about mobile SEO in Chapter 10.

Mobile Display and Pay-Per-Click Advertising

If you are doing display or PPC advertising (on mobile or traditional platforms), always promote your mobile content. Instead of linking to the home page of your mobile or traditional website, you can link directly to an optimized download page, application, video, or coupon. If you are doing PPC, include the name of your application and the platform it is built for, as well as the hook or call to action, in your keyword lists. Similarly, if you are doing display advertising, it might be a good idea to include a screen shot or illustration from your mobile application or website.

Mobile Applications

Mobile applications can drive a lot of awareness and even revenue for your company. In some cases, they will even be the central focus of your integrated mobile marketing campaign. Your mobile application and market place listing should always reflect the look and feel of the other collateral that is driving downloads, such as TV commercials and billboards.

As mentioned in Chapter 8, "Mobile Applications," it is important to optimize your download pages in the App Store to rank in the App Store search engine and promote your application with bloggers. Include viral incentives within your applications, perhaps by offering points or credits to users who recommend the application to a friend, and by allowing them to send text messages to friends inviting them to download the application. Also use traditional online social networks to promote your applications and other mobile offerings by creating fan clubs and social applications to encourage downloads, or posting mobile calls to action as tweets or Facebook posts.

Online Images, Videos, and Podcasts

Companies that create stellar images, videos, or podcasts usually put a lot of resources into making those assets great. To get the most out of your marketing dollar, be sure to make those assets available online. This means making them available on your website, the mobile Web, and vertical search engines that index images, videos, or audio files.

- **Video**—If you have TV commercials or other videos promoting your integrated campaign, submit them to YouTube, Google Video, SingingFish, Blinkx, Loomia, and MetaCafe. Also make them available for download in various traditional formats, such as MP4 video, QuickTime (MOV), and Windows Media Video (WMV); offer them in mobile video file types as well, such as Silverlight and 3GPP. When you're doing this, make sure that you use the appropriate MIME type in the file properties, to ensure that the file is downloaded and rendered appropriately.

- **Images**—If you have images, submit them to Google Image search, Yahoo! Image Search, MSN Live Image Search, Ask Image Search, Alta Vista Image Search, Pic Search, Pixy, and Imagery. This will help ensure that your images are widely available if people are searching for them online or on their mobile phones. It also should help your rankings for the pages containing the original images.

- **Audio**—If you have audio content, submit it as a podcast to iTunes, but also make it available in QuickTime (MOV) and Windows Media Video (WMV) formats, and consider offering it in mobile file types such as AAC and AMR. Make files available for download as MP3, WAV, and MIDI files (and, as always, use the appropriate MIME type in the file properties). It is also a good idea to submit files to traditional search engines such as Yahoo! Audio Search, Lycos Music Search, Alta Vista Audio Search, PodScope, Blinkx, SingingFish, and Loomia.

If you make these files available online, include a button to send download links to a user's phone via text message. This is a simple and easy way to drive mobile downloads and to make the experience more seamless for your users. When users input their number into the form field, an SMS or MMS can be sent to them immediately so that they're not forced to re-create the search that got them to the traditional Web page in the first place. You can also send them a follow-up text, asking if they would like to receive alerts or coupons on their mobile phone.

Mobile Social Networks

Social networking is a term we use to describe the activity of locating and interacting with other people who have interests that are similar to your own. Before the Internet, social networking happened in person, at mixers and other locations that were conducive to creating conversations. The Internet has taken social networking to another level by allowing people to interact socially, or to "socially network," without being tied to a specific location or time. Although online social networking is a very powerful force, online connections are rarely as strong or meaningful as in-person connections.

Mobile social networks provide an increased level of interactivity and personalization when compared to their traditional online counterparts. Many mobile social networks are location aware and allow users to discover and network with people in their immediate vicinity. In Asian countries, where mobile social networking is more common, content consumptions vary by age—80% of mobile social networking is done by those younger than age 34; news consumption on mobile handsets skews older.

The portable nature of the cellphone adds to the allure of mobile social networking because it enables users to connect with others online without having to be at a computer, and offers the potential for users to connect immediately with people offline as well. Although this type of social interaction is fascinating, it can be difficult for marketers to determine the best approach for marketing in these new venues.

U.S. vs. International Mobile Social Networking

The United States is distinctly behind the rest of the world in terms of adoption of mobile social networking. This is largely due to the slower networks and lack of flat-rate data pricing that is only recently being addressed by U.S. mobile carriers, but other important differences must be considered. In the United States, most people have access to a traditional computer on broadband networks, but this is not as common in the rest of the world. In countries Japan, China, and India, for example, access to a personal computer is less common, and this has driven social networking to the mobile phone.

The disparities in the social/technological ecosphere are causing many to postulate that mobile social networking will be quite different in the United Sates than it is in other countries. It is expected that the mobile social networks that succeed in the United States will simply be extensions of traditional online social networks that users are already members of. This is easier on participants because they don't have to set up and maintain profiles on multiple networks, and they can leverage the traditional computer to input information that will require a lot of typing or difficult formatting. Internationally, mobile social networks might be entirely mobile or might have a traditional component that is much less central to the experience.

Table 11.1 lists some of the top social networks and the regions they serve.

Table 11.1	Top Social Networks By Region		
United States	Buddy Beacon	JuiceCaster	Rummble
	Buzzed	Loopt	Strands
	Brightkite	MeetMoi	Twango
	dada.net	Mig33	WhosHere
	Facebook	Mobikade	Whrrl
	Fon11	MocoSpace	Xumii
	Frengo	MySpace	Zintin
	Groovr	Nrme	Zyb
	itsmy.com		
Asia	Cyworld (South Korea)	iBiBo (India)	MOBS (India)
	DesiMartini (India)	IndyaRocks (India)	Sequoia (India)
	EzMoBo (Taiwan)	MingleBox (India)	Tencent QQ (China)
	Frenzo (India)	Mixi (Japan)	TX.com.cn (China)
	Fropper (India)	Mobile Game Town (Japan)	Yaari (India)

Europe	aka-aki (Germany)	Faceparty (UK)	Mobiluck (France)
	BBC Communities (UK)	FriendsReunited (UK)	Moblog (UK)
			Next2Friends (UK)
	Bebo (UK)	GyPSii	NinetyTen (UK)
	Blyke (UK, Finland)	I'AM	Orange World
		Imity (Denmark)	

Social CPM Marketing

Many social networks make money almost exclusively through the sale of advertising on their sites. Although it remains to be seen whether this business model will be enough to keep all the social networks alive, you can be sure that it will always be a key element in the model. The simplest way for a marketer to reach out to potential customers on a mobile social networking site is to purchase ad placement within a cost per million (CPM) model. This is much the same as other mobile CPM advertising, but marketers work directly with the social networking company or their ad network to place and track the ads.

Advertising on traditional social networks was once thought to be the Holy Grail of online marketing because of the ability to target ads based on information that users volunteer in their online profiles. Unfortunately, many marketers were disappointed to realize that people access social networks to interact with their friends and rarely interact with the advertising on the site. When advertising on traditional online social networks, it is widely agreed that your primary goal should be to achieve an increase in brand awareness, because click-through and conversion rates are historically very low. How CPM advertising on mobile social networks will compare isn't yet clear.

Your best bet is to market mobile content or advertise local products and services with discounts and time incentives. Even on mobile social networks, CPM advertising should be considered a brand-awareness campaign more than anything. Many hope that the mobile nature of the experience will improve click-through and conversion rates of the advertisements. Traditional social networks were able to geo-target advertisements based on users' profile information, but in the mobile realm, advertisements can be hyperlocal, based on exactly where the user is at the moment. A majority of mobile social networking happens during downtime, while users are away from home, so this could make them more willing to click on ads. This is especially true if the ads are immediately redeemable, as with mobile coupons or redemption codes that can be used at stores or restaurants in the immediate vicinity. Ads can also be particularly valuable to the mobile audience if they offer some kind of short-term entertainment, to help the viewer pass time.

Branded Profiles on Mobile Social Sites

A more difficult but often more cost-effective way to interact with potential customers on a social network is to create a branded profile and participate as a member of the community. Many social networks allow companies to represent their brand and participate in the social network under a brand name, but if they don't, you can always create a profile based on a company mascot, a figurehead, or the CEO.

This type of marketing must be done very carefully. People who participate in social networking sites generally do not want to be marketed to, so it is important for your profile and your activities within the community to be genuine and community oriented, not self-serving and promotional. If you add value to the community, you will engender trust and affinity for your brand, and build friends and fans more quickly than if you are simply spreading a marketing message. Mobile social networks provide a variety of different types of interaction, but you must participate actively, especially by uploading photos, commenting on other people's profiles, and creating groups. When you are an active part of the community, it will be easier to market your product or service, because friends and fans will be more willing to listen.

Mobile Social Gaming

A different type of mobile social network that is popular in Asian countries is mobile social gaming. Much like Second Life for the cellphone, this type of social networking allows users to create avatars, or visual representations of themselves. Those avatars interact with other avatars within the social network. In some mobile social gaming networks, these avatars behave just as you would actually behave; in other mobile, social gaming networks, there is little relationship to reality—it's more like an online role-playing game.

Each social gaming network is different, but one commonality between all of them is the element of competition (hence, the gaming element). A popular mobile social network in Taiwan, called EzMoBo, encourages users to create avatars that look like themselves. Users participate in the community by interacting with other players, creating groups, and starting conversations. Participation on the site earns players points that can be traded for gifts, which users can send to a friend or keep as accessories for their own avatars. Users who don't have enough points to purchase what they want can spend actual money to present a friend or possible love interest with a gift for their avatar.

Product placement in this type of mobile social network can be powerful, especially for larger brands, because of the public nature of the avatar. Users who choose to purchase or gift your branded items on the social network are making a public declaration about their affinity for your brand. Don't underestimate this type of loyalty: It allows users to integrate your brand into their avatar, which is a public representation of who they are. It allows for conspicuous consumption, even for users who normally wouldn't be able to afford expensive branded goods in real life. Furthermore, it allows your brand to become integrated into their life as a publicly displayed aspiration, which will help create and increase the lifetime value of these types of customers.

Mobile Email

Mobile emailing came about at the same time WAP did, because the first mobile email clients used WAP to render emails. Mobile email was a luxury many people didn't use on smaller phones, because of the difficulty viewing the email on the small screen and the lack of a complete keyboard to respond with. As PDAs and smart phones came out with full QWERTY keyboards, more people began taking advantage of mobile email. Mobile email marketing hasn't really changed much in all the years it has been around.

Many mobile email clients have difficulty rendering full-HTML emails. You can do a couple things to improve how your email looks on mobile phones. The first mobile emails were simply text renderings of whatever came into your email box. This meant that if you received a text email from someone you knew, it rendered well, but if you received a marketing email from a company, the phone simply rendered the HTML as text, making the mobile version of the email almost totally useless. Many phones still are limited to the simplified text rendering of HTML that was present in the first mobile emails (especially BlackBerries).

The next advance in technology happened when the Palms, Treos, and Windows Mobile Devices began offering a more sophisticated mobile email client that could display pictures and render simple HTML. This made email marketing messages a bit easier to consume on a mobile device, but there were still many display problems.

The most recent evolution of mobile email marketing came with the iPhone (and now with the Palm Pre), truly offering a flexible rendering that looks exactly as it would on a traditional computer when displayed on the iPhone. This meant that recipients finally could get the full impact (almost) of the email marketing message when they were on the mobile phone, with the exception of having to zoom. The email marketing industry has not yet put significant effort into making emails more readable and compelling to mobile viewers on other types of phones. As email clients across all phones become more sophisticated, however, this might become less of a concern.

When sending mobile marketing emails, keep these points in mind:

- Include a link at the top of the email to a Web version of the email, in case people are having trouble viewing the email on their mobile phones. From this landing page, you can use browser detection and redirection to automatically send viewers to a version of the email that is optimized for their device. Also, if you include phone numbers in the text of your email, they will automatically become clickable when they are displayed on a mobile phone. If your campaign relies heavily on people calling in, it is important to include the phone number at the top of the email.

- Including your main navigation can cause problems in mobile rendering, because the buttons could be stacked vertically instead of horizontally, pushing all the promotional information lower, usually "below the fold" that the user can see when first opening the email. In the worst case, the link to each button and the path to each image will be displayed as HTML, pushing all the readable (non-HTML) content far down in the email. It is always a good idea to avoid including your main navigation in your email messages. Even in traditional email campaigns, many experts believe that it can take away from the main messaging of the email and distract the recipient from the main call to action.

- The best thing you can do to improve the rendering of your email campaigns is to test them on a variety of different mobile devices before you send them out. You will probably find that images and text will be stacked to make the email narrow enough to fit the phone. In some cases, images will also be shrunk to fit the phone. The best way to ensure that your images render correctly in mobile emails is to slice the images carefully when you are building the email, making sure that each image will be able to stand on its one, even if the surrounding images do not line up correctly.

- Even if you have not gotten your email campaign to render perfectly on all devices, you should loop email in to help promote your integrated efforts and your mobile offerings. Make sure your email campaign imagery and messaging reinforce the look and feel of the rest of the campaign. Then include links and screen shots of any mobile offerings, such as mobile applications, mobile coupons, or your mobile website. This will catch the viewer's eye and help her understand the value you bring to the mobile interaction. Once your email recipients request mobile downloads or coupons, you will have the opportunity to add them to your list of people who are opted in for mobile communication.

- In Asian countries, many people have email addresses that are specific to their phone, but in the rest of the world, mobile phones usually just pull in copies of messages that were sent to a traditional email address. When an email address is set up on an Exchange Server, users can automatically sync any activity that takes place on the email address, such as deleting or saving emails. If the email account is not set up on an Exchange Server, recipients are forced to delete and save emails twice, to maintain consistency of the account between devices. As phones improve, many email recipients are switching to Web-based email services, to avoid this burden.

Case Studies

The following case studies illustrate how you can create a cohesive marketing strategy that used mobile marketing to tie the on- and offline experience together. These great examples can be benchmarked by companies in a variety of different industries to make more successful marketing campaigns using mobile technology.

David's Bridal

In 2009, in an effort to reach out to teenage girls during prom season, David's Bridal created an integrated mobile marketing campaign that included SMS, MMS, mobile coupons, and mobile search (see Figure 11.8). When users opted in, they were sent text messages with links to the mobile site, where they could watch a slide show of the season's prom dresses. The mobile site also included a store finder and a "send to a friend" feature, which helped spread the campaign virally. Girls could vote for their favorite dresses and receive special discounts and tips, leading up to the big day.

The campaign was promoted on the traditional website and also in David's print advertising campaigns. The campaign helped drive foot traffic and sales in the stores, and gave David's Bridal a targeted list of opted-in recipients for future mobile marketing campaigns.

Figure 11.8 *David's Bridal used mobile coupons and mobile search to reach out to teenage girls preparing for the prom. Image courtesy of David's Bridal.*

Tahato

Japanese food company Tahato started an integrated marketing campaign called "World's Worst War." In the campaign, the company launched two new spicy snacks, Bazooka Deadly Hot and Burning Hell Hot. Both snacks were assigned an avatar representing them as the leader of an army in a mobile social gaming network. Using QR codes on the packaging of the snacks, purchasers could choose to join either of the armies, representing the snack of their choice. This created a massively multiplayer mobile role-playing game. Every night at 4 a.m. the armies would gather at one of 31 virtual locations to battle each other. Players met online to discuss strategies and improved their own rank in the game by recruiting new players. Text messages were sent to all players, giving them updates on the status of individual battles and the war as a whole.

Audi

Audi launched an iPhone application called Truth in 24, launched in combination with the documentary *Truth in 24* about the 24-hour Le Mans race. The application is a racing game that mimics the conditions of the race and gives the player a driver's view of the race track. It encourages players to monitor all elements of the racing experience, including the tire wear and fuel use. It was a great opportunity to create a unique branding message with an important demographic. Audi had determined that 95% of the traffic mobile traffic to its U.S. site came from iPhones and iTouches, so the company wanted to ensure that it was reaching out to the brand-loyal tech-savvy crowd to show that Audi was innovative and in touch with customers' needs.

QR Code Companies

The following is a listing of some QR code companies:

- ShortCode—www.shortcode.com
- Semacode—www.semacode.com
- Scanbuy—www.scanbuy.com
- TagIt—www.tagit.tv
- Kameleon—www.kameleon-media.com
- FuturLink—www.futurlink.com
- 509 Inc.—www.5o9inc.com
- Qwasi—http://qwasi.com

12

Mobile
E-Commerce

Mobile e-commerce, sometimes also called m-commerce or mobile commerce, describes any interaction in which a financial exchange or transaction is facilitated or executed with a mobile phone. In many ways, mobile e-commerce is the Holy Grail of mobile marketing because it closes the loop between marketing and its return on investment. Although many hurdles must be crossed before a robust mobile e-commerce system is adopted in the United States, the practice is being rapidly accepted in Asia and Africa and is growing in popularity in Europe. Consumer pressure is forcing carriers, credit card companies, banks, and brands to take notice and start working together to realize the mutual benefit that comes with mobile e-commerce. This chapter reviews important mobile commerce statistics and different business models that are beginning to incorporate mobile commerce.

Understanding how these mobile commerce business models work helps you develop strategies that monetize these mobile interactions with advertising, or learn more about your existing customer base through these mobile commerce interactions.

Figure 12.1 shows that, in the second quarter of 2009, consumers in the United States were warming to the idea of mobile payments and mobile commerce. In the eMarketer survey, 26% of respondents believed that it was "very safe" to make a purchase via a mobile phone, and 45% believed it was "fairly safe," combining as a total 71% of consumers who might be willing to participate in mobile e-commerce if they were convinced that the transaction would be secure. Only 22% of respondents felt that mobile e-commerce was "unsafe."

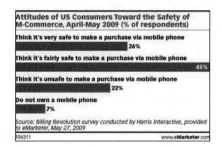

Figure 12.1 *eMarketer survey of what products people were willing to purchase using their mobile phones. Chart courtesy of eMarketer.*

A second study revealed that consumers in the United States who were willing to make a purchase on their phone were more willing to purchase goods and services that fulfilled a temporal or immediate need, such as food, entertainment, and travel needs (see Figure 12.2). In terms of food, many consumers were willing to purchase pizza and other fast food, but only 25% were willing to purchase coffee. Almost half of the respondents said they were willing to purchase hotel rooms or travel tickets. 58% said they were willing to purchase tickets for some type of entertainment, such as movies or concerts. Surprisingly, one of the smaller categories was digital content, with only 41% reporting that they were willing to purchase music, 34% saying they were willing to purchase games, and 24% reporting a willingness to purchase mobile video content over their phones.

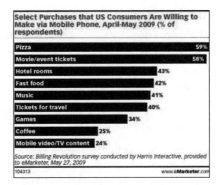

Figure 12.2   *eMarketer study that reveals what kinds of products or services people would be willing to purchase using their mobile phones. Chart courtesy of eMarketer.*

Finally, another study from eMarketer reviewed the purchases people made over their mobile phones at PriceGrabber.com, performed at the same time period (see Figure 12.3). This study showed slightly different results. This study revealed that, for those who made mobile purchases, 58% purchased digital content to be consumed directly on their mobile phone, 51% purchased consumer electronics, 37% purchased computer-related goods, 36% purchased books, 31% purchased clothing, and 20% purchased jewelry.

Although these results might not be entirely representative, they seem to indicate that when it comes to physical goods, consumers are willing to purchase a variety of different types of goods at a wide range of price points.

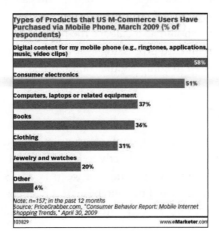

Figure 12.3   *eMarketer study that shows what types of products people purchased from PriceGrabber.com using their mobile phones. Chart courtesy of eMarketer.*

As it stands today in the United States, most mobile e-commerce is still completed via micropayments that are sent directly to the carrier in exchange for digital content such as ringtones, applications, music, and videos. Some key players, such as Google Checkout, Amazon Payment, and eBay, have begun to integrate mobile payment, but these services have not yet been widely adopted.

Mobile commerce covers a variety of activities that can be categorized as mobile payment or mobile banking. This chapter outlines a variety of different types of mobile e-commerce, as well as important aspects of mobile commerce implementation and security. This topic is evolving at break-neck speed, so when you begin to integrate e-commerce in your business, it is vital that you vet all your vendors and merchants, to ensure that your campaign complies with best practices and industry security standards.

Mobile Payment

Mobile payment is simply the capability to pay for a product or service using your mobile phone. Mobile payments can take place over the Web or can be completed in the offline world through contactless payment options such as Near Field Communication (NFC) and Radio Frequency Identification (RFID).

All mobile payments fall into one of two camps, micropayments or macropayments, depending on the size of the transaction and how the payment is processed. As in nonmobile commerce, processing credit card payments (especially macropayments) usually requires that the merchant pay the credit card company a fee for each transaction, usually between 20¢ and 50¢. Credit card processing thus cuts into the margins of many mobile commerce solutions and must be figured into your business plan. You should also balance the potential revenue from mobile commerce with the credit card processing fees, as well as other hard costs and overhead that will be required to complete the transactions.

Micropayments

Micropayments are small mobile commerce transactions that can be completed on a phone and, in many cases, billed directly to a user's mobile phone bill or to a credit card. These payments usually range between 1¢ and $5, and are useful for low-consideration purchases and the purchase of digital content. The most common types of micropayments are direct-to-carrier billing, subscriptions, and user accounts that are tied to credit cards.

Direct to Carrier Billing

One common instance of micropayments in the United States and around the world occurs when mobile carriers offer directory service (411) or premium SMS charges and downloadable mobile content such as ringtones or wallpapers. The carrier provides these goods and services, so they can be billed directly to your mobile phone bill. According to Wikipedia, 70% of all digital content in Asia, including traditional Web content, is purchased in this way. This type of mobile payment is ideal for the carriers. It is a simple and viable add-on to any mobile service plan and can be quite profitable. The carriers can bill customers directly instead of processing credit card payments and incurring merchant fees. Because credit card information does not need to be obtained, the processing of a purchase is quick and secure, and usually is completed within 10 seconds on a fast connection.

Subscriptions

Carriers and other mobile content providers offer subscriptions to SMS updates that are charged to the subscriber's bill in the same model. These subscriptions can be alerts about news, sports, weather, stocks, horoscopes, and the like, and the subscriber is generally billed for each text individually. These types of subscriptions are ongoing commitments, as with a magazine or a cable TV subscription, and subscribers must cancel or deactivate them if they want to stop incurring charges.

User Accounts Tied to Credit Cards

Other types of micropayments can be completed via accounts where credit card information is stored and validated with a PIN or a password. In the mobile world, the most common company that uses this type of service is iTunes; people download music or videos directly to their iPhones. This format of payment is also quite common in the gaming and adult mobile industries, where users can pay for downloads one at a time.

Macropayments

Macropayments are used for purchases that cannot be billed as a micropayment, usually for goods or services over $5. Prepayment, prompted mobile payment, full mobile Web transactions, and full brick-and-mortar transactions with proximity-based mobile payment are the four most common types of macropayments, and they are covered in more detail next.

Prepayment

A variety of different companies have begun to allow their customers to create pre-paid accounts that are debited each time charges are incurred and that stop working when the money in the account has been spent. This mobile payment option allows account holders to track their spending and prevent charges for excess use of the service, by avoiding overage charges. Prepayment accounts are most commonly used for mobile phone bills themselves, but can also be used with public transportation and fast food. With this method of payment, users create an account, usually online, and submit an initial payment to start the service. Periodically, users are sent text messages to inform them of their account balance or remind them to add money to their account, otherwise known as "topping-up." Because accounts have already been created, the customer has the option of repeating the payment amount and billing information of the last transaction, or adding different amounts or billing information to the account.

 Note

Prepaid mobile phones are relatively new in the United States but have been well accepted in the rest of the world for some time. In the United States, some of the major carriers have begun offering prepaid mobile phone service, but for a long time, the prepaid market was dominated by Cricket Wireless and TrackPhone. These services were ideal for people who were not old enough or did not have the necessary credit score to get service plans from the bigger carriers.

Prepaid subway and bus passes are also becoming more common. In this payment model, accounts are usually created online but are electronically tied to physical NFC or RFID chips stored in the hardware of the phone. The technology behind NFC and RFID is covered in more depth in Chapter 6, "Mobile Promotions and Location-Based Marketing." When customers pass through a subway gate or boards a bus, they simply swipe their phone over a sensor, and the fare is deducted from the account. Again, account balances and reminders are periodically sent to the customer via SMS.

Restaurants are also beginning to test prepaid accounts, although so far this has mostly focused on the larger fast food chains. This mobile payment model works in exactly the same way as the public transportation scenario, but it can be a bit more complicated to implement. In fast food restaurants, the exchange is simple because food is purchased directly at the register, where the phone can be swiped over an NFC or RFID sensor and immediately deducted from the prepaid account, just as it would be with a debit card.

In more traditional restaurants, where the waitstaff either takes a credit card to swipe at a processing terminal or processes the card at the table wirelessly, there is the expectation to tip. In this instance, the signal from the NFC or RFID chip owned by the restaurant must prompt a screen that allows the customer to enter a tip. This is a bit more of a hassle, but you can preprogram the system to precalculate common tip percentages for the patron, making the process easier and quicker to complete. See Figure 12.5 to get a better idea of how this type of transaction takes place.

Prompted Mobile Payment

Prompted payment is much like prepayment, except that the credit card on file is not charged until after the service is rendered. In this payment model, the service provider usually sends the customer an SMS with the total bill and asking permission to charge the credit card on file. Again, some carriers use this to remind their customers to pay their bill on time. In this scenario, the carrier sends a text message to the subscriber at the end of a billing cycle, notifying the customer of the total amount due and allowing him or her to respond with a preset PIN to pay the bill with the credit card information stored in the account. Prompted mobile payment is a great way to streamline bill payment or even charitable contributions because it can provide a cost savings over direct mail and can be used by a variety of different service providers, including home utilities, subscription TV services, and even childcare services.

Full Web Transactions

As on the traditional Web, entire transactions can be completed on the mobile Web without the need for an account or any kind of prepayment. Customers simply enter their credit card information, just as they would on the traditional Web. This type of mobile commerce is most commonly used by websites that offer some kind of mobile shopping experience. This method of mobile payment has been historically difficult, but it is improving with the market penetration of true Web-browsing phones and QWERTY keyboards. On WAP browsers in less-capable phones, the risk exists that the form fields for the payment information will be misaligned or that the JavaScript necessary to submit the form will not execute correctly. In the worst case, customers could hit the Submit button and reach the "thank you" page, but the actual order would never have made it into the system. The most common complaint with this type of mobile commerce is that if they don't have accounts set up, users must enter all their shipping, billing, and credit card information using the small keypad of their phone. This can be quite slow and cumbersome for the customers and can be a serious disincentive for a mobile purchase.

A couple tactics can make this mobile payment method more effective. All the best practices for mobile forms, discussed in Chapter 9, "Mobile Website Development," should be followed. The most important thing you can do when setting up this type of mobile commerce is to ensure that any problems cause by the mobile rendering do not prevent the completion of the sale. This includes providing users with a clickable phone number so that they can click to call if the phone is not working, allowing them to save their shopping cart or email themselves a link so that they can pay later when they get to their computer.

To limit the amount of scrolling that a user has to do to finish the form, sometimes it is a good idea to include the form input instructions in gray, inside the form fields, instead of above or beside the field. When a user clicks in the field, the instructions should disappear so that the field is ready to accept the information. This simply minimizes the vertical space that the text takes up, making the form appear shorter to the viewer. It is also a good idea to use check boxes and radio buttons whenever possible, to eliminate the amount of typing the user has to do on the phone.

When the user is submitting the form, you should minimize the information to include, limit the number of steps to finalize the purchase, and never require that a user account be set up to make a purchase. If user accounts are available on the traditional website, they should also be available on the mobile website so that users can log in to access their saved credit card and shipping information. When you are collecting their billing information, include a check box if the shipping address is the same as the billing address so that customers don't have to type their address twice. Clearly mark which fields are required and which fields are optional, and be as comprehensive as possible when creating the requirements for a successful submission. In the same process, allow users to create an account and save information to it if they would like to.

If the form submission returns an error, make sure the error page reloads the form with all the information the user has already input, and then scrolls exactly to the location of the field that must be updated. Place the error message directly above or below the field in red, with specific instructions about the requirements of the form. If a credit card is rejected or cannot be processed, offer the user the ability to re-enter it, but also provide an order ID and a clickable phone number so that the customer can click the phone number to be connected directly to a representative to complete the purchase over the phone. Some phone systems even enable you to transfer the order ID in the dialing sequence so that it is already in the system when a representative is reached. This is ideal, because once the phone is in calling mode, it will be hard for the user to switch back to the mobile browser to get the order ID off the browser screen.

If your customers are able to create accounts, you should test using HTML/JavaScript cookies to identify specific users when they enter your site. Not all mobile browsers accept cookies, but many do, and they can make it less daunting for your customers to complete a purchase on their mobile phone. The cookies should store their log-on information and shopping cart but, for security, should require customers to re-enter their password to access any billing or shipping information or to make a purchase.

Full Brick-and-Mortar Transactions with Proximity-Based Mobile Payment

Some credit card companies are beginning to work with mobile phone manufacturers, to make phones capable of Near Field Communication (NFC) and Radio Frequency Identification (RFID) proximity payment that bills directly to the user's credit card. With this payment model, the mobile phone can be used to pay for any goods and services on the spot, in a brick-and-mortar store, simply by swiping it over a sensor. A chip embedded in the mobile phone simply acts as a relay between the merchant requesting payment and the purchaser's credit card company. Systems like this are not yet common in the United States or Europe, but they are growing in acceptance, especially in Japan and Korea. (As mentioned, NFC and RFID technologies are discussed in more depth in Chapter 6.)

Both the customers and the retailers can benefit from the integration of LBS-style mobile payment. For the customer, it offers the convenience of shopping without having to carry credit cards, cash, or checks. For the retailer, it can streamline the checkout process, creating efficiencies that can even minimize the need for staff at payment registers.

In addition to a traditional brick-and-mortar purchase, this kind of mobile e-commerce can be leveraged by vending machines, street vendors, and even traveling merchants or promoters. In China and Japan, this kind of proximity-based mobile payment is even being used for transportation ticketing and paid-parking situations. In all cases, campaigns that integrate this type of mobile payment will see more success and uptake if they are integrated with other customer touch points that can add value to the transaction. Consider a couple examples where mobile proximity payment can be used.

Retail Locations

When retail locations integrate a proximity-based mobile payment solution with an existing coupon or promotion, they can encourage customers to test the new payment method to participate in the promotion or get the discount. A good example is a store that offers 20% off the final purchase if customers complete the transaction with their RFID- or NFC-enabled phone.

Vending Machines

Using proximity-based mobile payment in vending machines can help both the customer and the vending company. In this instance, mobile payment allows users to make a purchase even when they don't have cash on hand, and it enables vendors to remotely track the levels of stock in each machine. Switching to a mobile payment option also prevents service personnel from having to visit the machine before it is out of stock, simply to remove cash.

Street Vendors, Traveling Merchants, and Promoters

Wireless credit card payment and processing is quite popular in Europe but has not yet become mainstream in the United States. With this technology, service providers can carry a mobile device that can process credit card payments over a cellphone or WiFi signal. For instance, a train attendant could accept payments for train tickets, or waiters could accept payments for meals while walking around with this device. As it grows in popularity, mobile phone payment likely will be integrated with the wireless processing systems.

Figure 12.4 shows a wireless credit card terminal. This device enables a merchant to process credit card information over a cellular network so that it can move around in the course of work and not be tethered by a pay station or an Internet wire. This kind of payment processing can be especially effective for street vendors, traveling merchants, and promoters, but can also be quite useful for plumbers, maids, mechanics, valets, roadside rescue, locksmiths, and other business that require constant mobility.

Figure 12.4 *Wireless credit card terminals enable merchants to process credit card information over a cellular network.*

In the United States, credit cards use a magnetic strip to communicate with the merchant credit machines, but in Europe, they have transitioned to a system called "chip and PIN." With a chip and PIN payment, the credit card is usually inserted vertically into the payment device and left there for processing, rather than swiping the card as in the United States. The "chip" is an RFID chip that is used to automatically verify information with the card issuer. Figure 12.5 shows several screens from a chip and PIN device.

With any chip and PIN transaction, you are expected to enter a PIN and provide a signature as part of the verification process. Because of this added layer of protection, wireless credit card processing is much more common when a chip and PIN system is present. Instead of taking your credit card away to process when you are paying at a restaurant, waitstaff brings a small wireless processing terminal so that the credit card can be processed directly at the table.

Many companies are working to integrate this type of wireless mobile payment with mobile phones. In this model, a wireless mobile payment terminal could interact directly with a wireless phone through NFC or RFID in much the same way a credit card payment would be processed.

Credit card companies and banks actually tout RFID as a new layer of protection rather than a weakness or opportunity for abuse. Sophisticated RFID payment systems, such as those in chip and PIN credit cards, validate cards by randomly generating unique transaction numbers for each chip, and these change with each transaction. When a transaction is processed, the transaction number on the chip must match the transaction number in the card issuer's database. With this kind of assurance in place, even if thieves had access to a credit card number and an expiration date, they could not complete a transaction.

Travel and Entertainment Ticketing

In 2008, Juniper Research predicted that, by 2013, more than 400 million people in the world will be using mobile ticketing. The major benefit is that when tickets are sold electronically, staff does not need to work at the ticket counter, because tickets can also be delivered directly to

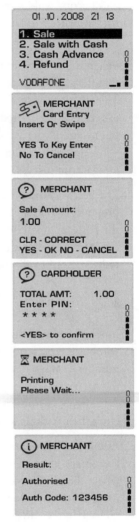

Figure 12.5 *Using wireless credit card terminals enables merchants to move around and not be tethered to one location.*

the mobile phone. Tickets can be purchased ahead of time, over a mobile Web or SMS payment system, or can be purchased as people enter the venue, when they swipe their phone over a sensor.

Mobile ticketing has seen the highest penetration in East Asia, where Japanese rail travelers and Indian cinema patrons are already purchasing tickets via their mobile phone. Presumably, adoption of this type of mobile commerce in the United States and Europe will follow the same patterns, so travel and transportation will be the first industries to truly embrace mobile ticketing, followed by entertainment and sports.

When mobile tickets are issued, they should include a barcode or redemption code that the attendant can enter directly off the phone at the door or the ticket booth. To make the most of this type of mobile commerce system and improve the user experience, it is incredibly important to give clear directions both on the mobile phone and in the physical area where patrons line up to redeem their tickets. This will help reinforce the efficiency of the process that you need to make mobile ticketing a true success.

The best way to encourage customers to take advantage of a new mobile ticketing program is to loop it in with other incentives or use it to create some efficiency in the customer experience; for example, you could create separate lines for mobile ticket holders, allow people with mobile tickets early entrance, or provide mobile-only coupons or discounts that can be redeemed within the venue.

Parking

Mobile payment can also be used to improve paid-parking opportunities, with or without the presence of a parking attendant. Mobile payment can be integrated in a number of ways, depending on the capability of the phone. Customers can text their parking spot number to a system that sends them a link for online payment. Alternately, customers can be prompted to visit a mobile website where they can enter their parking spot number and credit card information to pay.

Adding functionality to this type of mobile e-commerce is simple and useful for customers. You can send customers information and maps to remind them exactly where their car is parked, in case they can't find it later, or, if the parking spot is metered, the user can add time to the meter over the phone without even having to go back to the car.

Mobile Banking

Mobile banking has come to mean different things to different people, but it is essentially any activity that allows currency to change hands via a mobile phone.

Two types of currencies are usually described as being banked in discussion of mobile commerce: traditional government-issued currency (such as the dollars and pounds that many of us are used to keeping in our bank account), and mobile talk-time minutes, which can be traded for goods and services and then sold back to the carrier for traditional state-issued currency.

Using a mobile phone to complete a banking transaction has already become common in many places around the world, and the practice is growing quite rapidly, especially in the developing world. The functionality for mobile banking is improving because, as Ben Lorca from O'Reilly Radar explains (in his article "Mobile Banks in the Developing World Prove Simpler Is Better"), "Unencumbered by legacy software systems, business rules, and practices, mobile banks are innovating at a much faster pace than traditional financial services companies."

As mobile phones and service become more available in developing countries, mobile banking has been especially important to the development of the regions. It is being used to reach those who are described as the "unbanked": people who have never had a bank account and have always dealt exclusively in cash. Mobile banking also allows banks to reach a wide audience without as much reliance on expensive brick-and-mortar branches to serve their customers. In these areas, mobile phones are much more prevalent than computers, and many people live a long distance from the nearest bank.

Mobile banking began in developing countries as an informal trade of mobile minutes that were used and resold to others as a form of currency. In cultures where cash was the predominant or exclusive form of exchange, minutes were purchased with cash and then could be sent to other registered users via text message, and later sold back for cash all at corner shops. This method of transaction is commonly used by traveling laborers to send money back to their families in their village.

Mobile banking can be beneficial for both banks and their customers. It can decrease the overhead of the banks by either minimizing the reliance of human tellers or minimizing the need for brick-and-mortar branches in the first place. Mobile banking enables customers to manage their accounts, complete person-to-person money transfers, and set up bill payment without having to use a computer or go into a bank branch.

Institutions that offer mobile banking can provide their customers access to their accounts in a variety of ways. The method of account management that will be most successful generally depends on the type of handsets that are prevalent in the region the bank serves. If the customer base is using less capable phones with limited browsers, it is best to provide banking either through a WAP portal page or through SMS. If mobile Web access is limited in the region you are targeting, you might want to focus your efforts on SMS banking first.

In SMS banking, bank patrons register their phone number with their bank and are given a short code that they can use to direct bank requests. Requests can be submitted to receive account balances or transfer money between accounts. Bank patrons are given specific commands that can be entered in a text message, with money amounts associated with them. The bank system receives the request and executes the request, usually requiring a PIN confirmation, and then sends a transaction number back to the phone when the request has been completed.

In areas where mobile Internet access is more common but smart phones have low penetration, WAP sites are a good way to reach a mobile audience. WAP banking websites essentially offer a streamlined version of a traditional banking website. This is slightly more convenient for customers because they don't have to enter SMS commands, and the bank avoids the cost of maintaining the short code systems necessary for SMS banking. Whenever possible, the WAP website should provide all the functionality that the traditional website does, including the capability to transfer money between accounts and pay bills online.

If your target demographic is more likely to have smart phones and easy access to the mobile Web, it might work well to update your existing website to work on mobile phones or to create a mobile banking application that can be downloaded and installed on the customer's phone. In most cases, you can create a scenario in which customers need only authorize recurring payments, transfers, or other account modifications with a PIN, rather than inputting them each time.

Ideally, your solution will incorporate functionality that addresses each level of phone capability. Regardless of which type of mobile banking model works best for your company and your customers, it is important to fully integrate the offering with the rest of your existing services. Make it easy to access, and keep it top-of-mind. Promote it in your existing marketing channels, such as in TV and radio commercials, in brochures, in emails, and on the website. Let your patrons create and customize personal notifications about their account, such as when a balance gets to a certain level or when a bill is due; this helps create value and keeps the bank top-of-mind.

Usability is very important when it comes to online banking. In any mobile banking scenario, it is crucial to provide clear instructions on how to best manage the account from a mobile phone. If you are working with smart phone users, you can include a vCard with all the bank information so the user always has the phone number, website information, and even SMS commands handy if they are needed. If you are working with a demographic with a high percent of previously unbanked members, it is especially important to make all the interactions simple and to provide instructions whenever you can.

One of the best aspects of mobile banking is the capability to use your banking communication to learn more about your customers; this will enable you send them more targeted marketing over the phone. For example, if customers are constantly overdrawing their accounts, you can include ads for overdraft protection or bank credit cards whenever you send an SMS to let them know that they have overdrafted the account. Alternately, if customers appear to move large sums of money between accounts frequently, you can send them information about your financial planning services each time you send them a transfer confirmation. With this type of mobile marketing, you will reach your customers when they already have banking on their mind. For credit card promotions, financial advising, or insurance, you can even prompt them with a click-to-call phone number so that they can talk to a representative about the offer over the phone.

Security and Other Concerns

Obviously, security and risk management are the biggest concern for any company that wants to accept mobile payment or engage in mobile banking. Before you engage in any kind of mobile commerce, you should have a clear understanding of the risks it presents.

If any part of your mobile marketing campaign involves the input of financial information, it is vital for you to protect your users' privacy and ensure that the transmission of that sensitive data is as secure as possible. Working with a trusted mobile payment provider is crucial. These providers generally have the most knowledge about different types of mobile payment processing, as well as the laws and restrictions regarding mobile payment in different countries and with different carriers. Needless to say, the transactions should be encrypted and as secure as possible. The major risks associated with mobile e-commerce are phone theft, operator error, and hacking.

Mobile Commerce and Phone Theft Risks

In some ways, mobile payment can actually be more secure than traditional online transactions. This is because the biggest threat to online transactions is generally malware or viruses that collect users' sensitive information and transmit it to an external database over the Web, to later be used or sold by hackers. Mobile SPAM and spyware is covered in more depth in Chapter 13, "Mobile Marketing Privacy, Spam, and Viruses," but the general findings are that mobile phones are still relatively safe from that type of abuse. The lower threat of phone hacking actually gives mobile e-commerce a safety advantage over traditional e-commerce.

If you are selling products on a mobile site, you will generally be working with a mobile payment provider rather than creating the mobile payment system on your own. The mobile payment company that you work with should have a list of established clients that you can contact who report positive experiences with their services. They should also have lawyers on staff or on retainer who are familiar with the telecom and commerce laws of the region that you will be serving and who are willing to review your particular legal concerns. As an added protection, you might also want to hire your own lawyer to review the legal situation of each m-commerce platform or initiative before it launches.

The primary concern with mobile banking is that the banking information is generally stored on the handset, so if the handset is lost or stolen, all the accounts and information stored on the phone are susceptible to theft. This concern extends beyond financial information to other sensitive information stored on a phone, such as emails, documents, pictures, and videos, so many companies are coming up with "remote kill" features that back up all the information on the phone in the cloud and then block all access or clear all content from the phone memory remotely if it is reported lost or stolen. Savvy mobile payment companies will begin integrating their services with existing remote kill software companies, or will begin including it as a feature in their own mobile commerce platform.

Any company or institution that enables customers to create an account on the website must follow industry best practices before accepting payment or sending money. Just as on the traditional Internet, the best practice for mobile is to never display a full account number or passwords on the Web, but instead to just display the final four to six, with the rest of the numbers displayed as stars (*****-*****-1234) or x's (xxxxx-xxxxx-1234). This ensures that anyone who finds the phone does not have access to the account numbers, in case remote-kill features are not in place. It is also best to require that a PIN be entered for any account modification. If these safeguards are in place, a thief will have limited ability to make any real changes or do any damage without the PIN.

Mobile E-Commerce and Operator Error Risks

Other concerns about mobile commerce relate to the sensitivity or range of NFC and RFID readers. Because these types of payments are based on proximity, and phones need only be passed over a sensor, there is a risk of accidental payment based on proximity. A good example of the problem can be seen with a U.S.-based chain of gas stations: Before mobile payment became a viable option, the gas station tested payment key fobs that used contactless payment technology similar to RFID. After pumping gas, customers with key fobs could simply run them in front of a sensor on the gas pump to pay. It was a nice idea, but unfortunately, when customers walked past other gas pumps in the station, the sensors were so strong that they were accidentally charging customers with key fobs for other people's gas.

Newer technology has addressed many of these concerns, but even so, it is much easier to accidentally pass your phone over a sensor than it is to "accidentally" swipe your credit card through a credit card machine. The standard for contactless payment is about 4 inches or 10 centimeters. Now, ten years after the gas station's experiment, MasterCard, Visa, and American Express are all testing similar key fobs as contactless payment devices and are seeing great success. When these technologies are well tested and accepted, it will be only a small task to get the technology included in the hardware of a mobile phone handset.

Another mobile commerce concern is that when online payment transactions happen, the network could suddenly cut out and drop the connection while in the midst of transmitting a payment. In that scenario, users might think they paid, but sellers would never get the payment because the connection was lost. The website and payment system should be configured to send error messages if transmissions were not received correctly. The system should also be set up to send confirmation messages when transmissions were received and processed, to inform and assure the purchaser of the completed order.

Mobile E-Commerce and Hacking Risks

Outside of the more physical concerns about safety, debate in the mobile payment community swirls about different technologies and configurations. Although there have been no major reports of RFID hacking, the systems are not yet as secure as most of us would desire. There is unease regarding RFID card readers that can be created to access card information for malicious purposes rather than to simply execute a payment. The potential also exists for RFID readers in retail outlets to be "skimmed" by technology that can extract unencrypted credit card numbers and expiration dates as the reading is transmitting the data.

Because the technology is new and the potential unanticipated exposure is great, many groups that would like to establish standards and guidelines for companies that want to embrace mobile payment. The Global System for Mobile Communications (GSM Association, but originally, the Groupe Spécial Mobile) is pushing for a worldwide standard for mobile payment that it calls the Universal Integrated Circuit Card (UICC). This would be a standardized chip that would store all sensitive information in an NFC-enabled device. Other potential methods for securing mobile information include using Secure Digital (SD) cards to store the information, and storing the information on software in the phone memory instead of on a removable chip.

Because mobile payment is still evolving, there are bound to be pros and cons to each decision or technology along the way. Financial institutions and retailers would be wise to embrace security as much as possible and to model existing methods of traditional online payment, to develop and enhance the amount of protection they can provide for their mobile customers. Despite the concerns, mobile payment promises to be an important evolution of modern business and an important aspect of any mobile marketing campaign.

Mobile Marketing Privacy, Spam, and Viruses

The personal nature of mobile marketing is generally a great benefit, but it can also cause major problems for marketers who are not respectful of their customers' privacy. As with traditional computers, mobile phones are subject to attacks on privacy with spam, malware, and even viruses. For marketers to be truly successful in the mobile space, they must be able to leverage the personal nature of the channel without jeopardizing or compromising the customer relationship or the private information that it provides. The advice in this chapter will be particularly useful if you are building an interactive mobile website creating a mobile SMS campaign or using mobile technology to encourage the download of mobile content.

In the world of mobile marketing, trust is at a premium, so mobile marketers are generally forced to abide by laws and standards for both email- and computer-based marketing, as well as phone-based telemarketing restrictions.

That being said, the laws are frequently unclear or disparate, so mobile marketers in the United States are also forced to abide by federal as well as state laws that might impact their campaigns.

For the most part, laws that control marketing and messaging on the traditional Internet also apply to the mobile phone. SMS marketing and other mobile-specific communications that do not have a traditional computer counterpart are sometimes regulated by the local government or by the carriers. When spam is sent across multiple carriers or to recipients in multiple countries, it gets harder to enforce, so it is generally monitored and guided by agencies and associations. These agencies and associations create best practice documentation and codes of conduct to help marketers understand the mobile rules of engagement. However, many of these standards are not enforceable by any central body.

On the traditional Internet, pop-up advertising, spam, spyware, malware, and viruses began to hit the radar of the normal Internet user in the late 1990s and early 2000s. Just as Internet download speed increased and the medium began to take off as a marketing channel, some marketers began unscrupulous campaigns. Similarly, as we continue to see growth in the adoption of mobile communication, mobile commerce, and mobile marketing, we will also see some marketers trying to take it too far.

Some people will always try to push the envelope or blatantly disregard the best interests of their customers, but in some cases, it can be hard to tell when things have gone too far. Many countries have laws to protect the privacy of their citizens and prevent unsolicited marketing messages, but few countries have specifically codified *rules about mobile marketing. Until more specific laws are put into place, we must look to the best practices that are created by international associations such as the Mobile Marketing Association (MMA) and the Direct Marketing Association (DMA).*

Notions of privacy are culturally relative, and different regions have different laws that could affect your mobile marketing campaign. This chapter is meant to provide loose definitions and recommendations about the privacy implications of mobile marketing, but it is not meant to be exhaustive. Consult local experts whenever you have legal concerns regarding the deployment of a mobile marketing campaign. This is especially true if your campaign has elements that add to the legal risk, such as a target market under the age of 18 or the opportunity to win a prize. This chapter includes discussions and examples of mobile spam, malware, and viruses. It also discusses what carriers and marketers can do to protect their customers' privacy and their own best interest. Finally, it gives a brief overview of the major laws and mores regarding privacy in different regions around the world.

What Is Mobile Spamming?

The word *spam* is basically just geek-speak for untargeted digital marketing communication. The term was originally used to describe untargeted email marketing, but the definition has expanded to include all types of marketing communication that recipients have not consciously opted into. *Spam* is also used to describe marketing communication that is deceptive or obtrusive. Although email spam can be accessed on mobile phones, mobile spam generally describes unsolicited text, picture messages, or location-based marketing.

In the mobile world, spam can often be a bit more sinister than traditional email spam. The mobile medium is new enough that many users are eager to find new mobile applications or content and are unaware of the risks. They might be tricked by unsolicited SMS messages encouraging them to download a free ringtone; if they don't read the agreement, they might not know that by downloading the first free ringtone, they have opted into a subscription and will be sent weekly ringtones that are not free, but are automatically charged to their phone bill.

In the United States, unsolicited text messages are less common but more troublesome because carriers generally charge for both the sending and receiving of text messages. In other countries, unsolicited text messages are much more common and still a nuisance, but at least they do not directly impact the recipient's bill.

Mobile spamming can get much more insidious when it incorporates attempts to solicit private information under false pretenses, otherwise known as phishing. In March 2008, Brian Krebs of *The Washington Post* reported about a mobile phishing scheme that used a voice mail system (sometimes called vishing) to collect private banking information from its targets:

> The scams in this case took the form of a type of phishing known as "vishing," wherein cell-phone users receive a text message warning that their bank account has been closed due to suspicious activity, and that they need to call a provided phone number to reactivate the account. Victims who called the number reached an automated voice mail box that prompted callers to key in their credit card number, expiration date and PIN to verify their information (the voice mail systems involved in these sorts of scams usually are run off free or low-cost Internet-based phone networks that are difficult to trace and shut down).

The scam went on for about a month, with the perpetrators sending out millions of text messages, receiving 4,400 calls and full account information for 125 victims.

 Note

Phishing is a form of attack in which a thief uses email and the Web to pose as a legitimate company, such as your bank, and attempts to solicit your account information. The idea is that victims believe they are interacting with an actual company, when they're actually handing over private information to a thief. Vishing, on the other hand, is similar to phishing, in that the thief poses as a legitimate entity. However, instead of using the traditional Internet as a medium, vishing uses landlines as well as VoIP (Voice Over IP, or Internet phone service) to solicit private information, such as Social Security numbers, account numbers, and so on.

What the Carriers Can Do to Stop Spam

In many cases, mobile privacy and security is the onus of the carriers and the service providers rather than the marketers. We rely on them to secure and maintain their own networks, as well as work with other networks to prevent the spread of unsolicited marketing messages and malware. Mobile operators already block hundreds of millions of unsolicited text messages each month and are expected to have antispam included in all third-party contracts. They are also expected to provide customers with information and advice regarding the prevention of mobile spam, including mechanisms for reporting spammers.

The Groupe Speciale Mobile (GSMA), a European body that governs telecommunication communication, has created a Mobile Spam Code of Practice that asks carriers to voluntarily commit to the following:

- Providing a subscriber consent mechanism for the carrier's own marketing efforts

- Working cooperatively with other carriers, including those not yet committed to the code

- Including antispam conditions in all contracts with third-party suppliers

- Providing subscribers with the information and resources to help them minimize mobile spam

- Reviewing customer contracts, terms and conditions, and acceptable use policies to ensure up-to-date and relevant antispam conditions

- Encouraging governments and regulators to support the issue when necessary

Internationally, mobile spam is quite a large problem. In 2008:

- Forty percent of the SMS messages received in India were spam.

- Fifty percent of the SMS messages received in China were spam.

- Seventy percent of the SMS messages received in Japan were spam.

In the United States, many carriers have their own set of privacy requirements for mobile campaigns that are run on their network. Following are a few examples:

- **AT&T**—In SMS messaging, the recipient must opt into receiving text messages from the sender before they are ever sent; the sender must be identified in every message that is received.

- **T-Mobile**—T-Mobile requires that users opt in before receiving mobile messages and requires that advertisers submit a description of the message flow that the marketing campaign will take.

- **Verizon**—Verizon has a certification board to approve all Premium SMS campaigns or any changes in the prices of the service. Opt-ins are not required on the Verizon network, but this is expected to change soon.

What Mobile Marketers Can Do to Stop Spam

As a mobile marketer, the best thing you can do to stop mobile spam is to not send it yourself. Mobile marketing can give marketers a deep insight into their customers' lives. Although it is always best to track and measure as much as possible, you have to create a balance between the value you get from the information you collect and the risk that your customers might consider it an invasion of privacy.

Many of your potential mobile customers might be unaware of the level of tracking and targeting that is capable on a phone, but if they were aware of it, they might find it unsettling. Always be as transparent as possible with the people that you are marketing to, but at the same time, it is important to couch your transparency correctly, so as not to create undue concern.

Concern for privacy varies greatly among different age groups, cultures, and customer profiles. For instance, Figure 13.1 demonstrates attitudes toward mobile spam in Japan. The simplest way to address the concerns of all the various groups is to always consider mobile marketing a permission-based channel. Strive to acquire permission each time a new level of bond is created between your brand and its customers. This conservative mentality should keep you in the good graces of your customers and will do a lot to keep you on the right side of the law.

Also keep all marketing messages as relevant as possible to the recipient. Sending communication that is untargeted or irrelevant to the recipient will only increase the rate of people opting out of your messages. Messages that lack targeting can also drive up the cost of the campaign and decrease the potential ROI, not to mention expose you to more legal risks.

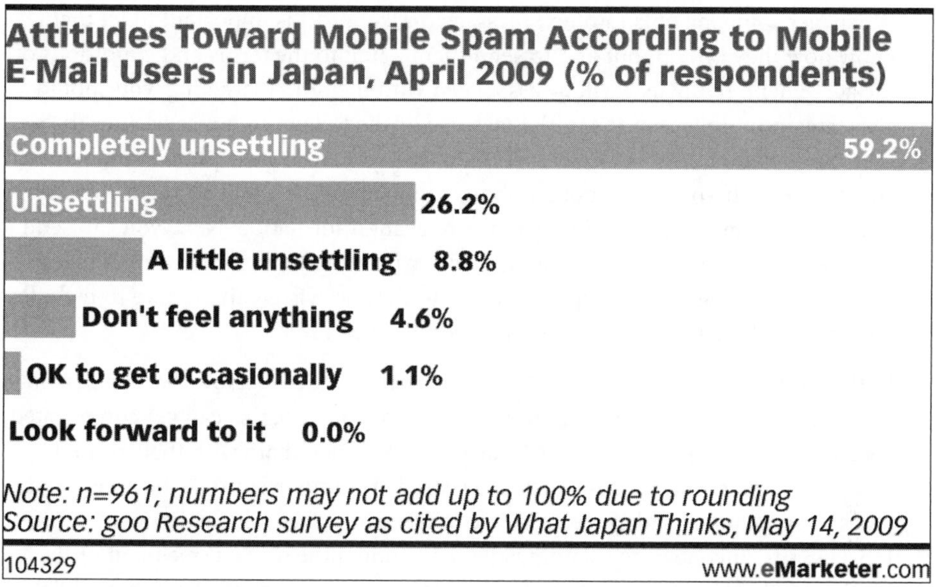

Attitudes Toward Mobile Spam According to Mobile E-Mail Users in Japan, April 2009 (% of respondents)

Completely unsettling	59.2%
Unsettling	26.2%
A little unsettling	8.8%
Don't feel anything	4.6%
OK to get occasionally	1.1%
Look forward to it	0.0%

Note: n=961; numbers may not add up to 100% due to rounding
Source: goo Research survey as cited by What Japan Thinks, May 14, 2009

104329   www.**eMarketer**.com

Figure 13.1   *Privacy concerns as they relate to mobile marketing vary among age groups, countries, and customer profiles. Japan's attitude toward spam is shown here. Chart courtesy of eMarketer.*

Joel Dichter of DMNews does a good job of summing up the legal requirements for SMS marketing in his article "Navigating the Legal Aspects of Mobile Marketing":

> In general, when promoting programs via mobile phones, content providers should ensure all material clearly indicates whether the service is a subscription. The program's terms and conditions, the pricing information, additional fees, the subscription term and billing interval also must be disclosed. Consumers should be informed whether the charge will appear on customers' mobile phone bills or will be deducted from their prepaid balances.

> For programs charging the subscriber a normal rate for text messaging, only a single opt-in is required. This single opt-in only applies to the specific program to which a customer subscribed and should not be construed as approval to market other products or services to the customer.

> For premium rate programs, a double opt-in is required. Where the premium service is a subscription service, the double opt-in must include identification of the service as a subscription and the billing interval. In addition, subscription periods should be no longer than one month, and prior to renewal of the service (or at least once a month) a renewal message must be sent to the subscriber.

Whenever someone opts into text message marketing, it is important to let them know how they can opt out and to send them a link to the terms and conditions of the agreement. If any fees will be associated with the SMS marketing, you should also explain those fees in the initial message or the follow-up message, after the users are opted in. In some cases, users will give you both their phone number and email address. If you do get both a phone number and an email address, you can send the user an email containing all the relevant information. Next, you can send a text message explaining how to opt out and explaining that more information about the text-messaging program has been sent to the user via email. Be sure to include the email address to which that information has been sent.

In the United States, the burden of proof is on the sender to show that the person has opted in to receive the communication. Unfortunately, this can get complicated because many companies use third-party lists that they share with their related companies and affiliates. When lists are shared, it is important that the appropriate types of agreements and protections are in place to protect all parties involved. In U.S. lawsuits, anyone in the sending chain, including the original recipient of the opt-in, the third-party sender, the SMS gateway, and the carrier, can be found liable for legal violations. In general, it is a good idea to consult with an attorney instead of relying on advice from the carrier, the SMS gateway, or the third-party list provider.

If people are using a traditional website to sign up for email and mobile alerts, you should send a separate message to their email address and mobile phone number, explaining that they opted in to receive communication from the website and requesting that they respond to confirm their decision. This is called a double opt-in, and it is required for many types of digital marketing. Even when the double-opt in is not required, most customers prefer it.

If you are participating in SMS marketing, you frequently need to work with a third-party SMS gateway company to collect opt-ins and send out SMS. In many cases, these companies can be great resources for understanding how best to protect your customers' privacy. However, it is important to make sure that the gateway company adheres to the letter *and intent* of the law. When working with an SMS gateway, it is always a good idea to ensure that it understands that your opt-in list is a private asset that belongs to your company and can never be resold to other marketers.

Some marketers believe that mobile SMS and MMS spam will never be as much of a problem as email spam because carriers charge an incremental cost for each message sent—unlike email, which can sent with no incremental cost. This difference might hold back spammers for awhile, but SMS gateways are being developed internationally that allow messages to be sent with little or no incremental cost.

Running Mobile Sweepstakes and Contests

A very popular method of developing an internal list of people who are opted into mobile marketing messages is to run a contest or sweepstakes in which participants opt in to participate. Legally, this can be a bit complicated because marketers are expected to abide by an additional set of laws and regulations. In the United States, this can be difficult because many contests or sweepstakes can resemble a lottery, and the only entities that can legally run a lottery are the individual state governments—take measures to ensure that your campaign cannot legally be considered a lottery.

Legally, the three elements that constitute a lottery are consideration, compensation, and chance. To create a legal sweepstakes or contest, you must remove one of these three elements so that you are not considered a lottery. Although you are required to remove only one of the elements, it is best to remove or mitigate as many of the elements as possible. Simple awareness in the planning phases of your contest or sweepstakes can do a lot to ease this stress:

- **Consideration**—The consideration element is the payment to participate; if it were a lottery, it would be the cost of the lottery ticket. If you are running a mobile sweepstakes, the best thing you can do to eliminate consideration is to make it free to participate in the contest. Because premium text-messaging services charge money, it is a good idea to allow users to freely participate online as well.

- **Compensation**—The compensation element represents the winnings; in a lottery, this is the payout for a winning ticket. If you are running a mobile sweepstakes, consider offering prizes that have no monetary value, such as having the winners' names listed on a leader board. However, if the prize is a cash prize (or a prize that has monetary value), it will be impossible to remove this element from your legal concerns and you will need to look closely at the laws that govern cash prize payouts.

- **Chance**—The chance element simply means that the winner is determined randomly; in a lottery, this is the chance that the right lotto balls are drawn. In mobile marketing campaigns, the best way to eliminate this element is to base winnings on skill rather than chance.

Location-Based Marketing and Privacy

Location-based marketing messages can also be considered intrusive or even an invasion of privacy. If you are using location-based marketing, first ask permission to send a marketing message, either with a short "push" request from the Bluetooth or WiFi beacon, or in a "pull" effort, using signage to encourage users to initiate the communication. After communication is initiated, in either scenario, it is important to explain what type of information you will be sending to people's phones and allow them to change their mind or save the communication to participate at another time.

 Note

> Location-based marketing is a form of marketing in which marketing messages are delivered directly to a user who is within broadcast range. For instance, a local eatery might broadcast nightly specials via Bluetooth to mobile users who have enabled their smart phones to receive Bluetooth messages. To learn more, see Chapter 6, "Mobile Promotion and Location-Based Marketing."

In the United States, the MMA has said that location-based Bluetooth marketing is permissible as long as you send an opt-in message to people who have set their Bluetooth devices to be discoverable. However, in the United Kingdom, the Direct Marketing Association believes that people should be opted in before they are sent a mobile marketing message via Bluetooth.

Respecting the Privacy of Children and Teen Mobile Users

The mobile Web presents unique challenges for those hoping to protect children's best interests. Most phones don't provide any means of implementing parental restrictions for what children can access on the phones—and carriers have yet to provide this as a service.

Children and teens can be a particularly lucrative target market for your mobile messaging, but many countries have established extra protections for their privacy and the types of mobile marketing they can receive. In general, do whatever you can to ensure that you are not targeting children with messages that are not appropriate for their age. This is especially true for campaigns that focus on adult content, gambling, alcohol, and tobacco.

No foolproof ways currently exist to protect minors from marketing messages that are not appropriate for them. The best way to ensure that you are legally marketing to people in the correct age demographic is to require them to input their birthday early in the communication. This means more than including a check box that says, "I am over 13 years old." Requiring the recipient to enter a specific date generates more accurate and honest responses. If participants are under 13, it is important not only to stop sending messages to them, but also to not collect or store any of their information in your system.

Children pose a particularly interesting problem because younger generations are less concerned about privacy than any other age group. They are usually active users of social networking sites and accept terms and conditions to use a website or download content without a second thought. This cavalier attitude might simply be a sign of the times, but it also illustrates how important it is for marketers to be explicit and direct when explaining how private information might be used.

In Europe, 26 carriers participate in the European Framework for Safer Mobile Use by Younger Teenagers and Children, which establishes the need for access control to adult content, making it more difficult for teen users to be exposed. Regulations created in this agreement are put in place at a national level through self-regulatory codes of conduct.

On-Site Privacy and Mobile Cookies

On traditional websites, cookies are frequently used in the back end of the website management system to carry or save information about the user from previous visits. They can be used to store preferences, keep items in a shopping cart, or simply identify users in a system log. Cookies work in varying degrees on different types of mobile phones, but the acceptance and storage of cookies is improving in each new generation of smart phones.

Cookies are apparent to the user when a website displays the user's name or location upon arrival to the site. Cookies are also apparent to end users if they allow the site to save their login information so that they are automatically logged into the site. This type of seamless experience can be great on a mobile device because it limits the need for typing, but it can also be considered an invasion of privacy if it is done without express permission.

Cookies make some computer users and mobile users uncomfortable because they can save information about users' past interactions with a website, and those cookies might eliminate the need for a username and password to access private information. This can be particularly problematic on mobile phones because they are more susceptible to loss or theft than traditional computers. If cookies on a mobile phone give access to things such as personal financial information, health information, or even sensitive business information, loss of a phone could be quite catastrophic.

The best practice for using mobile cookies is to always inform users when you would like to use them and give the user the option of not installing the cookies. Because cookies generally improve the user experience, many users will opt into the cookies, but those who are concerned will not do so. If you are using cookies on a sign-in form, you can include a "Keep me signed in" check box that the user can select if he or she would like the site to not require a username and password to be entered on each visit. To create the opt-in process for other aspects of the site, simply include a check box at the end of any form that users might fill out, asking if they would like the website to "remember this information for next time."

In some cases, you might want to require users to enter a password, even if they normally use cookies to access their personal information. This is especially true if you are allowing them to change or manipulate sensitive information, such as bank accounts, credit card information, travel confirmations, insurance, or health information. It is also a good idea to require that a password be entered whenever someone is submitting a purchase or making a change to a public-facing profile (such as a Facebook profile).

If you use cookies to control the session experience or to keep items in a shopping cart, it is important to test that the cookies are working on a variety of different phones. If you have mobile analytics in place, you should be able to find out what types of mobile devices are accessing your website the most. Then you can simply run tests on those types of handsets to ensure that everything is working correctly. If cookies are not working, the system can be changed to pass session variables in URLs instead of within cookies, but you must be careful to ensure that the URLs do not exceed the maximum length that the devices will handle.

 Tip

URL length is measured in bytes, and most mobile phones and browsers can handle a URL length of more than 100KB, which is quite long. Keep in mind, though, that incredibly long URLs can hinder load time and make adding bookmarks difficult.

Mobile Malware and Viruses

Mobile viruses and malware also threaten the efficacy of mobile marketing because they put doubt in the minds of consumers, making them question whether to trust your company or the content you are sending. Until recently, the only groups that were highly concerned with mobile viruses were the antivirus software companies, whose "fears" were motivated mostly by their desire to sell mobile antivirus software.

All types of viruses and malware exploit operating systems. Viruses and malware are much easier to create and spread on traditional computers (desktop and laptop systems) because there are relatively few operating systems. However, in the mobile world, it is much more difficult to write a virus that will affect a large portion of phones because so many different operating systems are available.

As the number of operating systems begins to consolidate and open-source operating systems become more common, the risk of mobile viruses and malware increases. A review of the different virus-related terminology is included here:

- **Malware**—An umbrella term for any malicious software, including viruses, Trojans, worms, and spyware.

- **Virus**—Code that inserts itself into another program and replicates when the host software runs. Viruses vary in potency from the relatively benign to the catastrophically destructive.

- **Trojan**—Otherwise known as a Trojan horse, this is a program that purports to be something the user would want to download, but actually harbors malicious code or viruses. In the mobile world, Trojans are usually masked as wallpapers, ringtones, or applications. It is important to note that sometimes Trojans attach themselves to legitimate programs and are installed when the legitimate program is installed.

- **Worm**—Worms are self-replicating viruses that automatically spread themselves across a network, usually taking advantage of a user's contacts or address book on an infected device. Worms can also spread via Bluetooth or WiFi.

- **Spyware**—Spyware is software that runs in the background of an operating system to collect and send private information about a mobile user's behavior to an unauthorized party. Information including private call logs, text messages, and picture messages can be distributed to a third party. Spyware infections can bring an otherwise healthy system to its knees because each spyware program is actually a small application that not only violates the user's privacy, but also hogs system resources from other legitimate applications.

Mobile viruses are a growing problem that threatens the efficacy of mobile marketing as an industry. As with viruses on traditional computers, mobile viruses can overwrite or delete system files, install corrupted applications, block antivirus software, block memory, or provide remote access to a user's phone. Mobile viruses are unique, in that they can be spread via a broader range of technology, including SMS, MMS, Bluetooth, WiFi, downloadable applications, and email. They can stop handsets from working properly or at all. Figure 13.2 shows the results of one such mobile virus.

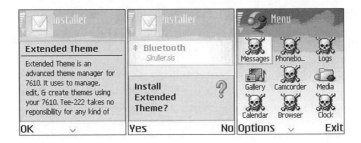

Figure 13.2   *Mobile viruses are a growing concern for mobile phone users because viruses can masquerade as legitimate add-ons, such as wallpapers, themes, or ringtones.*

Mobile Privacy and Spam Laws

Although regulations can make mobile marketing more complicated, they are very necessary. Unregulated and unrestricted mobile marketing practices pose a serious threat to mobile communication. As mobile marketers, we must do what we can to preserve the creditability and trust for the mobile channel and technology so that we can continue to benefit from it in the future. If we do a good job encouraging the right type of regulations and best practices, we will be able to bolster the medium and protect its long-term value. Strengthening the channel will also encourage the development of new, better technology. On the other hand, if regulations are ignored or the wrong regulations are put in place, we could be placing our companies and our customers at risk.

The following sections provide more specific information about international mobile privacy and spam laws; important agencies, governmental bodies, and documents; and companies that can provide services to integrate with your mobile marketing campaigns to ensure that your customers' privacy is respected.

United States and North America

- **Federal Trade Commission (FCC)**—The FTC and state attorneys general are in place to curb unfair and deceptive trade practices. Some of the laws and regulations that they pass apply to mobile marketing campaigns. The general guideline is that all material terms and conditions of the offer must be "clearly and conspicuously" disclosed to the consumer prior to the buying decision.

- **Federal Communications Commission (FCC)**—The FCC is an independent U.S. government agency, reporting directly to Congress, that regulates interstate and international communications by radio, television, wire, satellite, and cable. The FCC controls what information about mobile customers can be shared and how, but the guidelines have yet to be passed. The FCC has allowed mobile carriers to release data about their subscribers, but only upon the individual consent of the consumer. The FCC also has passed regulations that prohibit the use of autodialers to call or send text messages to mobile phone numbers. Many states have their own rules and regulations on these and other telemarketing issues. The FCC also regulates Voice Over IP (VoIP) and phone number porting (keeping the same phone number even if the user switches carriers), which both could affect a mobile marketing campaign. The FCC also prevents telemarketers from calling cellphone numbers.

- **Telephone Consumer Protection Act (TCPA)**—Congress passed the TCPA in 1991, restricting the use of automatic dialing systems, artificial or prerecorded voice messages, SMS text messages received by cellphones, and the use of fax machines to send unsolicited advertisements. Advertisers are not permitted to make solicitation calls before 8am and after 9pm local time, and may not ever make telemarketing calls using autodialers and voice recordings.

- **Telemarketing Sales Rule (TSR) and Amended Telemarketing Sales Rule**—The FTC established the TSR in 1995 but significantly amended it in 2004 as the ATSR. The most important thing this bill did was establish the National Do Not Call Registry. It is important to note that the rules established in this act cover all acts of telemarketing, whether the conversation is initiated by the telemarketer or the customer. This can come into play if you are using mobile marketing to drive phone calls to complete sales or make customer acquisitions.

- **Do Not Call Registry (DNC)**—Created in 2003, the DNC is a list of individuals' residences and phone numbers that would prefer not to receive telemarketing calls. It is illegal for solicitors to call these phone numbers. Business lines cannot be added to the registry. Charities and surveys are exempt, as are companies that you are doing business with or whom you have requested information from in the past three months.

- **CAN-SPAM**—This act was passed in 2003 to restrict commercial email by ensuring that mechanisms for opting out or contacting the sender directly are included. This law covers email on the traditional computer and on the mobile phone, but does not cover text messaging or other types of mobile messaging. It would be possible to add a Do Not Email Registry under this law, but the FTC determined that it would be too difficult to verify email account information, so this was not feasible.

- **M-SPAM**—This is a proposed U.S. Senate bill that would criminalize mobile SMS spamming in the same way CAN-SPAM criminalized email spam. As it is currently proposed, it would empower the FTC and the FCC to curb unwanted text messages in the United States. The proposed legislation might currently be too stringent, because it suggests the creation of a Do Not Contact type of registry, to block all text message marketing to some phone numbers. As it is proposed now, the Do Not Contact Registry will, by default, include all the phone numbers on the current Do Not Call Registry. This would prevent mobile marketers from ever sending text messages to those numbers, even if consumers later wanted to opt into a campaign.

  Many members of the mobile marketing community hope that a separate Do Not Text list will be created rather than grouping telemarketing protection and text message protection into the same list, because the two are very different. Alternately, some members of the community believe that any kind of list that blocks certain phone numbers from being contacted via text message would be too restrictive. In fact, some members of the mobile marketing community believe that a list such as this might actually prevent users from getting communication that they have explicitly opted into and actively want, such as SMS search from Google or Cha-Cha.

- **Children's Online Protection Act (COPA)**—The Children's Online Protection Act, otherwise known as COPA, prevents companies from collecting or storing information about people under 13 years old. This is important for mobile marketing, as many contests, sweepstakes, and other participatory initiatives are for products typically targeted at people in that protected age group.

- **Mobile Marketing Association (MMA)**—The MMA is an international group of mobile carriers, content providers, marketers, and other interested parties that helps establish the best practices in the industry. Although the MMA does have international representation, it is based in the United States, and most of its initiatives focus there first. None of the group's privacy guidelines are binding or enforceable, but the MMA is frequently referenced as providing accepted standards when clear-cut laws are not present. The MMA frequently publishes and updates mobile marketing best practice documentation, as well as industry reviews and articles.

- **Direct Marketing Association (DMA)**—The DMA is an international organization based in the United States that helps develop and guide direct marketing best practices. Although its focus is not exclusively mobile, the DMA is quite interested in the development of and adherence to privacy-related standards in the mobile marketing industry. The DMA has published a variety of articles, briefs, and codes of conduct related to mobile marketing.

United Kingdom

- **Data Protection Act (DPA)**—The DPA is the main legislation that protects personal information of individuals in the United Kingdom. Parliament passed this act in 1998, and it essentially limits how personal information, including email addresses and phone numbers, are used, processed, and protected in the United Kingdom. According to Wikipedia, it has the following eight principal requirements (many of these requirements are also echoed by the EC Directive, which sets forth similar expectations for all countries marketing throughout most of Europe):

    - Data may be used only for the specific purposes for which it was collected.

    - Data must not be disclosed to other parties without the consent of the individual whom it is about.

    - Individuals have a right of access to the information held about them.

    - Personal information may be kept for no longer than is necessary and must be kept up-to-date.

    - Personal information may not be sent outside the European Economic Area unless the individual whom it is about has consented or adequate protection is in place.

    - All entities that process personal information must register with the Information Commissioner's Office.

    - Entities holding personal information are required to have adequate security measures in place. Those include technical measures (such as firewalls) and organizational measures (such as staff training).

    - Subjects have the right to have *factually incorrect* information corrected.

- **Privacy and Electronic Communications Regulation (PECR)**—PECR created a directive known as the EC Directive that requires marketers to have opt-in permission or a prior commercial relationship with a person before they send a mobile marketing message. Marketers are also required to identify the sender of the message, provide a valid reply address, and make it easy for recipients to unsubscribe from future communication. The PECR does not require that Bluetooth marketing be opted into.

- **Computer Misuse Act**—This act makes it illegal for someone to knowingly use a computer to secure access to programs or data that is not lawfully theirs or to make unauthorized modifications to computer files or programs. It also makes it illegal for people to impersonate someone in email, chat, or a social networking site. The act was essentially put in place to make hacking and the creation and intentional spreading of viruses and malware illegal. Prescribed penalties range from a fine to five years in jail. The act does an adequate job of addressing digital privacy issues in the United Kingdom.

- **Information Commissioner's Office (ICO)**—The ICO is an independent agency in the United Kingdom, set up partially to protect citizens from unauthorized collection and distribution of personal information. The ICO is in charge of education, enforcement, and resolution of issues related to the Data Protection Act and the Privacy and Electronic Communications Regulations. This includes preventing unwanted solicitation via telemarketing, email, or mobile communication.

Important Mobile Agencies

The bodies below are official groups that help regulate and set guidelines about what is acceptable for mobile marketers. While none of these agencies have the ability to enforce their guidelines or Best Practices, governments look to them when developing laws and trying to police the market.

The Groupe Speciale Mobile (GSMA)

In 1982, the Confederation of European Posts and Telecommunications (CEPT) formed the Groupe Speciale Mobile (GSM) to design a European mobile technology. Over time, this has evolved to become the worldwide authority on mobile communication. The mission of the GMS is to "create value for operators and the mobile industry in the provision of services for the benefit of end users, so that those users can readily and affordably connect to and use the services they desire, anywhere, anytime." The group has led the way to develop worldwide initiatives to advance the adoption and development of new mobile technology to enhance communication and improve worldwide access to information. The GMS also helps represent the mobile technology industry to mobile regulators and policy makers, ensuring that mobile carriers, consumers, and content providers are protected evenly. The group has also created a series of world-renowned conferences, including the annual Mobile World Congress in Barcelona.

In addition, the GSM has created best practice documentation to help carriers respect and protect the privacy of their subscribers.

The Mobile Marketing Association (MMA)

In 1996, the Mobile Marketing Association was formed to help stimulate growth in mobile marketing by encouraging communication among mobile carriers, content producers, and handset manufacturers. According to the MMA mission statement, the group is:

> An action-oriented association designed to clear obstacles to market development, to establish guidelines and best practices for sustainable growth, and to evangelize the mobile channel for use by brands and third party content providers. MMA members include agencies, advertisers, hand held device manufacturers, wireless operators and service providers, retailers, software and services providers, as well as any company focused on the potential of marketing via the mobile channel.

The MMA describes its goals in the following terms:

- Providing an industry forum to meet, discuss, plan, and work cooperatively to resolve key industry issues

- Bringing together industry-wide global and regional work groups that focus on industry initiatives

- Providing representation for the mobile marketing industry to major legislative bodies worldwide

- Sharing perspectives on mobile marketing among Europe, Asia, Latin America, Africa, and the United States

- Fueling peer-to-peer interaction through seminars, conferences, and events

- Developing metrics for measuring ad delivery and consumer response

- Developing open and compatible mobile marketing technical and creative standards

- Defining and publishing mobile marketing best practices and guidelines on privacy, ad delivery, and ad measurement

- Providing the value and effectiveness of mobile marketing to advertisers, agencies, and consumers

- Serving as the key advocate on behalf of the mobile marketing industry

The World Wide Web Consortium (W3C)

The World Wide Web Consortium (W3C) is a nonprofit organization that creates specifications, guidelines, software, and tools to aid in the development of a better Internet and, in their words, "to lead the Web to its full potential." It has developed a variety of standards for coding languages, including mobile-compliant XHTML and WML.

The Direct Marketing Association (DMA)

The Direct Marketing Association is the leading global trade association of business and nonprofit organizations using and supporting multichannel direct marketing tools and techniques.

The DMA advocates standards for responsible marketing, promotes relevance as the key to reaching consumers with desirable offers, and provides cutting-edge research, education, and networking opportunities to improve results throughout the end-to-end direct marketing process. Founded in 1917, the DMA today represents more than 3,400 companies from dozens of vertical industries in the United States and 48 other nations, including half of the Fortune 100 companies, as well as nonprofit organizations.

Mobile Marketing Legal and Privacy Resources

- GSMA Europe's Safer Mobile Use—
www.gsmeurope.org/safer_mobile/index.shtml

- European Framework for Safer Mobile Use by Younger Teenagers and Children—www.gsmeurope.org/safer_mobile/european.shtml

- Safe Mobile Use by Younger Teenagers & Children, Implementation Report—
www.gsmeurope.org/documents/gsma_implementation_report.pdf

- The Privacy and Electronic Communications Regulations (EC Directive)—www.opsi.gov.uk/si/si2003/20032426.htm

- GSMA Mobile SPAM Code of Conduct—www.gsmworld.com/ documents/mobile_spam.pdf

- Guidance for Marketers on the Privacy and Electronic Communications Regulations of 2003 (the EC Directive)— www.ico.gov.uk/upload/documents/library/privacy_and_electronic/det ailed_specialist_guides/guidance_part_1_for_marketers_v3.1_081007.p df

- DMA-UK Guidelines for Bluetooth Marketing—www.consumer-preference.com/2007/10/bluetooth-marketing-ico-removes.html

MMA Mobile Privacy Code of Conduct

The Mobile Marketing Association Privacy Advisory Committee launched a code of conduct for mobile marketers in 2003 that covers six basic privacy concerns: choice, control, customization, consideration, constraint, and confidentiality. A summary of these six basic privacy concerns can be found at www.cellular.co.za/regulatory/code_of_conduct_for_mobile_marke.htm and is paraphrased here.

- **Choice**—Consumers must be given the option to opt-into all mobile messaging programs. Segmentation-based marketing is prohibited unless consumers opted-into the program.

- **Control**—Consumers must be able to easily opt-out of any mobile messaging program. If your program has multiple message strings, you must provide an opt-out option in each one.

- **Customization**—Since mobile messaging campaigns are most effective when targeted based on the consumers' interests, follow-up communi-cations with consumers should be confined to those areas specifically requested by the consumer.

- **Consideration**—You must offer the consumer something of value in return for agreeing to receive your messages.

- **Constraint**—You must manage the number of messages an individual consumer receives. Consumers must have the option to limit the num-ber of messages they receive even further if they wish.

- **Confidentiality**—You must not share consumer information gathered during your marketing with other companies except to provide prod-ucts and services requested by the consumer.

14

The International Mobile Marketing Landscape

Without a doubt, mobile marketing is an international phenomenon. Mobile Web traffic continues to grow worldwide, but not all markets are ready to receive sophisticated Web-based mobile marketing campaigns. Figures 14.1 and 14.2 show mobile advertising spending and mobile search advertising spending worldwide for the past three years, as well as anticipated spending for the next three years. Although most of this book focuses on mobile marketing strategy in North America and Europe, your understanding of the differences among the various regions can play a crucial role in the success of your mobile campaign if you are focusing on an international audience.

Mobile Advertising Spending Worldwide, by Format, 2007-2012 (millions)

	2007	2008	2009	2010	2011	2012
Mobile message advertising*	$2,560	$4,200	$6,440	$9,260	$11,960	$14,173
Mobile display advertising**	$52	$142	$338	$629	$945	$1,203
Mobile search advertising***	$83	$244	$597	$1,290	$2,345	$3,773
Total	$2,695	$4,586	$7,375	$11,179	$15,250	$19,149

Note: numbers may not add up to total due to rounding; *spending on placement in text messages, includes direct spending on message campaigns as well as spending on promotional coverage of end-user messaging costs; **spending on display banners, links or icons placed on WAP, mobile HTML sites or embedded in mobile applications such as maps or entertainment services (e.g. games or video); ***spending on sponsored display ads and text links that appear alongside mobile search results, as well as spending on audio ads played to mobile phone callers making a directory inquiry
Source: eMarketer, March 2008

092628   www.**eMarketer**.com

Figure 14.1 *Mobile advertising spending worldwide. Chart courtesy of eMarketer.*

Worldwide Mobile Search Advertising Spending, by Region, 2007-2012 (millions)

	2007	2008	2009	2010	2011	2012
US	$34.5	$107.4	$241.8	$530.5	$910.2	$1,484.2
Asia-Pacific	$26.0	$72.0	$189.9	$372.8	$732.4	$1,160.0
Western Europe	$18.4	$52.0	$140.5	$339.7	$614.1	$968.2
Rest of World	$4.4	$12.4	$24.4	$47.0	$88.6	$160.9
Worldwide	**$83.3**	**$243.7**	**$596.6**	**$1,289.9**	**$2,345.2**	**$3,773.2**

Note: includes spending on sponsored display ads and text links that appear alongside mobile search results, as well as spending on audio ads played to mobile phone callers making a directory inquiry; Western Europe includes France, Germany, Italy, Spain, UK; Asia-Pacific includes China, India, Japan, South Korea; numbers may not add up to total due to rounding
Source: eMarketer, February 2008

092113   www.**eMarketer**.com

Figure 14.2 *Mobile search advertising spending worldwide. Chart courtesy of eMarketer.*

Regional deployment of technology and mobile network infrastructure are important considerations when launching a mobile campaign. Also, cultural acceptance
and understanding of different mobile marketing channels can make or break a
campaign, so research must be done to ensure that your campaign will succeed.
This chapter offers a high-level outline of the key differences among regions and
how you can leverage those disparities to make the most of your mobile marketing
dollars.

 Note

> Statistics and methodologies vary dramatically between the different report-
> ing services. Use the charts and numbers in this chapter as a guide more
> than anything else.

Mobile Marketing in East Asia

Mobile marketing in East Asia is significantly different than mobile marketing in
the rest of the world. Figure 14.3 shows mobile advertising spending in the
Asia–Pacific region. The mobile programming language, WAP, was slow to take off
in Europe and the United States but was quickly embraced in Asia. The quick adoption in East Asia was likely the result of the high level of communication between
the mobile carriers, device manufacturers, and the mobile content creators. In most
other countries in the world, carriers did little to create incentive for Web content
creators to build out WAP content, so there was a dearth of understanding or
enthusiasm.

Mobile Advertising Spending in Asia-Pacific, by Segment, 2007-2012 (millions)						
	2007	**2008**	**2009**	**2010**	**2011**	**2012**
Mobile message advertising	$700	$1,229	$1,827	$3,100	$4,309	$5,320
Mobile display advertising	$12	$36	$91	$182	$293	$397
Mobile search advertising	$26	$72	$190	$373	$732	$1,160
Total		**$738**	**$1,336**	**$2,108**	**$3,655**	**$5,334**	**$6,877**

*Note: China, India, Japan, South Korea; numbers may not add up to total
due to rounding*
Source: eMarketer, March 2008

092636   www.**eMarketer**.com

Figure 14.3 *Mobile advertising spending in the Asia–Pacific region. Chart courtesy
of eMarketer.*

In East Asia, the WAP programming language was primarily used to create separate, mobile-specific websites on dotMobi domains that are represented as example-domain.mobi. In many instances, companies would have two domains, one traditional domain, and one dotMobi domain. This is quite different from the rest of the world, where WAP and thus dotMobi domains were slower to take off.

The debate about the dotMobi domain still rages on in the international sphere. Some people believe that a separate mobile experience on a separate domain extension is desirable, while others believe that the separate domain extension only causes problems and confusion. Many companies and individuals invested a lot of money in the dotMobi domain extension and in the development of dotMobi sites.

In East Asia, mobile access to the Web is considered fundamentally different from traditional access to the Web. Many users have email addresses that they use solely on their mobile phones (a system called mobile i-map), and businesses commonly have mobile-specific sites. In the rest of the world, especially in Europe and the Unites States, most Web content that can be accessed on a mobile phone is an extension of the existing Web instead of something fundamentally different.

One element of the accelerated adoption rate in East Asia relates to lack of choice. Much of the population in countries such as China and Taiwan do not have Internet access at home, so if consumers are interested in finding information, they must use their phone to do it. The quick spread of mobile marketing methodologies in East Asia can also be attributed to the size of the cohesive mobile landscape of these countries. It is much easier to create a common paradigm across large countries such as China, or countries with unified mobile standards such as Japan, than it is to do the same thing in a multitude of smaller countries that are geographically proximate but have different cultures, languages, carriers, and governments, such as in Europe.

3G access accounts for more than 80% of the mobile market in Japan, and carriers there are quickly deploying 4G technology. China owns the world's largest traditional telecommunication networks, but they are less advanced in mobile telecom, with a large portion of subscribers still relying on GSM networks. In 2008, the Chinese government set up and deployed many 3G networks for commercial launch in anticipation of the Olympic games, but many Chinese service providers are testing LTE technology instead. The Chinese government finalized the issuance of 3G licenses in the first week of 2009, and this should help advance the mobile marketing opportunity in China, but Chinese carriers may opt to focus on LTE and largely skip the deployment of 3G technology.

Prepaid mobile service is quite common in China, where the mobile networks are less developed. Prepaid mobile services are less common in Japan and Singapore. Singapore's first prepaid mobile network launched as recently as 2009, and it is targeted at tourists and business travelers. The service offers three-day unlimited data and voice packages for about $12.

Companies that want to launch mobile marketing campaigns in East Asia must be aware of rules and regulations regarding this type of marketing. In 2005, however, the Ministry of the Information Industry (MII) in China set up regulations about sending unsolicited text messages and disclosure requirements for companies who enroll customers in subscription services that have a recurring cost to the customer. Carriers enforce these regulations, but many worry that text messages that include content that the government deems inappropriate (possibly including dissenting political opinions) may be filtered, too.

In the Asia–Pacific region, there is a much more prominent demographic gap between those accessing the mobile Web on their phones. People under age 25 are more than twice as likely to access the Internet on their phones as their older counterparts. The younger age group is also twice as likely to have sent a picture message (MMS).

Mobile display advertising is more popular in Japan and China than anywhere else except the United States. More than 10% of online marketing budgets in Japan is already being spent on mobile ads, and this is expected to be worth more than $1 billion by 2011.

In Japan, a uniform platform standard called iMode, makes it easier for marketers to create and display ads across a variety of different devices, without having to duplicate the effort to make the same marketing work across a number of different platforms.

Studies show that 54% of Japanese mobile users consume ads, and 44% actively click on mobile ad links. Many mobile carriers have launched their own mobile advertising arm, such as D2 in Japan or Across in South Korea. When asked about the future of mobile advertising in China, Alvin Graylin, the CEO of China's largest mobile service provider, mInfo, said:

> "My prediction is that, within five to six years, mobile marketing will overtake online marketing in China because the user base will be so much more massive. It's not far-fetched when you look at 800 million Chinese mobile subscribers, compared with 300 million accessing the Internet through a PC."

Quick Response (QR) codes were actually developed by a car manufacturer in Tokyo. They are small, square dot matrices that can be scanned by a camera phone (like a barcode) and used to bring up text, phone numbers, ready-to-send text messages (SMS), or a phone number (see Figure 14.4). These codes can appear in a periodical, a flyer, billboards or just about any other printed medium. The use of QR codes is much more prevalent in Japan, China, North Korea, and South Korea than it is in the rest of the world, partially because most mobile phones in these countries come with QR code reading software already on the phone. They are particularly useful as a substitute for digitally typing information into a cell phone because many characters in Asian languages require 2.5 keystrokes to represent on a phone. More than 40% of mobile subscribers in Japan use their mobile phones to regularly scan QR codes in ads.

Figure 14.4 *QR codes can be scanned from a magazine, newspaper, billboards (as shown here) or other other advertisements with a camera phone to store information. Photo courtesy of Nicolas Raoul via Wikimedia Creative Commons License 3.0, a freely licensed media repository.*

SMS and MMS are also popular throughout the Asian continent, but SMS is between 35% and 75% more common than MMS (multimedia messaging). The prevelance of SMS marketing is very high; SMS is being used by 93% of subscribers under 25 in Singapore, 86% in Thailand, and 83% in Taiwan.

Mobile music has been important in China for some time because many carriers are offering mobile music services to their subscribers to help monetize their services. At the 3GSM World Congress in 2005, Wang Jianzhou, CEO of China Mobile, said, "The total revenue of mobile music in China last year surpassed the entire revenue of the traditional music industry. A single song was downloaded 15 million times over China Mobile's network in the last six months, a rate 15 times higher than a typical best-selling music CD."

Mobile gaming is also important in Japan; depending on your target market, it could be the cornerstone of a successful mobile marketing campaign. Whereas mobile gaming applications are all the rage in the Western world, mobile gaming websites are more common in East Asia. A Japanese survey of 15- to 29-year-olds in 2008 revealed that 79% play games on their mobile phones and 31% would be willing to pay a reasonable monthly price to play the mobile games. Payment for games may not be necessary, though: Mobile games can also be subsidized or sponsored with mobile marketing so that the game can be offered for free and still generate revenue. Role-playing games, puzzles, and table games are the most popular. Surprisingly, more women than men play mobile games.

East Asia's total interactive market will probably always be smaller than that of the United States, but its mobile component will be proportionally larger. Mobile technology is highly ingrained in the East Asian culture, and the people are quick to adopt and test new mobile technologies. Mobile video and mobile social networking are common in the region and offer great opportunities for marketing, branding, and customer engagement. Also, a program called i-mode FeliCa allows people in Japan to insert chips into their phones to turn their handsets into a payment device that can be swiped over a sensor at a point of purchase, for use much like a credit card. (In some cases, it can even be used as a home or office key.)

Mobile Marketing in Southeast Asia

The Southeast Asian markets lag behind the East Asian markets in terms of mobile broadband communication and the prevalence of mobile marketing. In this region, prepaid mobile service is popular, as is text message communication, because of its comparative cost savings over voice communication. Multi-SIM use, whereby users will have multiple SIM cards or phones that they use at different parts of the day to get the best calling rate is also common.

In Southeast Asia, the separation between the exclusively mobile Web and the exclusively traditional Web is still present but less prevalent. Mobile penetration rates in the Philippines are around 77%, but the penetration of broadband Internet communication is low, at around only 2%. In Malaysia, adoption of both types of communication is higher, with mobile penetration at 100% and traditional broadband communication at about 15%.

Mobile number portability (MNP) is a system that allows mobile users to keep the same phone number when switching from one mobile carrier to another, and it has been a major debate in this region. The debate still continues in the Philippines, where the government indefinitely postponed plans for MNP in 2008. In this case, the difficulty in transitioning to portable mobile phone numbers is due not to problems with voice communication, but to the difficulty of routing the massive amount of text messages that are being sent in India through a central hub and then out to the various carrier networks.

In Southeast Asia, mobile marketing is regulated but not generally well enforced, and is targeted at carriers instead of independent content creators. Malaysia has no major regulation, but in the Philippines, the National Telecommunications Commission (NTC) revokes the mobile license of any operator found guilty of breaking its guidelines on unsolicited broadcast messaging via SMS.

In Vietnam in 2009, the Vietnam Computer Emergency Response Team (VNCERT) issued regulations to reduce the number of spam SMS sent in the country. According to these regulations, networks must label outgoing bulk advertising texts as such, and customers must be given the chance to refuse the text before receiving it. Companies that send marketing SMS messages must register their content and notify subscribers about the costs of sending SMS to their premium shortcodes.

Although there have been large initiatives for the deployment of 3G networks in Southeast Asia (since 2005 in Malaysia), only 5% of Malaysia is on 3G networks and that number is even lower in the Philippines. SMS communication is considered an effective alternative for spreading news and information quickly, without the use of fast networks. Because SMS is so well accepted, it is also more appealing as a channel for mobile marketing. The spread of 3G technology is expected to push the growth of VoIP and mobile technology and adoption, but this will likely take a few more years.

Mobile Marketing in India

The situation in India is very different from that in the rest of Asia, so it should be considered separately. No major governmental regulations address mobile marketing, but a number of hurdles that are deeply rooted in the government and the culture that must be understood to really determine how mobile marketing can be used most effectively in India.

Infrastructural and cultural barriers have stifled the growth of broadband adoption and computing in India. Although the adoption rates for broadband computing are high in major cities, the rest of the country lags behind. In some cases, the electricity needed to power computers can be unstable, even in the most progressive states. Corporations such as Microsoft and Nokia are working with the Indian government and nongovernmental organizations to teach computer skills to all primary schools. This type of enculturation, unprecedented in India, should help drive demand for computing as a whole and especially for mobile computing because mobile handsets are cheaper and easier to get online than traditional computers or laptops.

India, like other countries with infrastructural barriers, will largely skip the copper-wired means of broadband communication because it is so prohibitively expensive for both users and service providers, especially in more rural areas of the country. Instead, wireless broadband will be the norm, and people will access it through mobile phones or laptops with wireless data cards or dongles. However, this will happen only if the government cooperates with telecom providers to hasten the availability of 3G communication.

The mobile penetration rate in India is still low, at only 27%, but the market has been growing at around 50% per year. It is expected to continue this rapid growth over the next two years. So far, this growth is all happening on the 2G network. The Indian government has not yet allocated the 3G network spectrum, but the auctions are expected to happen in 2010. Surprisingly, India's per-minute mobile rates are the lowest in the world, and handset prices are also very low. Some service providers even offer incentives such as a lifetime of free incoming calls for a one-time payment of about $21. But the lack of 3G penetration has slowed the adoption and sale of smart phones, which has prevented growth in access to the mobile Web.

Two official bodies must agree on decisions that involve the telecom industry: the Telecom Regulatory Authority of India (TRAI) and the Department of Telecom-munications (DoT), which is housed under the Ministry of Communications and Information Technology. The Cellular Operators Association of India (COAI) represents the mobile carriers' interests but is frequently at odds with the decisions of the TRIA and the DoT.

In general, the Indian government is reluctant to work with mobile carriers and tra-ditional ISPs. This resistance is probably to protect the profits of traditional cable-wire telecoms from further erosion and to provide fair competition. Unfortunately, the Indian government has even banned some types of VoIP, which can be seen as a serious detriment to a country that is trying to advance the adoption of new tech-nology and improve communication and education country-wide.

As a result of the many technological stumbling blocks, mobile marketing in India lacks the sophistication of similar marketing in the rest of the Asian continent. To date, mobile marketing in India has focused on simple text and picture messages, but the recent governmental approval of the operation of mobile virtual network operators (MVNOs) and the future deployment of 3G and WiMax networks prom-ises to change that situation quickly.

In terms of mobile marketing, the most effective channel is still text messaging. Before you send a message, you must check your list of recipients against the National Do Not Disturb (NDND) Registry. This registry, created by the TRAI in

2007, makes it illegal to send marketing messages to subscribers who are on the list and have not opted in to your marketing communication.

Mobile gaming is also popular in India, beating out email for top use of the mobile Web by 5%. This is likely a result of the lower percentage of people with email addresses in the country, but it may indicate a predilection toward more graphical interactive marketing when 3G networks are in place. Because of the less-capable mobile handsets, mobile gaming in India focuses on simple Web-based games and puzzles instead of downloadable applications. In many cases, there are display advertising opportunities on mobile game sites or within the mobile games themselves.

Mobile Marketing in the Middle East

Mobile penetration in some Middle Eastern countries is quite high, with countries such as Israel boasting more than 125% (people have 1+ phone[s] or SIM cards to get the best value out of various carriers pricing packages). Other countries have lower penetration rates that are still impressive: 85% in Turkey and 80% in Jordan. Recent increases in competition across the region have driven the cost of mobile service down and the level of service up.

Most Middle Eastern countries have instituted policies to drive competition within the market. Liberalization, privatization and the increase in competition have created a great benefit for the mobile community. Although most countries in the Middle East are still wrestling with more technological challenges, such as the desire for mobile number portability (MNP) and the potential to open the market to mobile virtual network operators (MVNOs), there is great promise.

The rapid growth and adoption of mobile phones has been achieved largely on 2 and 2.5G networks. Only about 25% of subscribers are on high-end phones because of the lack of 3G connections. The lack of rich mobile content available makes more expensive phones unnecessary. Mobile personalization services such as ringtones, logos, and desktops are popular, but they are downloaded over 2G networks. Mobile banking and news services are growing rapidly, and many interactive agencies are partnering with content and application service providers to secure technology and delivery capabilities now.

Direct marketing as a whole is less common in the Middle East than it is in Europe, and this may give mobile marketing companies that provide a more personal or tailored marketing message a serious leg up over the competition. More targeted communication should be approached very cautiously and directed exclusively at people who have opted in, to avoid offending potential customers who are not as used to such targeted messages.

Mobile Marketing in Africa

Africa is expected to be a leader in the growth of mobile broadband subscriptions from 2008 through 2012, and is expected to more than double its rate of mobile data consumption by 2014.

Some 3G networks were initially deployed in Africa in 2005. Now more than 30 operators are providing service throughout the major cities and are expanding their reach into the more rural regions of the continent. Despite the deployment of these networks, you still need a PC to reach broadband speeds, so network operators and private businesses have began opening Internet cafes that are run largely on cellular connectivity.

The situation in Africa is much like the situations in Southeast Asia and India, where access to traditional fixed-line Internet is prohibitively expensive or impossible for most people to access regularly, but mobile phones and access to data have seen a large uptake. Across the continent, 3G subscribers are quickly outpacing fixed-line broadband subscribers, and many are using data cards to connect to the Internet wirelessly on laptops or mobile phones.

Before the advent of mobile communication, many people in more remote areas in Africa had no home phone lines or computers. Mobile voice and mobile data have become the default means of communication. In more remote regions in Africa (and also in India), the mobile boom has created a large informal market for reselling mobile airtime: One or two people in a village purchase a cell phone and charge other villagers to use it.

Many other challenges threaten to stall the growth of mobile penetration. In Africa, the cost of mobile handsets is comparatively high, making having your own mobile device more of a luxury than it is in other places. Also, unstable electricity has made the development of stable mobile networks very expensive; operators need their own power generators to effectively serve their customer base. Those costs are passed directly to the consumer, increasing the cost of mobile voice and data service. To address these infrastructural problems, some companies, such as Erickson, have begun to install solar stations for recharging the cell phones and base stations.

Prepaid mobile access is the norm in Africa, and mobile marketing is still focused on text message marketing. However, advances in the technology and penetration are spawning new services such as micropayments, prepaid recharging, single-rate inter-regional roaming, and the uptake of m-commerce applications.

Mobile Marketing in Central and South America

Mobile penetration in Central and South America is well above average, with at least three countries at greater than 100% penetration. High prices and a lack of competition have stifled wired broadband access, so mobile phones have overtaken fixed lines in service. Paraguay leads the trend, with 10 mobile phones for every fixed line in service. GSM is the preferred technology by far, with a market share of around 69%, but Latin America is also at the forefront of global WiMAX deployment. Licensing of the 3G spectrum in Latin American countries is much cheaper when compared to the rest of the world, and the advancement of these technologies will further open the region to more sophisticated mobile marketing channels.

Countries in Central and South America generally have many more mobile carriers than other countries of a similar size, making mobile marketing challenging. No uniformity in advertising standards exists, making mobile marketing difficult. Working with the multitude of carriers in these regions can require diplomacy and patience.

Unfortunately, the mobile handset technology available lags behind that of other regions, so WAP sites and mobile Web access should be downplayed in your mobile marketing campaign. Mobile SEO is not yet relevant. Standard text and picture message marketing is more likely to be effective because mobile Web traffic is so low that content creators are not incentivized to create compelling content, and advertisers are not compelled to pay for mobile advertisement. Nonvoice features on the phone, such as text messaging, picture messaging, Bluetooth, and infrared, are used more heavily and are considered more important when choosing a phone.

In South America, mobile marketing is being used to foster interaction and create communities around well-established brands. The region is seeing growth in the consumption of mobile music and videos. Mobile ticketing, proximity marketing, and QR code marketing may be in the future for Latin America, but marketers will have to work diligently with carriers to make these possibilities realities.

Mobile Web marketing may not be as effective in South America, but mobile couponing and QR codes are well received, and mobile advertising is growing in acceptance. According to an article by the MMA in 2008:

> "Latin America continues to be a global leader in consumer adoption of mobile services," said Terence Reis, managing director, LATAM of the MMA. "Nearly two-thirds of mobile users in Latin America are at least moderately interested in mobile marketing and a quarter express strong interest in marketing programs."

Mobile Marketing in North America

Differences in infrastructure and the penetration of high-speed mobile networks cause noticeable differences between the use of mobile phones in the United States, Canada and Mexico. Over all though, the launch of the iPhone has done a lot to shape mobile marketing in North America, most notably making downloadable applications mainstream, vastly improving the mobile Web experience, and making streaming music and video a simple reality for many subscribers. The iPhone has drastically changed the expectations many North Americans have for their phone, but iPhones still make up only about 8% of the market. Although iPhones are now available in more than 88 countries worldwide, the acceptance and fundamental shift in thinking that the device has caused is most notable in the United States.

The United States were the first to build a nationwide network of mobile towers, speeding the overall adoption of cell phones. Unfortunately, the towers that were built were equipped to handle only slower analog and digital signals instead of the faster 2 and 3G connections. Until recently, the slower network speeds have prevented many subscribers from using their phones for anything other than calls and text messages. Much work has been done to improve mobile networks in the United States: In 2009, the penetration of 3G in the United States reached the same level as in Western Europe, at 28%.

Mobile number portability (MNP) became a reality in the United States in 2005, but multi-SIM card use is not the norm. Some subscribers do have more than one phone, but rarely because they are trying to save money; usually their employer provides a work phone and they keep a personal phone, for use when they are off the clock. Mobile calling and data rates in the United States are on par with those of the rest of the world, but in Canada, rates for both are much higher, which is proving to be a great disincentive for the consumption of mobile content.

The other thing that has slowed the adoption of mobile marketing in the United States and Canada is the carriers. Different carriers offer different services. They include different browsers on their phones, with different capabilities to reach "off-deck" content. Marketers have no uniform set of standards to follow to create a predictable mobile marketing experience across the different carrier platforms.

The interactive nature of the U.S. marketing space means that the United States offers far more opportunities for cross-media efforts than any other country in the world. The United States is the largest single market for mobile advertising, even though it lags behind both Europe and Asia in terms of mobile penetration (see Figure 14.5). Mobile marketing is not as developed or ingrained in the U.S. market as it is in East Asia, but it has promise. In 2008, about 23% of mobile subscribers in the United States reported seeing an advertisement on their phone, and about half of those reported that they had responded at least once to a mobile advertisement. Simple text and picture messages may be ideal for other regions, but the North American audience is expecting a richer, integrated experience that loops their mobile phone into existing marketing campaigns.

US Mobile Internet Users, Mobile Search Users and Mobile Search Advertising Revenues, 2006-2011 (millions)

	2006	2007	2008	2009	2010	2011
Mobile Internet users	27.0	31.1	36.0	42.9	52.3	64.8
Mobile search users	20.3	23.3	28.8	35.1	43.9	55.8
Mobile search ad revenues*	$2.1	$13.5	$48.1	$155.7	$307.4	$713.7

*Note: *earned from sale of display or text listings alongside mobile search results*
Source: eMarketer, July 2007

085441   www.**eMarketer**.com

Figure 14.5 *Mobile users and revenue in the United States. Chart courtesy of eMarkerter.*

Although the United States currently leads in mobile traffic and in ad spending, it is significantly behind European countries such as Italy and Spain in terms of 3G penetration. In recent years, the number of Americans accessing the Internet from their phones has grown significantly, as has the number of people performing Internet searches from their mobile phones. Mobile search was already important in 2008, when all U.S. carriers began offering flat-rate, unlimited mobile data packages. The United States represents 68% of the worldwide mobile searching, and with flat-rate data pricing, there is no disincentive to search when information is needed. It will be crucial for mobile marketers working in North America to learn how to leverage mobile search and mobile search engines.

Carrier decks and carrier search still play some role in shaping the Web activity of mobile users in the United States, but this trend is likely on its way out. The percent of U.S. on-deck traffic went from 53.4% in the fourth quarter of 2007 to 36.91% in the fourth quarter of 2008, but until recently, some carriers made it difficult or impossible for their subscribers to access content on the off-deck Web. Instead, they kept them on their deck, where they could potentially make money from partner advertising.

Despite the relatively advanced nature of the mobile landscape in the United States, not all mobile marketing will be well received. Americans have a deeper concern for privacy, which makes the idea of mobile marketing unappealing to many. The younger demographics are less likely to be offended by mobile marketing messages, but to avoid ostracizing potential customers, you should keep your messages highly targeted and short. Mobile marketing is largely unregulated in the United States, but advertisers are expected to follow guidelines set forth by the Mobile Marketing Association (MMA).

There is a variety of legislation currently being debated in the United States that might soon create more clear guidelines and expectations for mobile marketers. The most notable is them is the m-SPAM act of 2009, which is actually an amendment to the CAN SPAM Act of 1993. While the CAN SPAM Act of 1993 set forth expectations for email marketing, the m-SPAM Act creates rules preventing unsolicited text messages, and outlining how text message marketing can be legally conducted in the United States.

It is usually best to gauge the tolerance and level of mobile engagement that your North American audience will have by launching first with a mobile call to action from a traditional marketing channel such as TV, radio, or print. When people opt in, you can better identify the people who will be most willing to accept marketing messages on their phone, so you can avoid simply sending a marketing message to everyone in your customer database. Despite privacy concerns, 32% of mobile data users reported that they would be willing to receive mobile advertising if it traded off with a lower cell phone bill or the capability to receive more rich content on their phone.

Similar to the cultural difference regarding privacy, North Americans have a slightly different take on sexuality in marketing. Although Americans have gotten a bad rap for the commoditization of sexuality, internationally (especially in Europe, Asia, and South America), sexually explicit marketing is less taboo. Sex sells anywhere, but if you are marketing sexually explicit content, initially you must be a bit more discrete and understated in North America.

Mobile Marketing in Europe

The adoption of mobile marketing in Europe has gone more quickly than it did in the United States, largely because of the prevalence of high-speed mobile infrastructure and the availability of high-quality handsets (see Figure 14.6). As revenue for mobile voice in Europe has begun to decline, carriers rely more heavily on mobile data and on text and picture messaging to make their business profitable. Mobile telecoms have begun to actively engage mobile advertisers and content providers as a means of monetizing their investment in 3G technology, so this should also help advance the channel.

3G penetration is the highest in Italy and Spain, both at around 38%. The United Kingdom lags behind, at about 28%, and Germany and France rank at 24% and 17% respectively. Despite having a higher penetration rate than the United States, the percentage using the mobile Internet is slightly less across the board. In Europe, the United Kingdom leads in mobile Internet use, with 13% of mobile subscribers accessing the mobile Web. Spain and Italy both come in with 11% and 12% of mobile subscribers accessing the Internet.

Mobile Advertising Spending in Western Europe, 2007-2012 (millions)

	2007	2008	2009	2010	2011	2012
Mobile message advertising	$1,050	$1,502	$2,233	$3,100	$3,821	$4,353
Mobile display advertising	$5	$17	$51	$101	$170	$229
Mobile search advertising	$18	$52	$141	$340	$614	$968
Total	**$1,074**	**$1,571**	**$2,424**	**$3,540**	**$4,605**	**$5,550**

Note: France, Germany, Italy, Spain, UK; numbers may not add up to total due to rounding
Source: eMarketer, March 2008

092639   www.**eMarketer**.com

Figure 14.6 *Mobile advertising spending in Western Europe. Chart courtesy of eMarketer.*

The launch of the iPhone has also done a lot to drive growth in mobile marketing in Europe but the handsets are still not widespread, and they represent only 2% of the total market in the United Kingdom (see Figure 14.7). Complicated roaming charges have stifled some mobile penetration but have mostly driven subscribers toward multiple SIMs and prepaid mobile access. European carriers were among the first to offer flat-rate data pricing, which is driving a large portion of mobile marketing dollars to the mobile Web. The United Kingdom is just behind the United States in terms of mobile search, representing 13% of off-deck mobile search worldwide, so mobile SEO will also be important in Europe. Location detection will likely be more important to the mobile search algorithms than it is in the United States because of the proximity of countries with different primary languages.

Mobile Content Used by iPhone, Smartphone and Mobile Phone Users in the UK, January 2009 (% of total)			
	iPhone users	Total smart-phone users	Total mobile phone users
Accessed news/info via browser	79.7%	48.0%	19.8%
Accessed e-mail	75.4%	35.4%	13.1%
Listened to mobile music	65.6%	40.5%	22.6%
Accessed news or info via downloaded application	55.6%	22.1%	6.3%
Accessed weather	55.5%	26.1%	9.2%
Used Web search	55.1%	31.9%	12.3%
Accessed social networking site	54.8%	29.6%	12.7%

Note: based on three-month average for the period ending January 2009; ages 13+
Source: comScore Mobile as cited in press release, March 26, 2009

102709   www.**eMarketer**.com

Figure 14.7 *While iPhone users in the UK use their iPhones to access many media types, overall iPhone penetration has not increased at the same rate as in the U.S. Chart courtesy of eMarketer.*

Mobile music, especially ad-funded mobile music, is promising in Europe, expected to be worth $120 million by 2012 (see Figure 14.8). European marketers are skipping the middleman and are creating partnerships between carriers and labels—and even artists themselves—to provide subscribers with mobile music that they do not have to pay for. John de pre Gauntt, a senior analyst at eMarketer says:

> "Mobile works better as a marketing and customer relationship platform than it does as a retail sales platform. Bands and artists are increasingly using mobile to form direct relationships with their fans, which are then monetized through other means, such as tickets to live shows, merchandise, and fan clubs."

Mobile Music Spending in the EU-5, by Format, 2007-2012 (millions)	2007	2008	2009	2010	2011	2012
Mastertones, ringback tones and other*	$166	$258	$368	$532	$639	$740
Full-track downloads	$101	$172	$267	$435	$567	$740
Total mobile music spending	**$267**	**$431**	**$635**	**$967**	**$1,206**	**$1,479**
of which: ad-supported mobile music	$5	$22	$41	$77	$139	$170

Note: excludes monophonic and polyphonic ringtones; includes France, Germany, Italy, Spain, UK; *other includes music videos and streams
Source: eMarketer, July 2008

095967   www.**eMarketer**.com

Figure 14.8 *Mobile music spending in Europe. Chart courtesy of eMarketer.*

In terms of mobile marketing, Europe is very advanced and receptive. Mobile advertising is especially important, with an expected $614 million spent on mobile advertising in 2010. In Spain, 75% of mobile phone owners receive ads, while 62% receive them in France. Mobile mapping, video, and social networking are also very popular in Europe, and access to this type of content is expected to grow dramatically. These will also provide great means for reaching your demographic with mobile marketing.

Working with Mobile Carriers, Service Providers, and MVNOs

When you are launching a mobile marketing campaign, it can be important to understand the lay of the land in terms of what companies you will be working with. A mobile service provider, also known as a mobile network operator or a mobile carrier, is the company that has the power to acquire radio spectrum licenses from the government. These companies power and maintain the mobile cell towers and, in many cases, sell or lease mobile handsets to their subscribers.

If it makes sense to run your campaign through a particular carrier, you will need to know which carriers are available to work with, and in many cases, who powers their networks. Understanding who the service provider is can be more challenging than it sounds because service providers frequently operate under different names when they expand into new countries. Mergers, acquisitions, and joint ventures can also make this challenging.

Often service providers operate under their own name as well as other carrier brand names, called mobile virtual network operators (MVNOs). In this situation, a branded carrier leases network capacity from a mobile service provider and resells it under its own brand name. MVNOs can help carriers expand their network into new markets or reach new demographics without changing the strategy of their main brand. A good example of this is Boost Mobile, which was created as an MVNO of Nextel in the United States. The brand was targeted at urban youth and thus needed a much edgier appeal.

Carriers around the world follow different sets of regulations and advertising guidelines, so understanding how the different companies interact can help you assess which companies might be easiest to work with. If you are launching a campaign that you might later want to expand to other countries or regions, it can also help to understand which networks power various carriers internationally. Table 14.1 highlights the top carriers and service providers in different regions of the world.

Table 14.1 Major Carriers and Service Providers by Geographic Region

Africa
Etisalat
Globacom
MTN Group
Portugal Telecom
Safaricom
Telefónica
Telkom
Vivendi
Vodacom
Vodafone
Zain

Asia
Ayala Corporation
Celcom
DiGi
Grameen Telecom
KT Freetel
Maxis
New World Development
NTT DoCoMo
Orascom Telecom
Singapore Telecommunications
SK Telecom
Taiwan Mobile
Telekom Malaysia
Telenor
Telstra
True Corporation
Viettel Mobile
Vodafone

Australia
Optus Mobile
Telstra Mobile
Vodafone

Canada
Bell Mobility
Rogers Wireless
Telus Mobility

China
China Mobile (state owned)
China Telecom (state owned)
China Unicom (state owned)

Table 14.1   Continued

Europe	Middle East	South America
3	Asia Cel	Portugal Telecom
Cosmofon	Avea	América Móvil
Deutsche Telekom	Cellcom	bMobile
France Télécom	Free Float	Claro
02	Hamrah Aval	movistar
Orange	Mobilink	Telcel
Telefónica	Mobility	Telefónica
T-Mobile	MTN Irancell	Tigo
Vodaphone	Orange	
	Orange SA	**U.S.**
India	Orascom Telecom	AT&T
Airtel	Saudi Telecom Company	Cellular One
BSNL (state owned)	Telecom Egypt	Cricket Communications
Reliance	Telenor	Sprint Nextel
Vodafone		T-Mobile
	New Zealand	U.S. Cellular
Japan	NZ Communications	Verizon
au	Telecom	MetroPCS
NTT DoCoMo	Vodafone	
(50% state owned)		
SoftBank Mobile		

15

Looking into the Future for Mobile

We are already living in a world where our sneakers can interface with our phones (Nike) and our treadmill can Tweet our workouts (Netpulse), but the future promises to be even more exciting. Mobile technology such as networks and handsets will continue to improve, as it always has, but what is more interesting for marketers is how the heightened level of mobility will affect the way our customers think and the way they make decisions. Mobile connectivity will continue to change how we access information and make human connections in the same way that the traditional Internet did a generation ago. This change will give marketers an unprecedented opportunity to reach and understand their target market. To embrace the future of mobile marketing, you must understand how mobile technology addresses basic human needs, especially in terms of the mobility of human connection and the mobility of information.

The Future of the Mobility of Human Connection

The capability to connect people in a convenient and seamless way is one of the most powerful functions mobile technology provides. In Maslow's Hierarchy of Needs, safety and human connection or love are identified as foundational needs that humans have (just after physical needs such as air, food, and water), and mobile technology will continue to improve our ability to meet these needs.

Calling, texting, sending picture messages and emails, and participating in social networks are all activities that help us stay connected with the people we care about. These kinds of social activities are sure to grow as mobility continues to become more deeply integrated into our society.

Mobile technology has changed the way people use social networks, causing the social networks to adapt to meet the needs of an ever-present, real-time audience rather than interaction based on a user's willingness to participate on the social networking site in a more limited way. Although it went largely unnoticed, the addition of "What are you doing now?" prompts on social networks signaled this transition—and this is exactly what Twitter capitalized on to make its mark in the world of social networking.

Making specific predictions on how social interaction and human connection will evolve in the mobile space is difficult, but it is clear that integration with input mechanisms will be crucial. The mobility of social interaction has actually changed some people's self-perceptions to include the desire or even need to "live-report" their lives. The ability to upload a picture to Facebook or a video to YouTube using only a mobile phone is quite revolutionary, but it has become so simple that many people, especially those who consider themselves live reporters, do it daily or more. Interestingly, their posts are not ignored, but they actually help others feel more connected to them, no matter how mundane the updates or information appears to be.

On the other hand, the real-time access to social interaction via mobile devices has changed some people's self-perception to include more of a "perpetual voyeur" mentality. Mobile connectivity allows them to keep up-to-date on their friends, family, and community without active involvement. In some cases, these people are constantly reviewing the status updates of others; in other cases, they simply know how and where to find information about people or groups they are connected with, whenever they need it. In a way, they are using information stored in social networks as a collective social memory, a touch point that allows them to see how their loved one's day is progressing, to remember what someone looks like, or to remind them of someone's name.

To successfully leverage this dependence on social mobile technology, marketers need to be clever and unobtrusive. Any kind of service that helps people feel safe and connected will provide immense value to a mobile audience, and these needs will continue to be primary factors in the growth and reliance on mobile technology.

The Future of the Mobility of Information

After safety and love, Maslow suggests that self-esteem and self-actualization complete the hierarchy of human needs. When people need information, they search for it, and as we move into the future, we will continue to see changes in the way searchers discover new content on the mobile Web. Although the link is not explicit, self-esteem and self-actualization are both deeply related to a person's ability to access and process information. Self-sufficiency, authenticity, creativity, and meaning are all partially derived from a person's access to information or knowledge.

In the modern world, when people need information, they search—and the most common and accessible method of search frequently involves using an Internet search engine. Mobility extends our access to the unlimited amount of information on the Web, making it an ever-present life tool. Although some mobile search technologies hope to rival the dominance of mobile search engines, those mobile search engines will indefinitely maintain their prominence as the top method of accessing mobile information. Our reliance on mobile search engines will have a dramatic impact on mobile marketing in the future. Savvy mobile marketers must understand the imminent evolution of mobile search engines and the growing ubiquity of mobile search.

The Imminent Evolution of Mobile Search

The algorithms that search engines use to determine relevance and rank results are constantly changing. An antagonistic symbiosis exists between search engines and Internet marketers. Search engines will always try to give searchers the best results, and Internet marketers will always try to manipulate the results to make their websites look like "the best" in the eyes of the algorithm. Unintentionally, Internet marketers have done a lot to improve the search engines, by creating the need for a better algorithm. Updates to the mobile search engine algorithm will continue to make mobile search results more portable, more personal, and more intelligent.

More Portable Results

Mobile search engines currently enable you to specify where you are, and they will tailor your result set based on that location, but the location still must be manually set. Automatic location detection will soon become seamlessly integrated into the mobile search algorithm. Location-based search (LBS) is still in its infancy, but this will change quickly. More mobile phones are equipped with GPS technology (or assisted GPS), and soon the searcher's exact coordinates will become part of the search algorithm.

Because your cellphone is always on, the algorithm might even include information about how long you have been in one location. Hypothetically, a GPS-enabled mobile phone should be able to tell that you spend most of your time between two or three locations, usually home and work. So when you perform a mobile search, the algorithm could assume that you are relatively familiar with the local landscape when you are in those locations, but would adapt when you are not. When you arrive in a new city, the phone would know that you have not been in that geographic location for long, and local information would reasonably be given more priority in your search results to help you find your way around.

More Personal Results

Traditional and mobile search engines already tailor search results based on a user's past searches and click-throughs if searchers are logged into their search engine account. If you have searched and found what you were looking for (meaning you didn't immediately hit the Back button in your browser), the search engines can determine that your search was successful, and in future searches, they can assign a higher rank to the site where you found what you were looking for with that search. Conversely, if you perform a search and click on the results, only to immediately hit the Back button when you land on the site, the search engine will understand that you didn't find what you were looking for and will not rank that site as well in subsequent searches.

- As the world of mobile search progresses, we can expect many changes that will provide a much higher level of personalization. Because many computers are shared among multiple users, search engines can show personalized results only to users who are logged in. Because there is such a low chance that a mobile phone is a shared device, the search engines will be able to tie a user's search history directly to his or her phone number, eliminating the need to log in.

- In that same vein, mobile phone numbers might gain status as unique identifiers, as IP addresses are currently used in the traditional online space, or as Social Security numbers and driver's license numbers in the off-line world. Technology will become ever slimmer and quicker, and a majority of processing and data storage will become virtual—not hosted on any one device, but hosted somewhere on the Web or in "the cloud." Everyone will have a unique set of digital content that is device independent and accessible from a number of types of devices. This will make us much less reliant on the actual devices we purchase and more reliant on the Web and Web search, even if only to search within our own set of digital content hosted in the cloud.

More Intelligent Results

In addition to knowing where we are and what our normal search behavior is, future mobile search engines will understand and interpret context, and use that to influence the order in which search results are displayed. The device doing the search will become a much more integral part of the algorithm. Different devices have different intended uses that the search engine can easily determine:

- A person searching for "american eagle" on a traditional computer might be doing research on a bird, but a person doing the same search on a GPS might be looking for an American Eagle clothing store.

- Someone searching for "big head" on an MP3 player is likely looking for music by Big Head Todd & the Monsters, but someone searching for "big head" on a game system is more likely looking for a common cheat code that makes all the video game characters' heads appear humorously large.

This type of evolution to the algorithm won't be valuable only to differentiate among different types of devices, but it can also provide a different set of search results for different product models within the same type of device. When a query is sent, the search engines can see not only that it is coming from a cellphone, but also what type of cellphone it is, to provide results that are specific to the demographic that is associated with the specific handset:

- A person searching for Diesel on a push-to-talk cellphone is likely looking for fuel, but the same search from an iPhone is more likely looking for a store that carries the popular Diesel brand merchandise.

- Someone searching from a BlackBerry might want a different set of search results for a search on the word "nightlife" than someone searching from a Razr or SideKick.

Mobile Search Is Ubiquitous Search

One of the most important points to understand about the future is that mobile search is not just going to happen on mobile phone handsets. Many new portable devices are becoming Web enabled and will offer mobile search as an integral part of the device. Your mobile site will have the opportunity to rank in a number of other devices:

- **Game systems**—Video game systems increasingly enable you to play against friends via the Internet, but they also let you buy and download new games or game features, which creates a need for search. These devices can be portable or can be set up to work with your TV.

- **GPS**—The days of downloading updated maps and business addresses to your GPS are limited. Tapping into local Web search APIs for up-to-date maps and business listings is a more scalable solution that makes the devices much slimmer and more user-friendly; in fact, the three major search engines have already been brokering deals with car and GPS manufacturers around the world. BMW and Mercedes have already offered a limited fleet of cars with Web-enabled GPS in Germany.

- **MP3 players and HD radio**—Some MP3 players are already equipped to search and download music and album artwork from the Internet, but these are generally within the walled garden of the manufacturer. In the future, these walled gardens will likely be forced to open up, and some form of Web search will be included in all MP3 players.

- **TV and IP-TV**—In many cases, we can already set up recordings on our DVR via the Internet (TiVo), so we are already engaged in a search when we are looking for the right program to record. Mandatory digitalization of TV broadcasts in 2009 has taken this trend a step further, making it easier for companies to distribute and search for TV broadcasts in a Web environment.

With all these technologies, opportunities will arise to create and tailor a marketing message. Marketing dollars will always play a huge role in the development of new Web-based technology because they mitigate the development cost of the technology. Whether through carrier agreements with mobile gaming systems, search engine agreements with IPTV companies, or traditional mobile search results that are shown on your GPS, the opportunity to promote your products will be available.

With the plethora of new mobile technologies, search engines and Internet marketers will have a wealth of new information available to them. Search engine algorithms will be updated to provide better results, and this will make mobile search results more portable, personal, and intelligent.

Conclusion

Mobile marketing is changing at a break-neck speed, and the opportunities continue to expand and evolve. As in all marketing media, there will be a constant struggle for balance between the presence of marketing messages and the tolerance your target market has for the intrusion. Marketing that is understated or infrequent will not return the desired return; similarly, marketing that is overbearing and intrusive will not generate the desired response. Your best bet to leverage the future of mobile marketing could lie in your ability to understand and capitalize on how mobile technology helps people address their most basic needs, rather than simply focusing only on the more technical or flashy aspects of the practice.

Txtspk Definitions

Table A.1 provides some commonly used text speak (txtspk) and definitions.

Table A.1 Text Speak (txtspk) Definitions

Txtspk	Definition	Txtspk	Definition
:-(	Frown	AFK	Away from keyboard
:-)	Smile	AKA	Also known as
:(	Frown	Anom	Anonymous
:)	Smile	Apt	Apartment
)	Smile	Asap	As soon as possible
^5	High five	Atm	At the moment
8 (	Frown	Attn	Attention
8-(	Frown	Avg	Average
8-)	Smile	BB	Be Back
;)	Wink	Bbfn	Bye, bye for now
:D	Big smile	BBIAB	Be back in a bit
:x	Kiss	BBIAF	Be back in a few
:P	Bleh	Bbl	Be back later
QT	Cutey	Bbt	Be back tomorrow
>_<	Angry	Bc	Because
0_0	Stunned	B/C	Because
/W	With	B/f	Boyfriend
A/S/L	Age/sex/location	B/fs	Boyfriends
AFAIK	As far as I know	B/g	Background

Table A.1   Text Speak (txtspk) Definitions

Txtspk	Definition	Txtspk	Definition
B/gs	Backgrounds	Dl ing	Downloading
Brb	Be right back	Dnk	Do not know
Brh	Be right here	Dol	Dying of laughter
Bro	Brother	Drt	Dead right there
Btw	By the way	Dts	Don't think so
Btdt	Been there done that	Ext	Extension
Bwl	Bursting with laughter	Exts	Extensions
Bws	Big wide smile	Faq	Frequently asked questions
Cmon	Come on		
Congrat	Congratulations	Fav	Favorite
Congrats	Congratulations	Favs	Favorites
Cpu	CPU	Fb	Funny business
C/W	Class work	Fcol	For crying out loud
Cul	See you later	Fgt	Feeling great today
Cwyl	Chat with you later	Foc	Fell off chair
Cya	See ya	Focl	Fell off chair laughing
Degt	Don't even go there	Foomcl	Falling out of my chair laughing
Del	Delete		
Dgt	Don't go there	Ftbomh	From the bottom of my heart
Dif	Difference	Fwy	Freeway
Diff	Different	Fwiw	For what it's worth
DL	Download	Gday	Good day
D/l	Download	Gevening	Good evening
D/ls	Downloads	Gnight	Good night
D/ling	Downloading	G'Day	Good day

Txtspk	Definition	Txtspk	Definition
Gdr	Grinning, ducking, and running	Hciery	How can I ever repay you?
G'Evening	Good evening	Hf	Have fun
G'Night	Good night	Hhb	Hello, honey bunny
G/f	Girlfriend	Hnd	Have a nice day
G/fs	Girlfriends	Hoas	Hold on a second
Gfi	Go for it	Hoamp	Hold on a minute, please
Gfn	Gone for now	Hols	Holidays
GTG	Got to go	Holi	Holidays
G2g	Got to go	HQ	Headquarters
Gtgb	Got to go bye	Hrs	Hours
G2gb	Got to go bye	Hry	How are you?
Gg	Gotta go	Hty	Hugs to you
Giar	Give it a rest	Hwy	Highway
Gj	Good job	Iay	I adore you
Gdp	Good job, partner	Iayt	I adore you, too
Gmc	Getting more coffee	Ib	I'm back
Gmta	Great minds think alike	Icbw	It could be worse
Gtsy	Glad to see you	Ic	I see
Habo	Have a better one	Iddi	I don't doubt it
Hagn	Have a good night	Idk	I don't know
Hago	Have a good one	Idts	I don't think so
Hak	Hug and kiss	IIRC	If I recall correctly
Hatm	Howling at the moon	IMHO	In my humble opinion
Hawu	Hello all, what's up?	IMO	In my opinion
Hb	Honey bear	IMNSHO	In my not-so-humble opinion

Table A.1   Text Speak (txtspk) Definitions

Txtspk	Definition	Txtspk	Definition
IOW	In other words	lmc	Let me check
IRL	In real life	lmfao	Laughing my f****** a** off
Irmc	I rest my case		
Irt	In real time	lmho	Laughing my head off
ISTM	It seems to me	lmtal	Let me take a look
Iw	It's worse	loflol	Lying on the floor laughing out loud
Iwmy	I will miss you		
Iwywh	I wish you were here	lshict	Laughing so hard I can't type
Iyd	In your dreams	lsligt	Laughing so hard I got tears
Iykwim	If you know what I mean		
Iyo	In your opinion	lshih	Laughing so hard it hurts
Jacpm	Just a cotton-picking minute	lshmbb	Laughing so hard my belly is bouncing
Jas	Just a sec		
Jja	Just joking around	lshmbh	Laughing so hard my belly hurts
JJ	Just joking	lshmch	Laughing so hard my cheeks hurt
J/J	Just joking		
J/K	Just kidding	lshmsh	Laughing so hard my sides hurt
JK	Just kidding		
Jmho	Just my humble opinion	ltm	Laughing to myself
Jmo	Just my opinion	LTNS	Long time, no see
l8r	Later	lylab	Love you like a brother
latez	Later		
lol	Laughing out loud	lylas	Love you like a sister
lmao	Laughing my a** off	Mia	Missing in action

Txtspk	Definition	Txtspk	Definition
Min	Minute	Ottomh	Off the top of my head
Msg	Message	Pic	Picture
Msgs	Messages	Pics	Pictures
Mt	My time	Pkg	Package
Nb	Newbie	ppls	People's
N00b	Newbie	ppl	People
Ncto	Now, cut that out	pls	Please
Ne1	Anyone	plz	Please
Ngt	Not going there	Prob	Problem
Nm	Never mind	Probs	Problems
N/m	Never mind	Prolly	Probably
Nmh	Not much here	Rem	Remember
N/w	No worries	Rems	Remembers
Np	No problem	ROFL	Rolling on floor, laughing
N/p	No problem	ROTFL	Rolling on the floor, laughing
Nrn	No response necessary	ROTFLMAO	Rolling on the floor, laughing my a** off
Nsd	Never say die		
Nunya	None of your business	ROTFLMFAO	Rolling on the floor, laughing my f****** a** off
Nw	No way		
Ohd	Oh, happy days		
OIC	Oh, I see	RP	Role play
Oll	Only laughing a little	Rpg	Role-playing game
Omg	Oh my God!	Sec	Second
ootd	One of these days	Stfu	Shut the f*** up
OTOH	On the other hand	Sthu	Shut the h*** up
Otp	On the phone		

Table A.1   Text Speak (txtspk) Definitions

Txtspk	Definition	Txtspk	Definition
Swl	Screaming with laughter	Vid	Video
Syl	See you later	VR	Virtual reality
Temp	Temporary	WB	Welcome back
Tnx	Thanks	W/e	Whatever
Thnks	Thanks	W/o	Without
Thx	Thanks	Wk	Week
Tanx	Thanks	Wks	Weeks
TX	Thanks	WTF	What the f***
TTFN	Ta, ta for now	WTG	Way to go
TTYL	Talk to you later	Yr	Your

B

List of Vendors, Products, and Services

The following pages include a reference of different companies within the mobile marketing space. Companies included in this list are not necessarily companies that I have worked with or expressly recommend. Instead, they are companies that are known for their skill in a particular area, or companies that I found in my research for the book. The goal is simply to give you a place to start when you are researching different types of vendors for a mobile marketing project.

Mobile VoIP and Audio

Product, Vendor or Service	URL
HelloSoft	www.hellosoft.com
Melodis Corporation	www.melodis.com

Mobile Testing and Tools

Product, Vendor, or Service	URL
DeviceAnywhere	www.deviceanywhere.com
MobiReady	www.mobiready.com
W3C Mobile Code Checker	www.validator.w3.org/mobile
dotMobi Emulator	www.mtld.mobi/emulator.php
WinWap Smartphone Emulator	www.winwap.com/downloads/downloads
OpenWave Browser	www.developer.openwave.com/dvl/tools_and_sdk/phone_simulator/choosing.htm
Nokia Browser Simulator	www.forum.nokia.com/info/sw.nokia.com/id/d57da811-c7cf-48c8-995f-feb3bea36d11/Nokia_Mobile_Internet_Toolkit_4.1.html
Microsoft Pocket PC Emulators	www.msdn.microsoft.com/en-us/windowsmobile/bb264327.aspx
Online Mobile Simulator	www.emulator.mtld.mobi/emulator.php
Online WAP Browser	www.wapsilon.com
BrowserCam	www.browsercam.com

Mobile Tracking

Product, Vendor, or Service	URL
Adversitement B.V.	www.adversitement.com
Carrier IQ	www.carrieriq.com
Fli Digital, Inc.	www.flidigital.com
HipCricket	www.hipcricket.com
Medio MobileNow	www.Medio.com
MobClix	www.mobclix.com
Mozes	www.mozes.com
Qrme	www.qrme.co.uk/

Mobile Ticketing, RFID, and NFC

Product, Vendor, or Service	URL
AURA Interactive (Australia)	www.aura.net.au
CellTrust	www.celltrust.com
Qwasi	www.qwasi.com
TagIt	www.tagit.tv

Mobile Ad Design

Product, Vendor, or Service	URL
AditOn	www.aditon.com
Bluestar Mobile Group	www.bluestarmobile.com
Graphico New Media	www.graphico.co.uk
Medialets, Inc.	www.medialets.com
Wapple	www.wapple.net

Mobile eCommerce

Product, Vendor, or Service	URL
AirTight Networks	www.airtightnetworks.com
Bango	www.bango.com
CellTrust	www.celltrust.com
MCN, Inc.	www.mcn-inc.com
Mobile IQ, Ltd.	www.mobileiq.com
Mobile Media Production	www.mobilemediaproduction.com
Qwasi	www.qwasi.com
TagIt	www.tagit.tv

Mobile Video

Product, Vendor, or Service	URL
Amobee	www.amobee.com
Compera nTime (Brazil)	www.comperantime.com

Mobile Strategy Consulting

Product, Vendor, or Service	URL
Rank-Mobile	www.Rank-Mobile.com
Trend Mobility	www.trendmobility.com
ComperamTime	www.comperantime.com
iCrossing	www.icrossing.com

Mobile Industry News

Product, Vendor, or Service	URL
M:Metrics/ComScore	www.mmetrics.com
MediaPost	www.mediapost.com
MMA Mobile Marketing Forum	www.mobilemarketingforum.com
MobiAdNews	www.mobiadnews.com
Mobile Marketer	www.mobilemarketer.com
Mobile Tech News	www.mobiletechnews.com
Mobile Tech Today	www.mobile-tech-today.com
MobileBurn	www.mobile-tech-today.com
Mobile Marketing Magazine	www.mobilemarketingmagazine.co.uk
Mobile Technology Web Blog	www.mobile-weblog.com
Moco News	www.moconews.net
Nielson Mobile	www.en-us.nielsen.com/tab/industries/telecom
PC Magazine	www.pcmag.com
RCR Wireless	www.rcrwireless.com
Search Engine Land	www.searchengineland.com
Search Engine Watch	www.searchenginewatch.com
SearchEngineJournal	www.searchenginejournal.com
SearchMobileComputing	www.searchmobilecomputing.techtarget.com
SmartPhone Magazine	www.smartphonemag.com
Wireless Week	www.wirelessweek.com
PhoneScoop	www.phonescoop.com
Windows Mobile	www.windowsteamblog.com
Textually	www.textually.org

Product, Vendor, or Service	URL
SMSText News	www.smstextnews.com
Mobile Marketing Watch	www.mobilemarketingwatch.com/
Mobile Marketing Profits	www.mobilemarketingprofits.com
2D Code	www.2d-code.co.uk
GoMo News	www.gomonews.com
BeeTagg	www.beetagg.com
PC World	www.pcworld.com
MobiForge	www.mobiforge.com

Glossary

A

alternative input search   Search engine queries that are not based on direct entry of text into a Web search engine. Mobile phones have more options for inputting a search, such as voice, picture, and text messaging.

Amended Telemarketing Sales Rule (ASTR)   *See* Telemarketing Sales Rule (TSR).

Aztec Codes   *See* QR Codes.

B

Bluetooth   Technology that uses radio broadcast to allow multiple proximal devices to recognize each other and send information between them wirelessly.

branded profiles   A profile on a social network that is a representation of your brand and a means of communicating with your customers. Many social networks allow companies to represent their brand and participate in the social network under a brand name, but if they don't, you can create a profile based on a company mascot, a figurehead, or sometimes a CEO.

C

CAN-SPAM   Act passed in 2003 to restrict commercial email by ensuring that mechanisms for opting out or contacting the sender directly are included. This law covers email on the traditional computer and on the mobile phone, but it does not cover text messaging or other types of mobile messaging. It would be possible to add a Do Not Email Registry under this law, but the FTC determined that it would be too difficult to verify email account information and, thus, was not feasible.

carrier groups   In some cases it may be a good idea to segment your advertising campaign by carrier. This happens naturally if you are advertising on a carrier deck, but it can also be valuable for off-deck mobile advertising.

Cascading Style Sheets   Cascading Style Sheets are the rendering instructions that control how the content of your site is rendered. When a page is rendered, the browsers pull the style sheet to see how the page should be laid out and what fonts and colors to use when rendering it.

Children's Online Protection Act (COPA)   Legislation that prevents companies from collecting or storing information about people younger than 13 years old. This is important for mobile marketing because many contests, sweepstakes, and other participatory initiatives might be targeted at people in that protected age group.

Clearwire   A brand-name wireless Internet service provider (ISP) that operates in the United States, Ireland, Belgium, Spain, Denmark, and Mexico. It provides a unique wireless network that uses WiMax technology with 3G technology to provide 4G wireless network access.

click   A statistic that describes how many time users actually clicked on your advertisement. This is a measure or engagement rather than exposure.

code division multiple access (CDMA)   Subset of 2G technologies that relies on each phone being assigned a specific code, allowing multiple users to be put on the same transmission channel. Used in North and South America as well as Asia, CDMA still accounts for 17% of subscribers in the world.

compensation   Element that represents winnings. In a lottery, it would be the payout for a winning ticket. If you are running a mobile sweepstakes, you can consider offering prizes that have no monetary value, such as having the winner's names listed on a leader board. However, if the prize is a cash prize, it will be impossible to remove this element from your legal concerns, and you will need to look closely at the laws that govern cash prize payouts.

consideration   Element that is the payment to participate. In a lottery, it would be the cost of the lottery ticket. If you are running a mobile sweepstakes, the best thing you can do to eliminate consideration is to make it free to participate in the contest. Premium text messaging services charge money, so it is a good idea to allow users to participate for free online as well.

contextual mobile ads   Contextual mobile ads can be in the form of text or images and are displayed on a mobile website rather than in mobile search results. In this model, mobile site owners consent for relevant advertisements to be shown on their website in return for a portion of the profits that the ad network receives from those particular ads. The mobile ad network offers advertising opportunities through a bidding model that combines the advertisers' willingness to pay for position with the relevance of the ad to the content of the website it is being displayed on.

conversion and acquisition   Whenever a visitor to your mobile content takes an action that you want, such as buying something, downloading something, or signing up for something, that is a conversion and the visitor has said to have converted. If a visitor signs up for alerts or emails, or in some way indicates that he or she would like to receive messages from you in the future, that is considered a customer acquisition, frequently just called an acquisition.

cost per conversion (CPC) or cost per acquisition (CPA)   Ratios that measure the number of conversions or customer acquisitions that you received as a result of the advertising campaign, compared to the amount that you spend to place an advertisement. These are important statistics for understanding how much each you are spending on each conversion or acquisition. These statistics can be figured individually, for each conversion event, or aggregated, for all the possible conversions in the campaign.

cost per pair of feet (CPPoF)   The amount of money spent in marketing to drive each individual person into a brick and mortar store. The total cost of marketing divided by the number of visitors to a store over a specific time period.

cost per thousand (CPM)   (Also effective cost per thousand [eCPM].) Business model in which advertisers pay a certain price for an advertisement to be shown a thousand times or to have a thousand impressions. The M in CPM represents a thousand in Roman numeral form.

coupon applications   Applications dedicated to helping people save money. In some cases, that means coupons. People who download coupon applications and sign up with their services can receive coupons directly from the mobile application or through SMS, MMS, or email.

customer relationship management (CRM)   A computer database that stores information about individual customers. This information can include contact information, demographic information, and purchase behavior. The CRM is used to learn about customers and create marketing and customer service offerings that more closely meet their needs.

CSS   *See* Cascading Style Sheets.

CTR   Click-through rate. A relative measure of engagement based on the number of clicks per impression. A high CTR is valuable because it indicates that viewers are finding your advertisement compelling.

D

Day-parting   *See* Time Segmentation.

demographic segmentation   Grouping and targeting ad campaigns based on known demographic information like age, gender, income, or location.

direct marketing   The use of personal mass media as a marketing tool to elicit a direct response from the target market or people receiving the advertisements. It can include post mail, telemarketing, direct email, point of sale advertising, and online marketing. Direct marketing always has a measurable response so that effectiveness of the campaign can be determined and evaluated.

Direct Marketing Association (DMA)   An international organization based in the United States that helps develop and guide direct marketing best practices. Although the DMA's focus is not exclusively mobile, it is quite interested in the development of and adherence to privacy-related standards in the mobile marketing industry.

Do Not Call Registry (DNC)   A list, created in 2003, of residences and phone numbers for individuals who prefer not to receive telemarketing calls. It is illegal for solicitors to call these phone numbers, although business lines cannot be added to the registry.

dotMobi   (Also .mobi.) Top-level domain created to indicate that a website was developed specifically for mobile access. dotMobi domain names were first made available for purchase in 1996, designed to help distinguish mobile websites from traditional websites. They are not required, and frequently not desirable for mobile Web marketing, except in Asia.

E

effective cost per thousand (eCPM)   A representation of your estimated earnings for every thousand impressions of an advertisement. A means of comparing revenue across different advertising channels. *See* cost per thousand (CPM).

enhanced data rates for GSM evolution (EDGE)   A common 2.75G wireless network technology which improved the digital transmission speed of GDM and GPRS by 3x.

F

Federal Communications Commission (FCC)   An independent U.S. government agency, directly responsible to Congress, that regulates interstate and international communications by radio, television, wire, satellite, and cable. The FCC will control what information about mobile customers can be shared and how, but the guidelines have yet to be passed. The FCC also regulates VoIP and phone number porting, which could both affect a mobile marketing campaign.

Federal Trade Commission (FTC)   Organization that, with state attorneys general, is in place to curb unfair and deceptive trade practices. Some of the laws and regulations the FTC passes apply to mobile marketing campaigns.

FemtoCell   Technology used indoors to boost indoor mobile handset signals by converting a wired broadband signal into a radio signal that can be picked up by mobile phones.

full Web transactions   As on the traditional Web, entire transactions can be completed on the mobile Web without the need for an account or prepayment. Customers simply enter their credit card information, just as they would on the traditional Web. This is most commonly used by websites that offer some kind of online shopping experience.

G

Generated Packet Radio Service (GPRS)   The first improvement in mobile data transmission. GPRS achieves moderate improvements in the transmission of data by using TDMA to improve packet switching over the mobile network. Like many other technologies, after its initial deployment GPRS technology was later integrated into GSM. GPRS can be added to 2G, GSM, or 3G networks.

Global System for Mobile Communications (GSM)   A system developed to address some of the shortfalls of TDMA technology. It was originally created in Finland in 1991 but is now used around the world. It requires timing advance commands to be sent to the base station, which, in turn, sends signals to the mobile phone, telling it whether it should transmit the signal earlier and by how much.

Goog411   Service that text-messages your search results to you after you speak your query via phone.

Google Voice   Application that takes voice queries directly from an iPhone without having to call and returns live Web results to the iPhone within the application.

Groupe Speciale Mobile (GSMA)   An organization formed in 1982 by the Confederation of European Posts and Telecommunications (CEPT) to design a European mobile technology. Over time, GSMA has evolved to become the worldwide authority on mobile communication. Its mission is to "create value for operators and the mobile industry in the provision of services for the benefit of end users, so that those users can readily and affordably connect to and use the services they desire, anywhere, anytime."

H

handset groups   Groups of mobile handsets that have similar attributes like screen size, operating system or browser. Addressing groups of handsets rather than specific handsets can expedite the launch of any mobile marketing campaign or application deployment.

I

idle screen advertising   Mobile advertisements that are served while the user is waiting on a page or application to download or some other process to finish.

image Search results   Images that appear in regular search engine results, or image-specific search engines. All of the top search engines have indexes for cataloging images from the Web. To rank well in these search results, use alternative text, otherwise known as alt tags, to describe all your images and include the top keywords for each page. Also use keywords when naming your files, to ensure that the search engines understand what the image represents and can index the site appropriately.

impression   One instance of an advertisement shown online. The number of impressions can help evaluate the branding effect an advertisement might have, but it is a measure of exposure rather than engagement.

infrared (IR)   One of the oldest and most limited forms of broadcasting mobile messages. Some laptops and phones are equipped with infrared technology, but it has not been universally adopted by handset manufacturers. These limitations make it less desirable than other more universally accepted technologies available.

Integrated Digital Enhanced Network (iDEN)   A digital wireless standard developed by Motorola. It provides push-to-talk functionality like a walkie-talkie. The technology is used widely in the United States by Nextel.

Internet service provider (ISP)   An IP network designed to move data rather than voice communication. ISPs can replace mobile technologies such as GSM and CDMA or can simply be added to networks with GSM and DSMA to increase their capacity.

J

J2ME   Also known a Java Platform, Microsoft Edition or Java ME – this is a mobile application programming language that is commonly used for mobile game development.

L

local search results   Search results that feature business personal listings with addresses and other contact information. These can be included in regular search listings or local-specific search engines. Search results ranked based on traditional ranking factors as well as their proximity to searchers location or, in some cases, the city center. As geolocation factors become more closely integrated with mobile search, the actual area code of the phone doing the searching might even be integrated when other methods of geolocation are unavailable. Local results are also heavily weighted on star rankings, so reviews and comments from satisfied customers are important.

localization   Some search engines adjust search results based on the location of the searcher, so someone searching in New York will get different results than someone searching in Los Angeles. More dramatically, someone searching in Houston might get different results than someone searching from London, even if they are both searching from Google.com. This means that, again, just because you are ranking well in one place does not necessarily mean that you are ranking well in another place.

location-based Marketing   Marketing messages that are sent or received by users based on their physical location. These include digital signage, Bluetooth, WiFi, near-field, and infrared broadcasts.

location segmentation   Ad networks allow you to segment your ads based on the location of the recipient. This can be commonly be done by zip code, city, metro area, state, or even country. Segments are created in order to target advertising more effectively, measure advertising more effectively or both.

long-term evolution (LTE)   IP data network that optimizes the transmission of data packets (rather than voice). It is expected to be deployed in 2010 but competes with WiMax as the 4G standard of choice for network operators.

Loyalty Marketing   Marketing designed to add long-term value and brand affinity with existing or frequent customers. Common tactics are loyalty programs like punch cards, frequent shopper programs, or VIP clubs. These incentives encourage repeat purchases, and higher purchase values.

M

.mobi   *See* dotMobi.

macropayments   Used for purchases that cannot be billed as a micropayment, usually for goods or services over $5.

malware   Any malicious software, including viruses, trojans, worms, and spyware.

micropayments   Small transactions that can be completed on a phone and, in many cases, billed directly to a user's cellphone bill or credit card.

microsite   Term used to describe websites that are created to achieve a very specific goal that represents only a small portion of the company or brand's overall marketing goals.

MMA Mobile Privacy Code of Conduct   Code of conduct launched in 2003 by the Mobile Marketing Association Privacy Advisory Committee that covers six basic privacy concerns for mobile marketers: choice, control, customization, consideration, constraint, and confidentiality.

MMS   Multimedia Message Service. An extension of the SMS messaging standard, but uses the WAP coding language to display multimedia content.

M-SPAM   A bill that is currently being proposed in the U.S. Senate to criminalize mobile SMS spamming in the same way that CAN-SPAM criminalized email spam. As currently proposed, the act would empower the FTC and the FCC to curb unwanted text messages in the United States.

mobile affiliate marketing   Unique form of marketing in which other companies agree to help you sell your product or drive traffic to your website, in return for a portion of the profits from each sale they send.

mobile applications   Small programs that can be downloaded and added to a mobile phone to customize it for the users specific needs and wants. The major categories of mobile applications are games, entertainment, references, and productivity tools.

mobile banking   Using a mobile phone to complete a banking transaction. In some cases, this is a reference to pseudo-economies built on the exchange and transmission of mobile airtime minutes for cash. Minutes are transmitted and exchanged between people or even to businesses as a means of currency, and a replacement for cash. These practices are most common in Africa and Asia.

mobile directory submission   Directories are utility websites designed to help people find websites that are relevant to specific topics. They are organized in much the same way that a Yellow Pages book might be organized, dividing subjects by categories and subcategories. Within each category and subcategory are links to websites with more information on the topic.

mobile display Advertising   Graphics put on a page that consumers can click on, linked to a specific offer, or full-page advertisement. As with traditional banners, these are usually sold on a cost per thousand impressions (CPM) basis. Mobile site owners agree to show your advertisement on their site in return for payment from the mobile ad network. Mobile display ads can also be included in games and downloadable mobile applications for additional targeted exposure.

mobile email   Email that is rendered on a mobile phone. This is frequently the same emails that can be displayed on a traditional computer, though it is common in Asia for people to have email addresses that incorporate their phone number and are specifically designated to deliver to a mobile phone. Mobile email programs frequently have difficulty displaying HTML formatted marketing emails effectively but there are tactics for improving the effectiveness of traditional emails on mobile phones.

mobile landing page   The mobile page user are automatically sent to when clicking on a mobile advertisement.

Mobile Marketing Association (MMA)   An international group of mobile carriers, content providers, marketers, and other interested parties who help establish the best practices in the industry. Although none of its privacy guidelines are binding or enforceable, the MMA is frequently referenced as the accepted standards when clear laws are not present. The MMA frequently publishes and updates mobile marketing best practice documentation, as well as industry reviews and articles.

mobile network operator (MNO)   A company that has frequency allocations and the entire required infrastructure to run an independent mobile network.

mobile payment   The ability to pay for some goods or services with your mobile phone. Mobile payments can take place over the Web or can be completed offline through contactless payment options such as near field communication (NFC) and radio frequency identification (RFID).

mobile pay-per–click advertising   *See* pay-per-click (PPC).

Mobile Robots.txt   A search engine directive that tells mobile search engines which content they should crawl and index and which content they should not crawl. In some cases, mobile search engine crawlers may be blocked from crawling traditional websites, and traditional website crawlers may be blocked from crawling mobile Web content.

mobile search engine marketing (SEM)   A comprehensive term that describes any type of marketing that is sold by search engines and displayed in search results. It is usually a specific reference to advertising and placement that is paid for, but in some cases the term is used to describe all the wider aspects of search engine marketing including search engine optimization and website usability.

mobile search engine optimization (SEO)   Activity designed to improve the algorithmic search engine rankings of a website in mobile searches. Mobile SEO can be used to encourage mobile rankings for traditional websites (usually for rankings on smart phones) or mobile websites. Mobile SEO is not specifically a reference to optimization of '.mobi' domains or WAP websites. It is also an important marketing tactic for websites built in HTML and XHTML.

mobile search engine submissions   The act of requesting listings in a mobile search engine by providing the search engine mobile urls that should be included in their search results. Submission pages that allow other sites to request inclusion in mobile search results. This used to be a powerful strategy in traditional SEO efforts, but it has become less effective there. Luckily, it is still a good idea for mobile SEO because the mobile search engines are looking for valuable mobile-friendly content to index and rank.

mobile service provider   Also known as a mobile network operator or a mobile carrier. The company that has the power to acquire radio spectrum licenses from the government. Mobile service providers power and maintain the mobile cell towers; in many cases, these are also the companies that sell or lease mobile handsets to their subscribers.

mobile site map   A list of website urls that you explicitly request the search engines to rank in search results. Google allows webmasters to submit multiple mobile site maps based on the markup language that website is built in.

mobile social gaming   A type of mobile social network that is popular in Asian countries. Much like Second Life for the cell phone, this type of social networking allows users to create avatars, or visual representations of themselves. Those avatars interact with other avatars within the social network. In some mobile social gaming networks, these avatars behave just as you would actually behave, but other networks have little relationship to reality and instead act more like an online role-playing game.

mobile social networks   Social networking is a term used to describe the activity of locating and interacting with other people who have similar interests. This activity is one of the fastest growing uses of mobile technology word wide.

mobile spamming   Untargeted or unrequested digital marketing communication. The term was originally used to describe untargeted email marketing, but the definition has expended to include all types of marketing communication that recipients have not consciously opted into.

mobile subdirectory   A sub folder or division of a website that is specifically created for mobile content. It is generally represented as www.example.com/m or www.example.com/mobile.

mobile subdomain   A sub section of a website that is controlled from the server rather than in the file structure. It is generally represented as m.example.com or mobile.example.com.

mobile virtual network operators (MNVOs)   Branded carriers that lease network capacity from a mobile service provider and resell it under their own brand names. MNVOs provide mobile phone service but do not have their own license or the infrastructure required to provide mobile telephone service. Good examples of MNVOs are Boost Wireless, Cricket Wireless as well as the Disney and ESPN specific carriers that failed.

mobile Web portal   An entry page that provides immediate access to information and news without them having to search for it or go to multiple websites. Portals commonly bring in news, weather, and information from other sites, to aggregate it and make it easily accessible for their users.

N

near-field communication (NFC)   Technology that relies on high-frequency messages to be sent and received from two enabled devices, sending its own signal but also sometimes working with RFID.

news search results   Search results that are specifically designated as news either in regular search results or news-specific search engines. If your website frequently distributes news articles or press releases, it is important to be ranked in news search results.

O

off-deck   The Web-at-large when accessed through a mobile browser. Off-deck content is not controlled by the carriers, though in some cases it can be blocked or slowed by carrier proxies.

on-deck   Web content that is provided by the carrier though a branded portal, sometimes called a carrier WAP deck.

P

pay-per-click (PPC)   A business model in which advertisers are charged for an advertisement only when someone actually clicks on it. Frequently search engines provide ad networks, and ads are usually shown alongside search results in a search engine.

personalization   A search engine (especially Google) may use your previous search behavior to modify the search results it presents to you. If you have clicked on one listing frequently, the search engine may move it to the top of search results when you are searching for it; if you have never clicked on a result that ranks well, it may move it lower in the results.

PPC advertising   *See* pay-per-click (PPC).

prompted payment   A credit card on file with a specific company is charged for a recurring service after an SMS prompt is responded to by the recipient, giving permission for the charge. As an example, the carrier might send a text message to subscribers at the end of a billing cycle, notifying them of the total amount due and allowing them to respond with a preset PIN number to pay the bill with the credit card on file.

Q

QR Codes   Also known as Quick Response Codes, these are small square dot matrix bar codes that can be captured by a camera phone then decoded by software on the phone to execute a specific task, like opening a website, placing a call, transmitting a vCard or sending a text message. These are also sometimes called Aztec Codes or 2D Bar Codes.

R

radio frequency identification (RFID)   Technology that allows items to be "tagged" or tracked using radio waves. Some phones are equipped with RFID technology that can activate messages in offline mobile marketing like billboards and signs.

ROI (return on investment)   A measurement that incorporates all the costs associated with running the advertising campaign, including agency management fees, design fees, and the cost of the time the staff has spent managing the campaign. ROI is the success metric for mobile advertising because it allows advertisers to show that, for each dollar they spend on advertising, they are making more than a dollar back in value or return. ROI = (Gain from investment – Cost of investment) / Cost of investment.

S

SDK   An abbreviation for Software Development Kit. This is a tool set meant to help developers build applications for specific phones or operating systems.

short code   A five- or six-digit phone number that can be dialed as a destination for a text message. These must be registered and leased, much like a domain name.

SMS (Short Message Service)   Messages that can be sent from phone to phone or from computer to phone, or that can be sent from a phone to a common short code (usually abbreviated to simply *short code*).

social CPM marketing   Many social networks make money almost exclusively through the sale of advertising on their sites. Although this business model has not yet proven itself to be enough to keep all the social networks alive, you can be sure that it will always be a key element in the social network business model. The simplest way for a marketer to reach out to potential customers on a mobile social networking site is to purchase ad placement within a cost per million (CPM) model. This is similar to other mobile CPM advertising, but marketers work directly with the social networking company or their ad network to place and track the ads.

spyware   Software that runs in the background of an operating system to collect and send private information about a mobile user's behavior to an unauthorized party. Information, including private call logs, text messages, and picture messages, can be distributed to a third party.

T

Telemarketing Sales Rule (TSR)   Bill established by the FTC in 1995, but significantly amended in 2004; it then became the Amended Telemarketing Sales Rule (ATSR). The bill's most important accomplishment was to establish the National Do Not Call Registry. It is important to note that the rules established in this act cover all acts of telemarketing, whether the telemarketer initiates the conversation or the customer initiates the conversation. This can come into play if you are using mobile marketing to drive phone calls to complete sales or make customer acquisitions.

Telephone Consumer Protection Act (TCPA)   Act passed by Congress in 1991 that restricts the use of automatic dialing systems, artificial or prerecorded voice messages, SMS text messages received by cellphones, and the use of fax machines to send unsolicited advertisements.

text messaging   Otherwise known as Short Message Service (SMS). This is the act of sending a short 160 character message between phones using a short code or a traditional phone number.

time division multiplex access (TDMA)   An older method of wireless data transmission that is used to send digital signals that are divided into different time slots, rather than by codes in as in CDMA.

time segmentation   Segmenting your advertisements by time of day, otherwise known as "dayparting." This segmentation can be especially powerful for mobile advertising because it allows you to reach people when you can safely anticipate their needs, like sending a mobile coupon for food at or just before noon.

Trojan   Otherwise known as a Trojan horse. A program that purports to be something the user would want to download but actually harbors malicious code or viruses. In the mobile world, Trojans are usually purported to be wallpapers, ringtones, or applications.

Two-Dimensional (2D) Bar Codes   *See* QR Codes.

U

ultra-wideband (UWB)   Communication that uses a large portion of the radio spectrum to transmit broadband communication at a short range, requiring little radio energy. Ultra-wide-band transmissions can share a variety of different narrow-band radio signals without interfering with those transmissions. The uses of UWB are similar to those of Bluetooth technology, but UWB is less widely adopted.

unlicensed mobile access (UMA)   Similar to FemtoCell, UMA is deployed through a base station that uses WiFi signals to carry voice and data from mobile handsets to a base station. The base station provides improved access to GSM and GPRS by tapping into unlicensed aspects of the network spectrum. In the United States, this is being promoted by T-Mobile; in the United Kingdom, it is being promoted by British Telecom.

V

video Search results   When search results include videos either in regular search results or in video-specific search results like on YouTube. To be listed well in video search results, you must have videos on your website. Submitting videos and using a video site map helps search engines find and index the videos on your mobile website more efficiently. The video file types that can be included in your Google video site map are `.mpg`, `.mpeg`, `.mp4`, `.mov`, `.wmv`, `.asf`, `.avi`, `.ra`, `.ram`, `.rm`, and `flv`, but the most common mobile video formats are `.3pg` and `.mp4`. Flash (`.flv`) video files frequently do not work, so try to save your videos as `.mp4` or `.3pg` if you want them to rank well in mobile results.

virus   Code that infiltrates a host operating system with malicious intent, in some cases, replicating within the system to cause a crash or render the system useless.

VoIP (Voice over Internet Protocol)   A means of using a broadband internet signal to transmit voice, that can be pushed through a traditional phone handset, or conveyed with audio and video over computer programs like Skype.

W

WAP deck   A mobile website or portal built in Wireless Markup language for use as part of the Wireless Protocol. WAP decks focus on text and have minimal design or display features.

white label search engine   A search engine that can be leased and re-branded by companies who want to provide their users a search function. It is common for mobile carriers to use white label search engines to provide a search feature on their WAP decks or mobile portals. Users are generally unaware that the search engine is not actually owned or created by the brand name company that is displaying the results.

WiFi   A wireless local area network that uses high-frequency radio signals to transmit and receive data. WiFi is a trademark of the WiFi Alliance for certified products based on the IEEE 802.11 standards.

WiMax   Worldwide Interoperability for Microwave Access, a telecommunications technology that provides wireless transmission of data using a variety of transmission modes. The technology provides broadband speeds without the need for cables.

Wireless Action Protocol (WAP)   A mobile development protocol that is expressed in a markup language called WML or wireless markup language. Many older mobile sites are built in this protocol, and are usually designed for feature phones or mobile phones with text only browsers. 'WAP' deck is a reference to a website built for WAP.

wireless local area network (WLAN)   Internet access that is broadcast from wireless access points, otherwise known as wireless routers or hotspots.

World Wide Web Consortium (W3C)   A nonprofit organization that creates specifications, guidelines, software, and tools to aid in the development of a better Internet and "lead the Web to its full potential." The W3C has developed a variety of standards for coding languages, including mobile-compliant XHTML and WML.

worm   Self-replicating virus code that automatically spreads itself across a network, usually taking advantage of a user's contacts or address book on an infected device. Worms can also spread via Bluetooth or WiFi, and they do not work from the operating system. Worms are harmful to wireless networks, consuming inordinate amounts of bandwidth Worms can spread without any human interaction on the phone.

Index

H-I

U-V

Ubiquity, 2

UICC (Universal Integrated Circuit Card), 253

ULRs, length, 266

ultra-wide band (UWB), 119

UMA, 27

Unica, 48, 66

unified messaging, 216-217

United Kingdom
3G networks, 292
spam laws, privacy, 271-272

United States, 289
versus international mobile social networking, 230-231
spam laws, privacy, 268-271

Universal Integrated Circuit Card (UICC), 253

up-to-date users, 43

UrbanSpoon, 73, 78

user accounts, credit cards, 241

user agent detection, directing traffic, 177-178

user demographics, iPhone, 71-72

user psychographics, iPhone, 72
first wave of adoption, 72-73
second wave of adoption, 73-74
third wave of adoption, 74

User-Agent headers, 161

utility applications, 139

UWB (ultra-wide band), 119

V Festival, 17

ValueLabs, 151

vending machines, mobile payments, 246

vendors
mobile ad design, 313
mobile eCommerce, 313
mobile industry news, 314-315
mobile strategy consulting, 314
mobile testing and tools, 312
mobile ticketing, RFID, and NFC, 313
mobile tracking, 312
mobile video, 313
mobile VoIP and audio, 312

The Venue, 15

Verizon
3G, 24
stopping spam, 260

video, 172-173

integrating with mobile marketing, 228-229

Silverlight, 173

YouTube, 173

video results, mSEO, 211-212

Vietnam, mobile marketing, 284

Vietnam Computer Emergency Response Team (VNCERT), 284

ViewPoints, 152

viruses, 266-267

Visa, mobile advertising, 103

vishing, 258

VNCERT (Vietnam Computer Emergency Response Team), 284

voice recognition, iPhone, 78

VoIP (voice over Internet Protocol), 26

Vonage, 26

W-X-Y-Z

W3C (World Wide Web Consortium), 274

walled garden WAP decks, 97

WAP (Wireless Action Protocol), 155
East Asia, 279

WAP decks, 92, 155

WAP Input Format, 170

WAP2.0, 155

Web analytics, 55
comScore, 61
Google Analytics, 55-58
Omniture, 59-60
WebTrends, 60

web directories, integrating with mobile marketing, 226

Web portals, 129-131

Webkit, 154

WebMD, iPhone, 85-86

websites
integrating with mobile marketing, 226
promoting mobile applications, 148

WebTrends, 60, 64

WhatsOniPhone, 151

Whistler Ski Resort, mobile promotions, 121

WiFi, 26, 117-118
iPhones, 78

WiMax, 25

Windows Mobile, 140

Windows Mobile Catalog, 141, 152

Windows Mobile operating system, 30

Wireless Action Protocol. *See* WAP

Wireless Mark-Up Language (WML), 155

WLAN (wireless local area network) 26

WML (Wireless Mark-Up), 155

women, mobile phones, 39

World Wide Web Consortium (W3C), 274

worms, 267

writing descriptions for mobile applications, 146

XHTML, 165

XML mobile websites, 178

Yahoo! Go Mobile Multi-Application, 152

Yahoo! Mobile, 97
AirAsia, 102

YouTube, 173

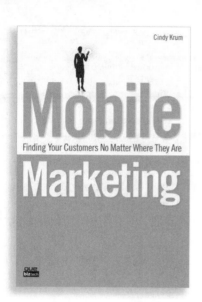

Cindy Krum

Mobile

Finding Your Customers No Matter Where They Are

Marketing

FREE Online Edition

Your purchase of **Mobile Marketing** includes access to a free online edition for 45 days through the Safari Books Online subscription service. Nearly every Que book is available online through Safari Books Online, along with more than 5,000 other technical books and videos from publishers such as Addison-Wesley Professional, Cisco Press, Exam Cram, IBM Press, O'Reilly, Prentice Hall, and Sams.

SAFARI BOOKS ONLINE allows you to search for a specific answer, cut and paste code, download chapters, and stay current with emerging technologies.

Activate your FREE Online Edition at
www.informit.com/safarifree

> **STEP 1:** Enter the coupon code: GEPTPVH.

> **STEP 2:** New Safari users, complete the brief registration form.
> Safari subscribers, just log in.

If you have difficulty registering on Safari or accessing the online edition,
please e-mail customer-service@safaribooksonline.com